ETHICAL DECISION MAKING IN SCHOOL MENTAL HEALTH

D1235179

ETHICAL DECISION MAKING IN SCHOOL MENTAL HEALTH

James C. Raines
Nic T. Dibble

Oxford Workshop Series

OXFORD
UNIVERSITY PRESS

2011

OXFORD

UNIVERSITY PRESS

Oxford University Press, Inc., publishes works that further
Oxford University's objective of excellence
in research, scholarship, and education.

Oxford New York
Auckland   Cape Town   Dar es Salaam   Hong Kong   Karachi
Kuala Lumpur   Madrid   Melbourne   Mexico City   Nairobi
New Delhi   Shanghai   Taipei   Toronto

With offices in
Argentina   Austria   Brazil   Chile   Czech Republic   France   Greece
Guatemala   Hungary   Italy   Japan   Poland   Portugal   Singapore
South Korea   Switzerland   Thailand   Turkey   Ukraine   Vietnam

Published by Oxford University Press, Inc.
198 Madison Avenue, New York, New York 10016

www.oup.com

Library of Congress Cataloging-in-Publication Data
Raines, James Curtis.
Ethical decision making in school mental health / James C. Raines and Nic T. Dibble.
p. cm. -- (Oxford workshop series)
Includes bibliographical references and index.
ISBN 978-0-19-973585-3
1. School children—Mental health services—United States. 2. School children—
Mental health services—Moral and ethical aspects. 3. School psychology—
United States. 4. School social work—United States. 5. School health services—
United States. I. Dibble, Nic T. II. Title.
LB3430.R34 2011
371.7'13--dc22
2010010495

Contents

Preface

This books aims to be different from most other books on ethics. There are three essential differences between this book and most others in the field of ethics. First, instead of focusing on specific issues, it focuses on the process of ethical decision making. New interventions and new technologies constantly create new ethical conundrums that require constant updating of ethical codes and legal guidelines. We believe that a solid process approach can withstand the test of time and equip practitioners to make good decisions regardless of the ethical issue at hand. Second, instead of writing for a specific profession, we wrote this book for all mental health professionals working in elementary and secondary schools. We especially hope that this book will be useful to both preservice and newly employed in-service pupil services professionals. Schools are a unique practice setting because mental health practitioners find themselves working in a host setting that may not share their therapeutic values. Even the U.S. Supreme Court has extended broader latitude to schools than would normally be allowed in American society (Negrón, 2009). Each of the professional codes of ethics developed separately can be informative and helpful for other professionals working in the same setting (see Box 2.3). Finally, most other authors of ethics books assume that they are writing for the individual ethical agent. We argue that the best ethical decisions are made in collaboration with others. Accordingly, we make a case for involving students, parents, and other school professionals in the ethical decision-making process.

Like one of our previous books, this title includes the phrase "school mental health." Some colleagues have objected that pupil services providers do not conduct mental health evaluations or treatment. They prefer to refer these concerns to community-based providers. While this may be ideal and actually achievable in many suburban communities, it is unworkable in many urban schools and rural communities. Sadly schools have become the default provider of mental health services for children and adolescents. It has been estimated that up to 20% of school-aged children need mental health services at some time between the ages of 5 and 18 years (Roberts, Attkinson, & Rosenblatt, 1998). Unfortunately, 70% of these children never receive any mental health services. Of those that do get assistance, schools are the primary providers (Burns et al., 1995; Rones & Hoagwood, 2000). Therefore, we believe that school counselors, school nurses, school psychologists, and school social workers are in a unique position to help. The fact that they work in a host setting whose primary mission is education creates inevitable tensions around the best way to assist these youth in becoming responsible and ethical citizens.

What can you expect to find in this book? The Introduction provides the ethical, legal, and clinical foundations on which this book is based. It also offers an overview of our ethical decision-making model. The next seven chapters each describe a major stage in the ethical decision-making process. Chapter 1 focuses on knowing oneself and your professional responsibilities, including your profession's ethical code and the relevant laws that govern your profession's practice. It presents four ethical orientations that practitioners commonly use to understand ethical issues. It also proposes a model for how to use your sense of self to categorize your reactions to clients. Chapter 2 centers on analyzing the predicament. It addresses such important issues as identifying stakeholders, organizational power, identifying the primary client, and identifying the values in conflict. Chapter 3 centers on the essential step of seeking consultation, specifically the ethical, legal, and clinical aspects. It also deals with two difficult issues, including what to do when ethics and laws conflict and how to ethically engage in civil disobedience. Chapter 4 focuses on identifying courses of action. It proposes that practitioners avoid polarizing alternatives, take a moral development approach, and engage in collaborative decision making. Chapter 5 focuses on managing the clinical concerns. It addresses three important issues: threat assessment, developmental decision making, and cultural differences. Chapter 6 centers on implementing the decision. It suggests making five final checks prior to implementation, justifying the decision, managing criticism, and documenting the process to establish a procedural standard of care. Chapter 7 focuses on reflecting on the process, including monitoring implementation, evaluating outcomes, re-engaging in the process, and improving the process for the future. An Appendix on U.S. Supreme Court cases related to school-based practice and a Glossary round out this volume.

Each chapter contains real-life scenarios based on our own practice or actual cases in the public domain, ethical guidelines for addressing key points, exercises, and relevant Internet sites. We hope that you will approach this material with an open mind and an open heart. Overall, we hope that the book is both intellectually stimulating and ethically useful in your daily practice.

Introduction

This introduction sets forth our moral and legal foundations for ethics, our clinical foundations for practice, and provides an overview of our decision-making model. We use the term "ethics" to refer to the set of norms, both obligatory and aspirational, that guide our behavior in accordance with our shared values.

In November of 2008, the Gallup Poll released their annual ethics ratings of several common professions. Nurses were at the top with 84% of respondents giving them a high or very high rating. Bankers had slipped the most, down from a high of 41% in 2005 to just 23% in 2008. Lawyers were in the bottom 10 with only 18% of respondents giving them a high or very high rating. It seems ironic that those to whom we entrust the fair and unbiased application of the law are so consistently seen as unethical. Unfortunately, counselors, psychologists, and social workers were not part of the telephone survey. Before we give too much credence to the findings, however, it is interesting to note that Gallup never felt the need to define the term "ethical." Apparently, they thought that most Americans shared the same understanding (Saad, 2008).

Ethical Foundations

There are two foundations that undergird this book. The first is the moral foundation of the Golden Rule found in all the major religions and many ancient philosophies. The second is the legal importance of the fiduciary relationship.

The Golden Rule

From where do ethical values originate? Philosophers and theologians have debated this for centuries, but most point to a common-sense idea known as the Golden Rule. The most well-known version of the Golden Rule comes from the Judeo-Christian commandment to "love your neighbor as yourself" (Leviticus 19:18 and Luke 6:31). Philosopher of religion John Hick (1996), however, points out that this moral principle is taught by all the great religions. Confucius wrote, "Do not do to others what you would not like yourself"

(*Analects*, 12:2). In Taoism, we find that the good person will "regard [others'] gains as if they were his own and their losses in the same way (*Thai Shang*, 3). Hinduism's *Mahabharata* states, "One should never do that to another which one regards as injurious to one's own self. This, in brief, is the rule of Dharma." (*Anushana parva*, 113:7). In Islam, Mohammed says, "No one is a true believer unless he desires for his brother that which he desires for himself" (*Ibn Madja*, Introduction, 9). Zoroastrians posit, "Nature only is good when it shall not do to another whatever is not good for its own self" (*Dadistan-i-dinik*, 94:5). The Jains agree that one should treat "all creatures in the world as he himself would be treated." The Buddhist *Way of the Bodhisattva* reads, "Just as I defend myself from all unpleasant happenings, however small, likewise I shall act for others' sake—to guard and shield them with compassion" (8:110).

Theologian Hans Küng (1976) argues that in theocentric religions (e.g., Christianity, Judaism, and Islam) such a view of our neighbor stems naturally from the view of God as a universal parent:

> God can be rightly understood only as the Father who makes no distinction between friend and foe, who lets the sun shine and the rain fall on good and bad, who bestows his love even on the unworthy (and who is not unworthy?). Through love human beings are to prove themselves sons and daughters of this Father and become brothers and sisters after being enemies. God's love for all men is for me then the reason for loving the person whom he sends to me, for loving just this neighbor. (p. 220)

Not all theologians, however, agree that the Golden Rule is a sufficient basis of human ethics. Paul Tillich (1955), for example, objects that the Rule fails to tell us what we should wish for ourselves or others. As we shall see later, this criticism also receives some support from a philosophical perspective.

Does a person have to be religious to affirm this moral principle? The ancient Greeks used reason or logic as their source (Berchman, 2009; Wattles, 1996). For example, in 800 B.C., Homer put these words on the lips of Calypso when she promised not to harm Odysseus as he journeyed toward home, "I will be as careful for you as I should be for myself in the same need, I know what is fair and right" (*The Odyssey*, Book V, vv. 184–191). When Plato was formulating laws for property ownership, he wrote, "May I be of a sound mind, and do to others as I would that they should do to me" (The Laws, Book XI, v. 913 in *The Dialogues of Plato*). According to the ancient biographer Diogenes Laértius, Aristotle is credited as saying that we should treat friends "as we should wish our friends to behave toward us" (*Diogenes Laertius*, Book V, §11). Modern humanitarians have also pointed to reason as the source of their belief in the Golden Rule. For example, the famous Russian humanitarian Tolstoy (1896/2005) wrote:

> Tradition—the collective wisdom of my greatest forerunners— tells me that I should do unto others as I would that they should do unto me. My *reason* shows me that only by all acting thus is the highest happiness for all people attained. Only when I yield myself to that intuition of love which demands obedience to this law is my own heart happy and at rest. (p. 71, emphasis added)

Most recently, the United Nations' (1948) *Universal Declaration of Human Rights* begins with the following assertion: "All human beings are born free and equal in dignity and rights. They are endowed with reason and conscience and should act towards one another in a spirit of brotherhood" (Article 1). Philosopher Alan Gewirth (1978) details how the Golden Rule can be rationalized. He identifies two common criticisms of the traditional formulation of the Golden Rule. First, the actor's desires for himself may not accord with the recipient's desires. A literary example of this would be the police inspector Javert in *Les Misérables*. His belief in justice is so tenacious that he must track down Jean Valjean regardless of the latter's rehabilitation and generosity. There is no room for forgiveness in his view and, in the end, he must commit suicide rather than accept Jean Valjean's mercy. Second, the actor's desires may not accord with accepted social mores. A political example would be the alleged corruption of former Illinois governor Rod Blagojevich, who is reported to have sought a bribe in exchange for Barack Obama's vacant Senate seat. Since Blagojevich may have been willing to bribe others, he may see no problem with eliciting such a bribe from others. His claims that he did nothing wrong and will ultimately be vindicated may even rest on such a perversion of the Golden Rule! The problem with both distortions of the rule is that too much credence is given to the actor's desires rather than the will of the recipient. Singer (1963) suggests that the solution to this conundrum is to "take account of the interests and wishes of others in my treatment of them" (p. 300). A simple inversion of the rule—"do unto others as they would have me to do"—gives too much credence to the recipient's desires rather than the will of the actor. A literary example of this would be the character Ishmael in

Moby Dick. After being invited by Queequeg to join in pagan worship, he ponders:

> And what is the will of God?—to do to my fellow man that what I would have my fellow man do to me—that is the will of God. Now, Queequeg is my fellow man. And what do I wish that this Queequeg would do to me? Why unite with me in my particular Presbyterian form of worship. Consequently, I must then unite with him in his [worship]; ergo, I must turn idolater. (Melville, 1967, p. 54)

Just as many a store clerk has reflected on the absurd notion that "the customer is always right," we must recognize that any such inversion of the Golden Rule gives too much power to the recipient. Neither the single perspective of the actor nor the single perspective of the recipient can provide a reasonable basis for ethical behavior.

Gewirth's (1978) philosophical solution to such criticisms is to focus on the "spirit" of the law or its inherent principle of reciprocity so that it is rationalized as follows: "Act in accord with your recipient's rational desires as well as your own." (p. 138). He argues these "rational desires" should be interpreted as the natural rights that should extend to every citizen, namely freedom and well-being, because they establish the ground for all other actions. We would point out that the U.S. Constitution sets forth similar "unalienable rights" in terms of "life, liberty, and the pursuit of happiness." In this case, life becomes a right of being that forms the ground for the other two rights of action. Gewirth concludes with a "principle of generic consistency" that recommends that people should "act in accord with the generic rights of your recipients as well as yourself" (p. 140). Obviously, this formulation of the Golden Rule is general rather than particular. It aims at a general principle rather than at specific application. This does not mean, however, that society cannot apply this precept. The application of such a principle can occur in two ways. First, it can be applied indirectly to create fair laws and systems of jurisprudence. Second, it can be applied directly to specific situations involving transactions between individuals. Wherever a conflict might occur between the two applications, the former application would take priority.

Does this mean that the Golden Rule is both necessary and sufficient for moral action? We suggest that the Golden Rule is a necessary, but insufficient foundation for a code of ethics. There remain three common problems. First, the actor's right to freedom may conflict with the recipient's right to well-being. For example, I may have a right to walk past an injured person who needs help, but that person's right to health may take precedence. In this case, society would have to be the arbiter of justice. Second, the actor's right to freedom may conflict with her right to well-being. For example, children may have a right to be free from restraint, but this may conflict with their well-being near a busy street. Thus, both laws and codes of ethics constantly try to find a balance between one person's rights and another's rights. They also recognize that even single-agent actions may conflict with that agent's best interests, such as when a person is deemed a danger to himself. Third, the Golden Rule assumes that the two actors are moral equals, but when adults work with children this is usually not the case. There are differences in maturity and power that are not recognized by the rule. Thus, the Golden Rule is a starting point, but not a terminal point for moral discussions. For example, Hook and White's (2001) module on the American Nursing Association's (ANA) *Code of Ethics for Nurses with Interpretive Statements* specifically refers to the Golden Rule in the Preface:

> The concept of human dignity, flowing from the principle of respect, is expressed in numerous ways when nurses go about their work. The idea is based on the principle of respect for persons and is derived from… the Judeo-Christian texts, that *people should treat others in the same manner in which they desire to be treated.* (pp. 4–5)

The Fiduciary Relationship
The fiduciary relationship is a common law concept that serves as the foundation for many types of professional relationships, but the common denominator is they all involve confidence, belief, and good faith (Kutchins, 1991). *Black's Law Dictionary* defines a fiduciary as "a person who is required to act for the benefit of another person on all matters within the scope of their relationship; one who owes to another the duties of good faith, trust, confidence, and candor" (Garner, 2009, p. 702). The *Code of Federal Regulations* defines an occupation that involves a fiduciary relationship as "a profession in which the nature of the services provided causes the recipient of those services to place a substantial degree of trust and confidence in the integrity, fidelity and specialized knowledge of the practitioner" (5 C.F.R. §2636.305). The professional relationship can be established by an explicit agreement of the parties, by statute, or by state law. Establishment of a fiduciary relationship

can be done orally or in writing or simply implied by the nature of the relationship. *Black's Law Dictionary* states that such relationships typically arise under any of four conditions:

> (1) when one person places trust in the faithful integrity of another, who as a result gains superiority or influence over the first, (2) when one person assumes control and responsibility over another, (3) when one person has a duty to act for or give advice to another on matters falling within the scope of the relationship, or (4) when there is a specific relationship that has traditionally been recognized as involving fiduciary duties. (Garner, 2009, p. 1402)

There are many professional relationships that require a fiduciary duty: accountant–taxpayer, attorney–client, banker–depositor, doctor–patient, engineer–builder, priest–penitent, real estate agent–homeowner, stockbroker–investor, and therapist–client. Ordinarily, the relationship involves a power differential between the two parties. *Burdett v. Miller* (1992) states, "Common law imposes 'fiduciary duty' when disparity between parties in knowledge or power relevant to performance of undertaking is so vast that it is reasonable inference that had parties in advance negotiated expressly over the issue, they would have agreed that agent owed principal fiduciary duty because otherwise principal would be placing himself at agent's mercy, as for example, relation between guardian and minor ward or between lawyer and his client" (p. 1378).

How is the fiduciary relationship to be expressed? The federal court case *Brown v. Wells Fargo Bank* (2008) states that:

> "Fiduciary" and "confidential" relationships are relationships existing between parties to a transaction wherein one party is duty bound to act with the utmost good faith for the benefit of the other. Such a relationship ordinarily arises when one party reposes a confidence in the integrity of the other, and the other voluntarily accepts that confidence. (p. 28)

Thus, the key element of such a relationship is trust in the beneficence of the fiduciary agent toward the client. In at least two federal cases, the fiduciary relationship is linked to the Golden Rule. For example, in *Market Street Associates Ltd. Partnership v. Frey* (1991), it states, "Fiduciary is required to treat his principal *as if principal were he*, and therefore he may not take advantage of principal's incapacity, ignorance, inexperience, or even naiveté"

(p. 593, emphasis added). *Burdett v. Miller* (1992) reiterates, "Fiduciary duty is the duty of an agent to treat his principal with the utmost candor, rectitude, care, loyalty, and good faith—in fact to *treat the principal as well as the agent would treat himself*" (p. 1381, emphasis added). In the former example, case law is proscriptive—it clearly delineates what the professional may not do. In the latter example, case law is prescriptive—it clearly defines what the professional must do. These delimitations circumvent the vagaries of simply using the Golden Rule as a guide for moral behavior. Thus, we posit that the Golden Rule as a moral basis and the fiduciary relationship as the legal basis taken together form a solid foundation for professional ethics.

Clinical Foundations

This section will address two broad clinical perspectives that undergird this book. These include the ecosystems perspective and the strengths perspective.

Ecosystems Perspective

This viewpoint has received the attention of school counselors (Carns & Carns, 1997; Green & Keys, 2001; Lambie & Rokutani, 2002), school psychologists (Bartell, 1996; Power & Bartholomew, 1987; Sheridan & Gutkin, 2000), and school social workers (Germain, 2006; Monkman, 2009; Winters & Easton, 1983). Ecological theory and systems theory began as two different perspectives.

Ecological theory holds the basic idea that organisms adapt to their environmental niche. Organisms that fail to adapt will not survive. The basic assumptions of ecological theory are that (*a*) human beings are both biological and social in nature; (*b*) they are dependent on their environs for essential sustenance (i.e., air, food, and water); (*c*) they are interdependent on other human beings; (*d*) the human life cycle imposes time as both a constraint and a resource; (*e*) human interactions are spatially arranged; and (*f*) human behavior can be understood only by looking at both the individual and the related population (White & Klein, 2008).

Applying these assumptions to students in schools, we would posit several propositions. First, children come to school with biological and social-emotional needs. Schools should address the needs of the whole child, not just the intellectual part (McCabe, Tollerud, & Axelrod, 2006; Norris, 2008; Woodrich, 2004). Second, they are dependent upon the school environment for getting those needs met. Adequate assessment includes both the classroom and school milieus (Chafouleas, Riley-Tillman, & Sugai, 2007; Nelson & Bustamante, 2008; Sink & Spencer, 2007). Third, we need to build school climates where students engage in peer-to-peer helping networks. This can take the form of peer-assisted learning within the classroom or older-to-younger peer mentoring outside the classroom (Foster-Harrison, 1995; Karcher, 2008; Logan & Scarborough, 2008). Fourth, they are only enrolled in school for a defined period and schools should try to understand the child's circumstances prior to his or her enrollment. Behavior that seems maladaptive was probably once adaptive in the child's home environment; it has simply outlived its usefulness. Once we understand behavior as a form of nonverbal communication, we can determine the function of misbehavior and redirect the child's efforts (Crone & Horner, 2003; Raines, 2002; Steege, Mace, & Brown-Chidsey, 2007). Fifth, the spatial arrangements of a school have a real impact on children's behavior. Overcrowded conditions and high pupil-to-staff ratios have a deleterious effect on students' conduct (Devine, 2004; Opotow, 2006). Finally, we can only assess a child by examining both the individual student and their peer-adult context. Many of our students live in both a minority culture, where one set of norms applies, and go to school in a dominant culture, where a different set of norms apply (Ford, 1987; Freed & Pena, 2002). Helping students understand and bridge this cultural divide should be part of their education.

Systems theory holds the basic idea that all parts of a system are interconnected. Like a hanging mobile, one cannot change one part without affecting the whole and vice versa. The basic assumptions of systems theory are (a) that understanding is only possible by viewing the whole which is greater than the sum of its parts; (b) there is a feedback loop between any system and its environment; and (c) systems are models and should not be regarded as material entities (White & Klein, 2008).

Applying these assumptions to students in schools, we hold three propositions. First, classroom and school systems are greater than the students and teacher involved; together they create a "culture" that has its own norms for behavior. As the National Association of School Psychologists' (2000) *Practice Guidelines* state:

> School psychologists demonstrate their knowledge of schools (or other institutional settings) as systems when they work with individuals and groups to facilitate structure and public policies that *create and maintain schools and other systems as safe, caring, and inviting places for all persons in that system.* (Guideline 6, emphasis added)

Second, there are no simple cause-and-effect explanations for student behavior. Johnny is not naughty simply because he is a bad boy; behavior has both antecedent and consequential conditions that serve to maintain it or diminish it. If our efforts focus solely on the child and do not address the conditions under which that behavior occurs, then our efforts will be doomed from the start (Crone & Horner, 2003; Raines, 2002; Steege, Mace, & Brown-Chidsey, 2007). Finally, while students, families, and classrooms can be considered as systems, they should never be equated with systems—to do so would mean losing the human element. People are not just cogs in a machine; they have free will and the right to seek their own well-being. Individuals can and occasionally should "buck the system."

Strengths Perspective

The strengths perspective has also garnered the attention of school counselors (Day-Vines & Terriquez, 2008; Dixon & Tucker, 2008; Galassi & Akos, 2007), school psychologists (Buckley, Storino, & Saarni, 2003; Jimerson, Sharkey, Nyborg, & Furlong, 2004; Terjesen, Jacofsky, Froh, & DiGiuseppe, 2004), and school social workers (Edwards, Mumford, Shillingford, & Serra-Roldan, 2007; Franklin, Gerlach, & Chanmugam, 2008; Gleason, 2007). School nurses have also recently come aboard (Concepcion, Murphy, & Canham, 2007).

Saleebey (2002) identifies six general principles of the strengths perspective. First, all individuals, groups, families, and communities have strengths. This does not mean that practitioners should be Pollyannas and see only the good in others. It does mean that we should not focus solely on the deficits. For example, Graybeal (2001) recommends a ROPES assessment, where practitioners focus on clients' resources, opportunities, possibilities, exceptions, and solutions. Second, abuse, disabilities, illness, problems, and traumas may be difficult, but they do not have to be debilitating. We should help clients see their setbacks as opportunities for growth and maturity. Third, it is dangerous to believe that we know the limitations of a client's capacity to change; it is helpful to harness a client's hopes and dreams. Fourth, we serve clients best when we treat them as partners in the process. Collaboration and consultation are key skills to employ when helping students. Fifth, every environment has resources. These may be formal or informal sources of aid. These may include hard services (e.g., food, clothing, or shelter) or soft services (e.g., counseling, health care, or legal aid) (Raines & Ahlman, 2004). Identifying and referring to community-based programs is an efficient use of time for busy school professionals. Finally, caring for each other promotes human dignity and well-being. Much of psychopathology involves too much focus on the self; people are helped as they reach out to others in need. Engaging students in service-learning not only helps the community, it helps the students as well (Leming, 2001).

Applying these principles to schools has several implications. First, we must discover and employ assessment instruments that focus on students' strengths more than their deficits. Jimerson et al. (2004) and Gleason (2007) do an excellent job identifying some of these scales. Second, a solution-focused approach can help students and their families overcome their problems and reach their own goals (Murphy, 2008; Sklare, 2005; Teall, 2000). Third, many students suffer from low expectations; we can empower them by engaging them (and their parents) in the process of school reform (Day-Vines & Terriquez, 2008). Fourth, we should recognize that our role in the lives of students is supplemental to their families who will support and care for them over the long haul. If we come alongside families with the goal of equipping them as caregivers, we will do more good than if we see ourselves as surrogate parents in the school system (Giles, 2005; Mueller, Singer, & Draper, 2008; Seitsinger, Felner, Brand, & Burns, 2008). Fifth, we must be culturally sensitive in our assessments of families and communities. If we use our own ethnicity as the norm, we will do our families and their communities a disservice. We must learn to assess school environments from their perspectives (Nelson & Bustamante, 2008). Finally, we must engage and empower the natural networks of student care. As the American School Counselors Association's (2004) *Ethical Standards* state, a professional "respects the rights and responsibilities of parents/guardians for their children and endeavors to establish, as appropriate, a collaborative relationship with parents/guardians to facilitate the student's maximum development" (§B.1). This may also mean using more mutual aid techniques, such as family, group, or pair therapies (Day, 2005; Dennison, 2008; Selman & Schultz, 1998; Webb & Brigman, 2007).

Ethical Decision-Making Models

Most Codes of Ethics assume that they have limited utility in resolving all of the ethical quandaries that practitioners will face. For example, the National Association of Social Workers (NASW) *Code of Ethics* (2008) states:

> The NASW Code of Ethics does not specify which values, principles, and standards are most important and ought to outweigh

others in instances when they conflict. Reasonable differences of opinion can and do exist among social workers with respect to the ways in which values, ethical principles, and ethical standards should be rank ordered when they conflict. Ethical decision making in a given situation must apply the informed judgment of the individual social worker and should also consider how the issues would be judged in a peer review process where the ethical standards of the profession would be applied. (p. 6)

All mental health professionals who have practiced for any length of time have faced ethical predicaments. Strom-Gottfried (2008) lists five circumstances under which ethical quandaries may arise: (1) when the application or boundary of an ethical standard is unclear, (2) when standards conflict with institutional demands, (3) when there are conflicting loyalties, (4) when a professional finds it difficult to adhere to an ethical standard, and (5) when good solutions seem unattainable.

A variety of people have developed and shared specific models to help mental health professionals resolve ethical predicaments. Some of these target mental health professionals, in general, while others are more focused on pupil services professionals in schools. Still others target a specific pupil services profession (i.e., school counselors, nurses, psychologists, or social workers). It is important to note that, to date, no one has established an empirical foundation that supports any of these models as being more effective than the others. However, many share a great deal of common steps.

Goals

The primary reason it is important for pupil services professionals to understand and utilize an ethical decision-making model is to maximize the likelihood that the practitioner will make the best possible decision, given the circumstances. As school-based mental health professionals, we have a primary ethical and fiduciary responsibility to our students. As such, we must take all reasonable steps to ensure that when we face an ethical quandary, we are acting in the student's best interests. Utilization of an ethical decision-making model is a process all of us have the capacity to do.

Ethical predicaments, by their very nature, may not be able to be resolved in an ideal manner. That is why they are predicaments. Practitioners may receive formal or informal complaints about their decisions and actions. In extreme situations, a lawsuit may be filed. Reamer (2005b) identifies a standard of care that is used in court hearings: What would an ordinary, reasonable, and prudent person with similar training have done in a similar situation? Use of an ethical decision-making model can help a pupil services professional involved in litigation to meet this standard of care.

Effectively managing ethical quandaries accomplishes a variety of desirable goals: (1) the student is protected and better served, (2) the pupil services professional avoids possible disciplinary action for unethical conduct, and (3) the profession avoids "bad PR," since a serious error by a pupil services professional made public reflects poorly on the entire profession and makes practice by other pupil services professionals more challenging because of the loss of credibility.

Ethical Competencies

Jacob and Hartshorne (2007) offer seven ethical competencies for school psychologists. These can be helpful when applied to any ethical decision-making model: (1) sensitivity to the ethical implications of school psychological services; (2) familiarity with ethical and professional standards, as well as laws related to service delivery; (3) commitment to anticipating and preventing ethical dilemmas through a proactive, rather than reactive, stance; (4) ability to apply a systematic procedure for making decisions about ethical issues; (5) awareness of one's attitudes, values, and feelings, as well as the potential impact on decisions; (6) acknowledgment of the complexity of ethical decisions and the likelihood that multiple courses of appropriate action are possible; and (7) willingness to take action and to accept responsibility for actions taken in response to ethically challenging situations. We believe these competencies should apply to all pupil services professionals working in schools.

Our Ethical Decision-Making Model

Our model consists of seven steps with numerous substeps to consider at each stage. The next seven chapters in the book describe our model and reasons behind it. Our steps include (1) knowing yourself and your profession's relevant ethical and legal parameters; (2) analyzing the predicament; (3) seeking consultation; (4) identifying the courses of action; (5) managing the clinical concerns; (6) implementing the decision; and (7) reflecting on the process. The steps we have chosen for the ethical decision-making process in this book are based upon an extensive review of the literature and the authors' many years of experience providing consultation and training to pupil services professionals (Dibble, 2006; Raines, 2004, 2009). As stated earlier, there is no empirical proof in the literature that would establish any model as being superior to any others (Cottone & Claus, 2000). While we strongly recommend that practitioners consider all the steps discussed in this book, we also recognize that the order of the steps we recommend in this book is not sacrosanct. Which models (or steps within models) best facilitate ethical decision making may depend in part upon the individual practitioner, the ethical quandary, and the practice setting. We recognize that ethical practitioners may disagree and remain ethical practitioners. Our goal in this book is to help the reader adopt an ethical decision-making process that will result in the best possible services for students and enhance professional pupil services practice.

At this point, we would like to provide a brief overview of our ethical decision-making model using the following scenario:

> A 16-year-old Hispanic student seeks out the school nurse and shares that she is pregnant. The student has a previous history of substance abuse and poor decision making. The school nurse previously worked with the student and her family to help the student successfully access substance abuse treatment. The student states she wants to give the child up for adoption, but she is concerned her parents will not allow it. Her parents do not yet know about the pregnancy. From her previous work with the family, the school nurse anticipates the parents would vigorously resist adoption. Finally, the student shares she is "using" again but does not want to return to treatment.

Step 1: Knowing Yourself and Your Professional Responsibilities
The school nurse needs to be self-aware and understand what her ethical preferences are, so they do not inappropriately influence her health care services to her student. Does she tend to err on the side of student self-determination? If so, this ethical preference should not allow the unborn child to be seriously harmed by the student's substance abuse. Or does the school nurse tend to err on the side of concern for the student's health and well-being? If so, this ethical preference should not usurp the student's right to determine personal courses of action.

If the school nurse has any personal values about adoption, either for or against, it will be very important for her to be aware of these values and not allow them to interfere with her services to this student. If her personal feelings about adoption are particularly strong, she may choose to refer this student to another qualified pupil services professional. Similarly, if the school nurse has worked with other students regarding adoption, with either very positive or negative outcomes, these previous experiences should inform the school nurse but not inappropriately affect how she provides services to this particular student.

The school nurse needs to be familiar with the state laws regarding this minor student's right to place a child for adoption. In addition, the father of the unborn child may have rights as well (i.e., the father may have to consent to the adoption, as well as the mother). While this student has the right to access confidential health care services (see Chapter 4), depending upon the circumstances of sexual contact with others, there may be requirements to report the student's pregnancy as possible sexual abuse or assault.

Step 2: Analyzing the Predicament

There are many issues that need to be considered in analyzing this predicament. Most immediate is that the student is pregnant and abusing substances again. This could lead to permanent harm to the unborn child. While the student is the client, the school nurse should consider what responsibility she has to the unborn child.

The school nurse should identify who, other than the student, will be affected by the management of this ethical predicament. At minimum, the student's parents and the father of the unborn child are important stakeholders who may have very strong opinions about what is done.

While the student claims she wants to give the child up for adoption, her current substance abuse and history of making major life decisions that she later regrets brings into question whether the student has thought through this choice. Being familiar with the family's personal and cultural values from previous contacts, the school nurse knows the parents may attempt to forbid their daughter to give the child up for adoption. Clearly, the parents have an important role in helping to guide their child, but the school nurse is concerned their influence will go far beyond guidance. While the school nurse may have a supportive role in helping this family, this support should not interfere in the family's private life.

The school nurse does not yet know the circumstances that led to the student's pregnancy. However, if the student is abusing substances again, it may be that the student is having sexual intercourse while under the influence, rendering the student incapable of voluntarily participating in sexual contact. The school nurse needs to determine whether a report to child protective services or law enforcement is necessary. Finally, some states require a report be made to the authorities if a pregnant woman is abusing substances that may cause serious harm to the unborn child. The school nurse needs to determine the extent of the substance abuse and whether a report is required under the law. If so, the clinical relationship between the student and school nurse needs to be actively managed and preserved as well as possible.

Step 3: Seeking Consultation

The school nurse may wish to consult with a licensed substance abuse treatment provider with expertise working with adolescents. The combination of a pregnancy and substance abuse makes this situation urgent.

If the school nurse is not familiar with the state's adoption laws, she will want to seek out others with more expertise. There may be a state adoption information center that summarizes this information in easy-to-understand language for consumers. The school nurse needs to take care to seek out information from objective sources (i.e., not organizations that are biased for or against adoption).

If the school nurse is unable to independently determine whether a report to the authorities is required under the law, she could contact either child protective services or law enforcement for input. At this stage, it would not be necessary for her to share the name of the student, but simply the circumstances of this ethical predicament.

The school nurse may wish to consult with another professional who is more knowledgeable about Hispanic culture and how this ethical predicament can be best managed with respect for the family's culture.

Step 4: Identifying Courses of Action

Failing to identify all possible courses of action may artificially create more challenging ethical predicaments. Practitioners should avoid "either-or" thinking that leads to only two possible courses of action, which may be diametrically opposed.

In this situation, courses of action need to be explored regarding the student's renewed substance abuse, the student's decision about adoption, family involvement in this decision, and the possible need to report the student's sexual contact with another person. Some of these courses of action are driven by ethical and clinical concerns, while others are more influenced by laws.

The school nurse should attempt to project the outcomes of the different courses of action that are generated. Effects on stakeholders, as well as the student, should be anticipated.

The student can be engaged in a collaborative decision-making partnership that empowers the student while also helping to provide guidance for an important life decision, consistent with the student's developmental readiness. For instance, if information is available online about adoption, the school nurse and student could explore the Web site together. Other stakeholders, such as the parents, can be involved collaboratively as well.

Step 5: Managing the Clinical Concerns

One of the clinical concerns in this predicament is the student's renewed substance abuse. A referral to a licensed, substance abuse assessment specialist may be warranted to determine the extent of the abuse. Ideally, a community-based treatment provider who has previously worked with this student will conduct the assessment so that the recommendations are well informed.

While the student may have the right to elect to put her child up for adoption independently of her parents, the school nurse knows the family's personal and cultural values do not embrace adoption as an alternative. The school nurse is also concerned that if the decision making is not managed well and does not involve the parents' input, it may create a permanent rift between the parents and their daughter.

Step 6: Implementing the Decision

Prior to implementation, selected course(s) action can be "tested" to help ensure that the ethical predicament is managed to produce the best possible outcomes and any unanticipated, adverse outcomes are avoided by asking the following questions:

- If I were the student, is this what I would want for myself?
- Would I treat other students in the same way?
- Who is my primary client?
- Would I feel comfortable if my professional colleagues found out how I handled this situation?
- Would you recommend a professional colleague handle a similar situation in the same manner?

The school nurse should document the decision-making process she used, including whom she consulted with and was involved in selecting the course(s) of action. In addition, she should be prepared to justify the selected course(s) of action, knowing that other courses of action may have resulted in less satisfactory outcomes for the student and others.

Step 7: Reflecting on the Process

Many ethical decision-making models end at the point the practitioner implements the selected course(s) of action, but we believe that another step is necessary for ethical practice. The fact that the practitioner is struggling with the ethical predicament means there is the real possibility of less than positive outcomes for the student or other stakeholders.

We believe that to fail to monitor the decision and its outcomes is not ethical. Additional services may be necessary to meet the needs of the student or manage unintended, adverse outcomes. In addition, conducting a postanalysis of the ethical predicament and how it was managed can help prepare the practitioner to better manage similar situations in the future.

Exercises

1. The Golden Rule

Use the Web site listed under the Golden Rule Curriculum below and browse through the different versions of the Golden Rule. Which one appeals to you more? Why? If none of them appeals to you, how might you paraphrase the Golden Rule for yourself?

2. Fiduciary Relationships

Since there are many kinds of fiduciary relationships, think about those you currently have where you are *not* the fiduciary agent, but the client in a dependent position (e.g., depositor, patient, or taxpayer). What expectations do you have of the fiduciary agent—proscriptively and prescriptively? How would you feel if the fiduciary agent betrayed your trust? What action would you take?

3. Ethical Decision-Making Steps

Which of the steps do you employ the most? Which particular steps are you most likely to skip? What helps you make ethical decisions? How do you determine when the ethical decision is the right one? How often do you reflect on your past decisions?

Internet Resources

Golden Rule Resources

Committee for the Golden Rule
http://patriot.net/~bmcgin/golden.html
Golden Rule Curriculum for Schools
http://www.scarboromissions.ca/Golden_rule/school_curriculum.php
Prof. Harry Gensler's Golden Rule page
http://www.jcu.edu/philosophy/gensler/goldrule.htm#Li
United Nations' Universal Declaration of Human Rights
http://www.un.org/en/documents/udhr

Ecosystems Perspective

Human Ecology Review
http://www.humanecologyreview.org/
Inquiring Systems
http://inquiringsystems.org/index.php
School 2.0–Learning Ecosystem
http://etoolkit.org/etoolkit/map
Social Psychology
http://www.socialpsychology.org/

Strengths Perspective

Strengths Institute
http://www.socwel.ku.edu/Strengths/mission.shtml
Penn Positive Psychology Center
http://www.ppc.sas.upenn.edu/index.html
University of Cambridge Well-Being Institute
http://www.cambridgewellbeing.org/
Solution-Focused Brief Therapy Association
http://www.sfbta.org/
National Resilience Resource Center
http://www.cce.umn.edu/nrrc/index.html
Ethical Decision Making in School Mental Health

I

Knowing Yourself and Your Professional Responsibilities

Ethics requires self-knowledge on the part of the ethical agent. Some professional associations make this goal explicit. The American Counseling Association (ACA) *Code of Ethics*, for example, states, "Counselors also explore their own cultural identities and how these affect their *values and beliefs* about the counseling process" (2005, p. 4, emphasis added). This self-knowledge can be broken down into three categories: knowing one's own ethical orientation, knowing one's values, and knowing one's countertransference issues. Ethics also requires an in-depth knowledge of one's professional responsibilities. These are covered in each profession's respective code of ethics as well as in laws sanctioning that profession's practice.

Ethical Orientations

Here we will address the two dominant ethical theories of deontological and consequentialist ethics (Congress, 2000; Francis, 2002; Linzer, 1999). Then we will add two more ethical theories that can be seen as corrections to weaknesses in the dominant theories. These include virtue ethics and the ethics of care (Banks, 2008).

Deontological Ethics

Deontologists believe in a moral code that defines the prescriptions (oughts) and proscriptions (naughts) of people living together (an ethnic group) or working together (a profession). It aims to produce fundamental principles of right and wrong and how these led to ethical practice. Deontologists tend to view these fundamental principles as either self-evident through logic or jural through legislation. Modern skepticism has questioned whether any principles are self-evident, leaving most deontologists to the jural ground for moral principles. The original jural justifications were religious (Deigh, 1999). For example, in the Ten Commandments we find both prescriptions (e.g., proper worship, keeping the Sabbath, and respect for parents) and proscriptions (e.g., against lying, stealing, adultery, and murder).

After the Enlightenment, two other forms of jural justification emerged: formalism and contractualism. Kant, the founder of formalism, formulated his first Categorical Imperative as follows: "I ought never to act in such a way that I could not also will that my maxim should be a universal law" (1785/2002, p. 203). He then identifies the corollary of this law for human relations: "Act in such a way that you treat humanity, whether in your own person or in any other person, always at the same time as an end, never merely as a means" (1785/2002, pp. 229–230). While the former imperative requires that universality be the guiding principle, the second requires humanity to be the primary concern (Hill, 2006). According to Kant, all rules for human behavior ought to be able to apply to all people and should never treat any human being as the means to another end. Ross' (1930) deontological ethics, however, would argue against universality on two points. First, it posits that special relationships have a claim on our loyalties so that we must keep certain promises that are not due to everyone. For example, clients have a claim that the general public does not. Second, it claims that such an overall imperative makes every decision too derivative, and he argues for a plurality of moral principles. Contractualism can be traced back to Locke and Rousseau, but it gains its fullest exposition from Rawls (1971). In this view, it is the social contract that determines the terms of ethical behavior. Rawls posits that justice is determined by regarding everyone in a society as equals with each person taking on a "veil of ignorance" with regard to individual differences, such as wealth, social status, talents, and religious affiliations. This leads to two principles. First, certain liberties are basic—liberty of conscience, freedom of thought, freedom of association, integrity of the person, and the rule of law—because they enable us to engage our "moral powers" of reason and justice seeking. Second, certain differences are permissible—wealth, income, power, and position—because they are open to all in a fair competition and because they may indirectly benefit the least advantaged by increasing the general well-being of society. In general, deontological ethics posits three propositions. First, there are moral principles that contain proscriptive duties, for example, murdering innocent people. Second, there are duties of special relationship that are "agent relative," such as duties owed to family, friends, and clients (Constable, 1989). Third, there are permissible duties; we have a right to decide whether the cost to us outweighs the benefit to others. For example, we may determine not to impoverish our children in order to feed the hungry children in Africa.

Most codes of ethics reflect some form of deontological ethics by beginning with certain principles regarded as fundamental to the profession. The American Psychological Association (APA) *Code of Ethics* (2002), for example, begins with five general principles: (*a*) Beneficence and nonmaleficence, (*b*) Fidelity and responsibility, (*c*) Integrity, (*d*) Justice, and (*e*) Respect for people's rights and dignity. Similarly, the National Association of Social Workers (NASW) *Code of Ethics* (2008) begins with six core principles: (*a*) Service, (*b*) Social justice, (*c*) Dignity and worth of the person, (*d*) Importance of human relationships, (*e*) Integrity, and (*f*) Competence. For other examples from pupil services professional associations, see Box 1.1.

We wish to emphasize two important points about these deontological principles. First, despite the similarities between the two professions mentioned previously, it is notable that only half of these overlap: Justice, Integrity, and Human dignity. Does this mean that social workers do not value Beneficence or Fidelity or that psychologists do not value Service, Human relationships, or Competence? It is our view that such moral principles are illustrative, but not exhaustive. We believe that these principles complement each other more than they conflict. The implication of this conclusion for

---

Box 1.1 Ethical Values in Three Pupil Services Professional Associations

ASCA	NASN	NASP
Respect and dignity of others	Client care	Advocacy for students
Self-direction and self-development	Professional competency	Nonmaleficence ("Do no harm")
Right to understand choices	Professional improvement	Competence
Right to privacy and confidentiality		

ASCA, American School Counselors Associations; NASN, National Association of School Nurses; NASP, National Association of School Psychologists.

---

pupil services professionals is that we have much to learn from each other. While we believe that practitioners should consult their own code of ethics first, we also believe there is much to be gained by a thorough examination of the other professional codes. The NASW (2008) *Code of Ethics* makes this recommendation explicit:

> In addition to this Code, there are many other sources of information about ethical thinking that may be useful. Social workers should consider ethical theory and principles generally, social work theory and research, laws, regulations, agency policies, and *other relevant codes of ethics*, recognizing that among codes of ethics social workers should consider the NASW Code of Ethics as their primary source. (p. 6, emphasis added)

The ACA (2005) concurs, "Counselors understand the ACA Code of Ethics and *other applicable ethics codes from other professional organizations*" (p. 18, emphasis added).

Second, the principles are aspirational rather than obligatory. The APA (2002) *Ethical Principles* clarifies this:

> General Principles, as opposed to Ethical Standards, are *aspirational* in nature. Their intent is to guide and inspire psychologists toward the very highest ethical ideals of the profession. General Principles, in contrast to Ethical Standards, do not represent *obligations* and should not form the basis for imposing sanctions. Relying upon General Principles for either of these reasons distorts both their meaning and purpose. (p. 3, emphasis added)

Despite these two delimitations, awareness of ethical principles is important because there is no code of ethics that will provide guidance for every ethical conundrum we face (Pope & Vasquez, 2007). It is in these gray areas that we most need to return to our ethical principles.

Even proponents of deontological ethics admit to four common problems. First, it seems improbable that different cultures and ethnic groups can all agree on the same universal ethical principles (Houser, Wilczenski, & Ham, 2006). While we think the Golden Rule comes close given its appeal to a wide variety of times and places, we cannot state unequivocally that it is universally accepted (Healy, 2007). For example, Francis (2002) points out that international codes of ethics are considerably shorter than national codes of ethics. Second, there are philosophers who deny that moral reasons are rational. They would object that all moral reasons are tied to religion or tradition if traced back to their origins. Third, there is no algorithm for determining which principles are primary. Principles often conflict in real-life situations (e.g., love vs. justice) and even people who agree on which principle should be primary may not agree on how it should be applied. Fourth, there is no uniform list of moral principles. For an example drawn from multiple sources (Loewenberg, Dolgoff, & Harrington, 2000; NASW, 2008), see Box 1.2. As we have seen previously, different professions gravitate toward certain favorites, but there is no standardized catalog (McNaughton & Rawling, 2006). Different professionals will have different moral absolutes.

Box 1.2 Rank Your Ethical Principles

Below you will find a baker's dozen of ethical principles. Rank the following principles in importance from 1–13, with 1 = highest value and 13 = lowest value.

—— *Truthfulness and Full Disclosure*—Practitioners should be completely honest with their clients.

—— *Dignity and Worth of the Person*—Practitioners should treat each person in a caring and respectful fashion.

—— *Privacy and Confidentiality*—Practitioners should only seek to acquire relevant information and should keep that material sacrosanct.

—— *Social Justice*—Practitioners should pursue social change, particularly with and on behalf of vulnerable and oppressed individuals and groups.

—— *Protection of Life*—Practitioners should seek to protect and prolong a person's biophysical life.

—— *Service*—Practitioners should seek to help people in need and address social problems above any self-interest.

—— *Equal Treatment*—Practitioners should treat persons in similar circumstances in a similar manner.

—— *Importance of Human Relationships*—Practitioners should seek to strengthen relationships among people to enhance the well-being of families, groups, and communities.

— *Least Harm*—When faced with two or more negative outcomes, practitioners should choose the least harmful, least permanent, or most reversible option.

— *Integrity*—Practitioners should behave in a trustworthy manner, congruent with professional values and ethics.

— *Quality of Life*—Practitioners should seek to promote the highest quality of life for both the individual and his or her environment.

— *Competence*—Practitioners should practice within their areas of knowledge and skills, constantly striving to develop and enhance their expertise.

— *Autonomy/Freedom*—Practitioners should respect an individual's right to control or contribute to decisions that affect him or her.

Pair and Share

1. Share your top three principles when working with children and explain why you picked them.
2. Ask your partner whether there are any circumstances under which these would change.
3. Share your lowest three principles when working with children and explain why these were less important.

Consequentialist Ethics

If deontologists claim that an action is right if it accords with a moral principle, then consequentialism holds that an action is right if it promotes the best result. Generally, the best result is defined teleologically as the most good for the most people. This, of course, begs the question, What is "good"? Within consequentialism, there are three kinds of value theorists: hedonists, desire theorists, and perfectionists. Jeremy Bentham's utilitarianism was an Enlightenment version of hedonism that defined good as the maximization of pleasure and minimization of pain (Harrison, 1983). Among modern hedonists (Nozick, 1989; Sumner, 1996), good can be defined as either

     Ethical Decision Making in School Mental Health

simple pleasures (physical sensations) or complex pleasures (contentedness in the Epicurean sense). Desire theorists argue that people should be allowed to determine their own needs. The good then becomes what satisfies or what will lead to satisfaction for the most people (Griffin, 1986). Accordingly, there are instrumental goods such as money and intrinsic goods such as happiness. Perfectionists define the good as our highest aspirations, such as knowledge or achievement, because they integrate multiple subordinate goals (Hurka, 2006). Like deontological ethics, there is a lack of consensus on whether these goods can be precisely ordered or finitely measured so that a hierarchy of goods can be determined. There is also a lack of consensus on whether an ethical actor has "agent-relative" duties (e.g., loyalty) or whether he or she must always aim for the common good. Rule consequentialists object that any agent-relative duties interfere with the rule of impartiality (Hooker, 2000).

Most codes of ethics also draw two important implications from consequentialist ethics. These include clinical foresight and balancing client rights versus their best interests.

First, mental health practitioners must exercise some degree of foresight in their relationship with clients. Most codes of ethics commend some kind of risk–benefit analysis at different points in the therapeutic relationship. For example, the ACA (2005) *Code of Ethics* recommends that this type of scrutiny begins with every counseling relationship: "They inform clients about issues such as, but not limited to, the following: the purposes, goals, techniques, procedures, limitations, *potential risks, and benefits of services*" (p. 4, emphasis added). The APA (2002) *Ethical Principles* are cognizant that psychologists must sometimes mislead clients to get an accurate assessment (e.g., the use of social desirability scales) and warns, "In situations in which deception may be ethically justifiable *to maximize benefits and minimize harm*, psychologists have a serious obligation to consider the need for, the possible consequences of, and their responsibility to correct any resulting mistrust or other harmful effects that arise from the use of such techniques" (p. 3, emphasis added). The ACA (2005) *Code of Ethics* suggests that this cost–benefit analysis should also occur during consultation: "Counselors use clear and understandable language to inform all parties involved about the purpose of the services to be provided, relevant costs, *potential risks and benefits*, and the limits of confidentiality" (p. 11, emphasis added). The NASW (2008) *Code of Ethics* argues that foresight is especially important when considering whether to violate a client's confidentiality: "The general expectation that social workers will keep information confidential does not apply when disclosure is necessary to prevent serious, *foreseeable, and imminent* harm to a client or other identifiable person (p. 11, emphasis added). The implication is that practitioners should not only be able to foresee the future but also how close that future might be. The APA (2002) *Ethical Principles* also recommend that cost–benefit analysis occur toward termination: "Psychologists terminate therapy when it becomes reasonably clear that the client/patient no longer needs the service, *is not likely to benefit, or is being harmed* by continued service" (p. 16, emphasis added). The NASW (2008) *Code of Ethics* echoes this at two similar points. When social workers leave an agency, they "should inform clients of appropriate options for the continuation of services and of *the benefits and risks* of the options" (p. 14, emphasis added). Likewise when receiving a transfer client, "social workers should discuss with potential clients the nature of the clients' current relationship with other service providers and the implications, including possible *benefits or risks*, of entering into a relationship with a new service provider" (p. 18, emphasis added). Obviously none of us have 20-20 foresight, but the ethical codes do expect us to exercise prudent care. For example, the APA (2002) *Principles* clarify that "the term reasonable means the prevailing professional judgment of psychologists engaged in similar activities in similar circumstances given the knowledge the psychologist had or *should have had at the time*" (p. 2, emphasis added).

Second, practitioners must balance what is best for the client versus the client's right to self-determination. For example, Fry and Veatch (2000) recognize that nurses may discover that there is often a conflict between rights versus goods. "Many situations faced by the nurse pose the problem of the rights of the patient conflicting with benefits to the patient; that is, one course seems to protect the patient's right [to autonomy] while *another course would produce more good for the patient*" (p. 32, emphasis added). This is especially true for minors where schools are sometimes expected to operate under the principle of *parens patriae* (lit. "parent of the nation")—sometimes called *in loco parentis*, meaning "in place of parents." Both doctrines allowed schools to make decisions in the "best interests" of children who are not ready to make important decisions for themselves (Corrao & Melton, 1988; Weiss, 1990). The APA (2002) *Principles* state that for all persons legally ineligible to give informed consent, the practitioner must find a balance between "such persons' preferences and best interests" (p. 7). Practitioners should be warned, however, that the doctrine of *parens patriae* has been severely curtailed by the U.S. Supreme Court's (1967) decision, *In re Gault* (Ichikawa, 1997; Williams & Baumeister, 1988).

Consequentialism also has four common drawbacks. First, there are often conflicts between the "most good" and the "most people." Should school administrators expel disruptive students to avoid inconveniencing the majority of people in the school? This may sound extreme, but consider the story of Joe Clark in Box 1.3. Second, there may be a conflict between the ways to aggregate "most people." Should we take an additive approach to define

---

Box 1.3 Joe Clark: America's Toughest Principal

Joe Clark was one of the most colorful figures in education during the 1980s. After making the cover of *Time* magazine in February of 1988, *People* magazine declared him the "most famous high school principal in America" (VanBiema & Moses, 1989, p. 52). Morgan Freeman played his character in the Warner Brothers hit film *Lean on Me*. Born in Georgia and raised in Newark, New Jersey, he worked as a drill sergeant in the army. After earning degrees at Columbia University and Rutgers, he worked his way up to principal at an elementary school in Paterson, New Jersey, a small city of 140,000 in northern New Jersey. The school district was on the verge of bankruptcy and most students came from poor minority families, with a third of them on welfare (Rimer, 1988). Eastside High was infested with drugs and gang violence when Clark took the helm in 1982. He began his first year by taking a law-and-order approach to school management. He walked through the school carrying a baseball bat and talking through a bullhorn. He banned loitering in the hallways, instituted a dress code, and chained the doors shut so drug dealers could not sneak in. By the end of that year, he claimed to have "expurgated" 300 students for being absent, late, or disruptive without due process or approval by the school board (Davis, 1988). From 1984 to 1987, over 600 students dropped out or were kicked out, a rate nearly twice as high as other Paterson high schools (Rimer, 1988). When the school board objected that only they could expel students, the conflict drew national attention.

William Bennett, then U.S. Secretary of Education under Ronald Reagan, famously quipped that sometimes schools "need Mr. Chips, sometimes you need Dirty Harry," an allusion to Clark (Hyman, 1989, p. 20).

Was Joe Clark effective as a principal? It depends on whom you ask. The mayor and district superintendent supported Clark's methods, but the city council and the school board opposed him. Many parents and community leaders admired his "tough love" approach, but half of the teachers left during his 7-year tenure and the teacher's union filed 44 grievances against Clark (Davis, 1988). There was probably a good reason: in June of 1985, he sent a memo to union delegates that read, "I invite you to purge yourselves of the demons that make you so dangerous to the very institutions and ideologies to which you should be dedicating your professional lives or to purge the Paterson school system by leaving it" (Rimer, 1988, p. 2). More objective measures were mixed. According to Davis (1988),

> While math scores are up 6% during Clark's reign, reading scores have barely budged: they remain in the bottom third of the nation's high school seniors. While a few more students are going to college—211, up from 182 in 1982—Clark has lost considerable ground in the battle against dropouts: when he arrived, Eastside's rate was 13%; now it is 21%. (p. 55)

Legal experts pointed out that the U.S. Supreme Court's 1975 ruling *Goss v. Lopez* found that the 14th Amendment's right to due process applies to state laws about student suspensions and expulsions (Jennings, 1988). Principals and school boards cannot act capriciously when meting such severe punishment. A contemporaneous poll by the Carnegie Foundation, however, found that 25% of teachers thought that up to 20% of their students did not have what it takes to finish high school (Norman, 1988). Hyman (1989) concludes that Clark epitomizes those who are willing to suspend the civil liberties of the few to raise the test scores of the majority. In the final analysis, the principal "rationalizes that the end justifies the means" (p. 20).

Discussion Questions

1. Clark and community leaders claimed that Eastside High was out of control the year he arrived. What immediate actions would you have recommended?

2. In your opinion, under what circumstances should students be expelled from school?

3. What options do expelled students have for the future?

4. Where do you think most of these students eventually end up?

5. How should schools balance the rights of a disruptive student and the best interests of the majority who come to learn?

6. Clark employed a retributive model of school discipline. What would a restorative model of justice look like in schools (Varnham, 2005)?

"most people" or an average approach to define "most people"? Consider three examples. Should schools allow overcrowding so that the "most students" get an educational opportunity or will this significantly decrease the educational opportunity of the average student? How long should students be required to remain in school? An additive view would suggest as long as possible (despite diminishing returns); an average perspective would propose as long as the regular student obtains an optimal educational benefit. Should schools support students' giftedness in different specializations or aim for the well-rounded student (e.g., academics, arts, and athletics)? Third, how should we define "good"? There are likely to be conflicts between educators, parents, students, and taxpayers about the final (teleological) outcome. Does consequentialism infer that the majority rules? This can lead to a tyranny of the majority and disempowerment for minority stakeholders whoever they may be (e.g., age, race, or language group). Fourth, how do we institute any checks or balances on such an axiomatic rule where right action is defined so simply? Ultimately, consequentialism supports the idea that "the end justifies the means," but most of us shudder at the implications of such an ethic.

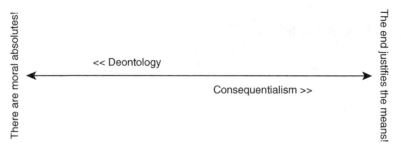

FIGURE 1.1 Deontological vs. Consequential Ethics.

All of us probably gravitate toward either the deontological or consequentialist point of view. Look at the continuum in Figure 1.1; where do you see yourself on this spectrum? Osmo and Landau (2006) conducted an interesting study in which they asked Israeli social workers to identify their general ethical positions prior to being confronted with three ethical vignettes. While most social workers aligned with the deontological position in theory, they moved to the consequentialist position in practice. Their study serves as a cautionary reminder that ethical decision making is more complex than simply ascribing to a theoretical position.

New Ethical Approaches

There are two recent developments in ethical theory that deserve mention. These include virtue ethics and the ethics of care. We will begin with the oldest view and work our way forward.

Virtue Ethics

The concern with virtue permeated classical Greek discussion of ethics, but this faded away after the rise of deontology and consequentialism. Annas (2006) defines virtue as a disposition to do the right thing for the right reasons. What differentiates a virtue from mere self-control is that the virtuous person does the right deed in a wholehearted manner. Obviously, virtue is not inborn; it is learned. A person gradually becomes virtuous in two ways. First, the person adopts some people as role models or mentors about ethical behavior. Second, the person begins to make ethical decisions and *reflect* on these choices in such a way that he or she becomes more integrated over time. We often think of a person with such traits as having *integrity* as a result.

Over time, the virtuous person becomes both more sensitive to ethical quandaries and insightful about the nuances of each situation. The ultimate goal of being virtuous is what the Greeks called eudaimonia or flourishing. Flourishing is the fulfillment that comes from a life lived in accordance with our deepest values. How does living virtuously help us become more ethical? The focus on virtue requires that we constantly and consciously aspire to be better than we are. It is greater than simply conforming to a professional code of ethics. Most codes of ethics have two aims. First, they aim to provide a set of rules applicable across a wide variety of situations. Second, they aim for application of the rules by both virtuous and nonvirtuous persons without resort to moral wisdom. Very simply, a virtuous person is one who consistently strives to go "above and beyond" what is merely required. So while virtue ethicists admit that virtues (and vices) tend to have corresponding rules, they resist prioritizing these rules into a code of ethics. As Hursthouse (1999) states, "Any codification ranking the virtues, like any codification ranking the rules, is bound to come up against cases where we will want to change the rankings" (p. 57). This does not imply that generalizations are not possible, only that they are at best a combination of specificity and flexibility. Virtue ethics primarily relies on the "moral wisdom" of the virtuous person (see Box 1.4).

The emphasis on virtue as a character trait has two important implications for professional ethics. The first implication is that we must seek to understand the person in the ethical decision-making process (Mattison, 2000; Pipes, Holstein, & Aguirre, 2005). The ACA (2005) *Code of Ethics* alludes to this when the Preamble states, "Inherently held values that guide our behaviors or exceed prescribed behaviors are *deeply ingrained in the counselor and developed out of personal dedication*, rather than the mandatory requirement of an external organization" (p. 3, emphasis added). This principle has two corollaries. First, it is important to know oneself as an ethical agent. Part of this self-knowledge is developmental (Sherwood, 2003). Thoughtful and experienced practitioners will not only embody more coherence in their ethical decisions, they will also tend to see ethical conundrums with greater complexity than novices. Scheffler (1992) agrees that morality is a developmental task in which people grow in "moral sensitivity, perception, and imagination" (p. 43). It is our hope that school professionals will return to this book at many points over their career and glean something different from it each time. Second, we must strive to provide an ethical education for our clients. Most of the predicaments we face as professionals are

Box 1.4 The Virtuous School Social Worker

Jane Buri was born on March 12, 1924. She grew up in St. Louis during the Great Depression. She was an only child and her father owned a small cigar shop. She got her first position as a school social worker in 1954, earning just $3,800 per year. Like many survivors of the Great Depression, she was frugal with her money—clipping coupons, wearing costume jewelry, doing her own hair, driving an old Chevy, and sharing a house with her parents. She wasn't miserly though; she donated regularly to Catholic charities, took trips to California and Europe, and splurged on a baby grand piano. Her sister-in-law explained why she never dated or had a boyfriend: "I think she was so into her school [social] work. Just the people in themselves were enough for her" (Hunn, 2009, p. 2). She co-authored an article on school truancy in 1962 (Earl-Brooks, Buri, Byrne, & Hudson, 1962). In the late 1960s, she was one of the founding members of the Midwest School Social Work Council. In the early 1970s, she became the supervisor of school social work in St. Louis Public Schools overseeing a department of 70 workers. When she was awarded the Missouri School Social Worker of the Year in 1989, the minutes remarked that "this award is long overdue, chiefly because she refused to accept the award until 1989" (School SW of the Year 1989, p. 5). She retired at the end of that school year in 1990 but kept in touch with her former colleagues. Sidney Edwards Cole recalled seeing her at a retirement party in 2007 and described Jane as follows: "She always had a smile and wanted to know how you were doing and wishing you well. She was always very helpful and resourceful." Jane died March 18, 2008, leaving $1.3 million to beloved friends, relatives, and charities (Hunn, 2009). While everyone was surprised at the amount, no one was surprised by her generosity.

Discussion Questions

1. Have you ever known a secret "millionaire next door" like Jane Buri?
2. What is your reaction to people who are so frugal with their money?

3. What is your reaction to people who are so generous with their money?
4. Who do you consider to be your role model in your profession?
5. What kinds of issues would you consult them about?

shared predicaments. We do our clients a disservice if we think only of ourselves as the ethical agent. Clients can and should be encouraged to grapple with the ethical conundrums of their lives. This facilitates their growth into persons of virtue (Chamiec-Case, 2010). The second implication is that we must understand the importance of the mentoring relationship in the process (Constable, 1989). As Hursthouse (1999) observes, most of us faced by a difficult ethical issue naturally turn to someone we respect for advice. Sometimes this mentor will be someone within our chosen specialization; sometimes the consultant will be someone in a related field of practice. There are pros and cons in both relationships, and we will discuss this in more detail in Chapter 3. We hope that this book will be helpful for both the consultant and the consultee in the ethical decision-making process.

Ethics of Care

The ethics of care is sometimes seen as a variation of virtue ethics, but its proponents view it as a distinct ethical theory. It does have similarities with virtue ethics, such as its view of caring as both an action as well as a disposition. Caring is an action because it involves responding to the needs of others. It is a disposition because our interpersonal actions should exemplify the values of sensitivity, trust, and reciprocity. Held (2006) identifies five major features of the ethics of care. First, its primary focus is the need for responsiveness toward those for whom we have responsibility. Thus, our relationships with intimate others make compelling demands on us that may not extend to everyone. Second, the ethics of care embraces emotion over neutrality. Reflecting on feelings through empathy actually enables the ethical agent to clearly see the best ethical decision. As Held states, "Central to caring are close attention to the feelings, needs, desires, and thoughts of those cared for, and a skill in understanding a situation from that person's point of view" (p. 544). Third, it respects the possibility—even the probability—that specific others have ethical claims on our choices that abstract universal

---

principles cannot require. Our friends and family, for example, have a right to expect more from us than total strangers. Universal principles may work for justice systems, but they are often ineffective for family systems. Fourth, it rejects the traditional divisions between the public and private spheres of life. Domestic violence and child abuse do not occur in a societal vacuum; they are given tacit permission by a society that is indifferent to inequity and sees violence as a legitimate way to resolve conflict. Finally, the ethics of care primarily conceives of persons as relational. The goal of human development is not independence, but interdependence. Our relationships define our identities—we are partners, parents, siblings, and neighbors. Our ethical predicaments are encumbered by and embedded in our family and social relationships (Keller, 1997). We cannot make an ethical decision without a definite and direct effect on our relationships.

The ethics of care also has two important consequences for ethical decision making. First and foremost, it serves to remind us that it is relationships that matter. The NASW (2008) *Code of Ethics* states one of its core values this way:

> Social workers understand that relationships between and among people are an important vehicle for change. Social workers engage people as partners in the helping process. Social workers seek to strengthen relationships among people in a purposeful effort to promote, restore, maintain, and enhance the well-being of individuals, families, social groups, organizations, and communities. (p. 8)

We may have strong disagreements with our clients about which ethical decision is the correct choice, but if they feel cared for during the process it is likely that our relationship will not be disrupted due to the dispute (Constable, 1989). Each ethical quandary provides us with an opportunity to deepen our relationships—with administrators, colleagues, parents, students, and teachers—because it means sharing our deeply felt values and our inner conflicts. Each predicament allows us to share who we are and facilitate the self-disclosure of others. Second, it beckons us to pay attention to our feelings during the process. We may find ourselves angry, confused, disgusted, saddened, or worried about our clients. Rather than reject certain feelings because they are "biased," "negative" or "inappropriate," we must embrace these emotions as informative on a gut level. The source of our countertransferential reactions may be our own past, the client's influence, or some combination,

Ethical Decision Making in School Mental Health

but we will never know the source unless we are willing to reflect on it (Staral, 2003). Once we have sorted out the message that our feelings convey, we can sensitively share them with the client (Raines, 1996a). Generally, this has the effect of deepening the emotional bond between practitioners and their clients.

Use of Self

Abramson (1996) and Mattison (2000) have emphasized the importance of self-awareness in ethical decision making. This self-awareness includes countertransference issues (Jennings et al., 2005). We are mindful that the term *countertransference* has often been used negatively to refer only to those issues originating in the therapist (e.g., racial prejudice) that impede treatment. We are using the term in the broader totalist sense to include those issues which are commonly shared responses to the client (e.g., protectiveness of the client's vulnerability). In other words, countertransference is both an unavoidable and potentially useful aspect of therapeutic work (Brandell, 1992; Dubé & Normandin, 2007; Wishnie, 2005). Here we build on Racker's (1968) seminal work, in which he differentiates between concordant and complementary identifications. *Concordant* identifications occur when we identify primarily with the client. *Complementary* identifications occur when we identify with significant others in the client's environment (Tansey & Burke, 1995; Ursano, Sonnenberg, & Lazar, 2004). Either type of identification can lead to disjunctive "acting out" by therapists unless they are able to analyze their own emotional response and use it productively to understand their clients (Kraft, 1986; Palombo & Berenberg, 1997; Towbin & Campbell, 1995). As Boland-Prom and Anderson (2005) state, it is vital for ethical practitioners to recognize "countertransference based distortions in professional perspective" (p. 498).

Pope and Vetter (2003) found that one of the most troubling ethical issues has been blurred, dual, or conflictual relationships with clients or their significant others (e.g., parents). In their survey of psychologists, it ranked a close second behind confidentiality issues. About a fifteen years ago, Raines (1996a) wrote a seminal article on how practitioners could categorize their reactions to clients along two dimensions and communicate them in a helpful way (Bridges, 2001; Satterly, 2006; Strean, 2001). This model has since received partial empirical support from factor analytic research (Friedman & Gelso, 2000). It has also been adapted by Hepworth and colleagues (2006) for their widely used textbook on direct practice. The first dimension is the level of involvement. Raines suggested that practitioners may be overinvolved or underinvolved with the client. The second dimension was the therapist's attitude. Raines posited that clinicians could hold positive or negative feelings toward the client. Treating these as orthogonal dimensions allows therapists to create typology of responses (see Fig. 1.2). As Bridges (2001) observes, such communication is not without risk:

> The fiduciary principle must be honored and informs therapists' decisions regarding disclosure. Therapists guard against excessive disclosures, disclosures that shift the focus away from the patient, or disclosures that might harm monitoring the effect of such interventions on the patient and the treatment process. (p. 22)

We suggest that a practitioner's emotional response to an ethical quandary can be useful information in the process of managing the problem. After describing each of these countertransferential positions, we offer a sample set of self-questions for the clinician to consider. For complementary sets of self-questions, see Table 1 in Nagy (2005) or Table 1 in Strom-Gottfried (2007).

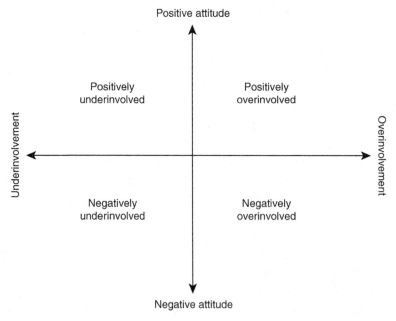

FIGURE 1.2 Typology of Practitioner Responses.

Negative Underinvolvement

Sometimes the clinician feels underinvolved about the quandary. Detert, Treviño, and Sweitzer (2008) refer to this as a form of moral disengagement. Their research found that trait cynicism and chance locus of control contributed significantly to moral disengagement. *Trait cynicism* is the tendency toward disillusionment and distrust of other people. People with this characteristic are more likely to displace their ethical responsibilities onto others whom they believe are deserving of their fate. While locus of control has traditionally been bifurcated into either internal (self-governing) or external (other-governing) loci, Levenson (1981) found that the external locus of control could be further divided into a chance locus or power locus. Whereas believers in the latter hold that powerful others (e.g., God) are really in charge, believers in the *chance locus of control* deem that luck is in control or that one's fate is randomly determined. People with this locus of control separate themselves from ethical issues because they do not think any consequences can be predicted. It makes no difference what the ethical agent might do because the result cannot be foreseen.

While we doubt that many school mental health practitioners would possess these traits as stable characteristics, they can occur by emotional contagion. Sometimes our clients are so depressed or live in such chaotic circumstances that we begin to wonder if any issue is worth the effort. Recognizing these as ego-dystonic states is the first step toward realizing that we have been infected by their disillusionment and their turmoil. Our momentary detachment about the hopelessness of resolving an ethical predicament is a clue to what our clients are feeling and a way to connect with them on a deep emotional level. If we do not reflect these feelings back to the client, there is a strong possibility that they will disown them after having projected them onto us.

Self-Questions About Negative Underinvolvement

1. Do I have a lack of interest in this student's ethical issue?
2. Do I feel hopeless about the outcome of this student's predicament?
3. Do I feel like this conundrum is so convoluted that I cannot make sense of the chaos?
4. Would I rather let someone else in the building handle this situation?
5. Do I find myself changing the topic when this student brings up this issue?

Positive Underinvolvement

While this may initially sound like an oxymoronic category, there are times when practitioners are overly confident in a client's ability to resolve an ethical quandary independently without sufficient assistance by the ethical agent. As with the previous situation, the practitioner may be reluctant to engage the moral issue, but for a different set of reasons. Perhaps it is because the client has heretofore been making excellent progress and the professional does not anticipate a momentary setback. Perhaps it is because the client has been primarily sharing his strengths and is reluctant to share his weaknesses and the professional inadvertently "buys in" to the client's false self-esteem. Clinicians may even rationalize positive underinvolvement as respect for the client's self-determination. As Hepworth and colleagues (2006) state:

> While generally focusing on client strengths and having a positive attitude toward clients is consistent with social work values, the possibility of under-involvement alerts us to ways that attention to strengths could be exaggerated and not completely helpful in some circumstances. (p. 545)

Self-Questions About Positive Underinvolvement

1. Am I overestimating the student's ability to handle this problem on his own?
2. Does the student's physical maturity mislead me about her moral maturity?
3. Does the student's age give me the wrong impression about his developmental stage?
4. Am I asking questions that the student feels incapable of answering?
5. Am I giving advice that this student feels incapable of following?

Positive Overinvolvement

Positive overinvolvement probably occurs more often than underinvolvement due to the desire of most practitioners to understand and help their clients (Amundson, Daya, & Gill, 2000; Steadman, 2004). Sometimes this overinvolvement takes the extreme form of boundary violations of either a sexual or nonsexual nature (Gabbard, 2006; Knapp & VandeCreek, 2006;

Reamer, 2003), but these are the external symptoms of an internal process that starts long before. This process often begins as concordant identification with what the client is experiencing. Because all of our clients are children and adolescents and all pupil services professionals have been students themselves, it is natural for us to put ourselves into their shoes. Chances are that we, too, experienced similar ethical predicaments. Being older and wiser than our students, this sympathy often leads to paternalism (Clark & Croney, 2006). Left unchecked, this paternalism can lead us to take ownership of the problem, subtly coercing the student to handle her quandary the way we think it should be resolved. Clinicians may even rationalize positive overinvolvement as commitment to the client or acting *in loco parentis*. An anecdote may illustrate this temptation (see Box 1.5).

This type of professional influence can take mild forms of persuasion, interpersonal leverage, and inducements (Szmukler & Appelbaum, 2008). Let's describe each of these tactics of influence. *Persuasion* can use either logic or emotion to influence the client. This is the least problematic form of pressure because the client can use logic or emotion to present her own perspective. Furthermore, this kind of give-and-take discussion or debate can lead to a compromise. *Interpersonal leverage* is stronger and often more subtle. The practitioner may look disappointed at the client's choice, shake her head, and wonder aloud where things will go from here. If the relationship has been helpful, the client may feel compelled to change his mind in order to seek approval and maintain the relationship. *Inducements* are the most coercive of these tactics because they involve conditions: if the client complies, then the professional will do something. This something can include mystery motivators, extra time, food, points, or even a special outing.

Self-Questions About Positive Overinvolvement

1. Am I taking too much ownership of this problem because I care about this student?
2. Am I thinking about the predicament outside of my normal work hours?
3. Do I overidentify with this student because of our similarities (backgrounds, faith, race)?
4. Am I taking shortcuts to resolving this problem without fully exploring the options?
5. Do I think about seeing this student outside of school hours to help her even more?

Box 1.5 A Young Girl's Dilemma

When one of our daughters was in seventh grade, she informed us that one of her best friends was involved in drinking alcohol alone at home. Her friend's parents had been through a nasty divorce and her estranged father was constantly trying to manipulate the girl into taking his side. While the friend had revealed her tendency to get drunk, she also warned that if my daughter told anyone they would never be friends again. Needless to say, my daughter felt trapped; she wanted to help her friend and keep her secrets, but she couldn't do both at once. Fortunately, she sought advice from her father, who, knowing the value she placed on her friendship, only reflected that "sometimes friends tell." Even though I knew the girl's mother, I left the ultimate decision in my daughter's hands. She waited 24 hours, hoping that her friend would tell a grown-up, and then went tearfully to the school counselor to share her concerns. The counselor immediately contacted the friend's mother who was shocked, but relieved to know the truth. She told her daughter that the disclosure was a sign of true friendship and, by the weekend, the girls reconciled and spent an overnight together. Afterwards, it was discovered that her friend had also disclosed the problem to the school nurse, who agreed to keep the drinking confidential.

Discussion Questions

1. Which pupil services professional did the "right thing" in your opinion?
2. What factors may have influenced each one?
3. Which of the four countertransference positions did each professional exhibit?
4. Was there a collaborative way to handle this problem? How would you describe it?
5. Which of the four positions are you most likely to take in working with students?
6. What does this suggest about seeking clinical consultation around such issues?

Negative Overinvolvement

While most overinvolvement is probably of a positive valence, there are times when practitioners have a negative attitude toward a client. This often occurs due to complementary identification with other persons in the client's ecological niche. Perhaps the client is a bully and the counselor was once a victim. Perhaps the client is a braggart and the psychologist grew up with a relative who had similar tendencies. Perhaps the client is a delinquent and the social worker hates to see scoundrels get away with their misdeeds. Any of these situations can lead the professional to abuse her own power in order to "level the playing field" between such clients and those who have been harmed by their actions. In these situations, the clients often do not feel any ethical or moral compunction about their behavior. Their lack of scruples leads us to own the predicaments for them. Clinicians may even rationalize negative overinvolvement as respect for law and order in the school or society.

Here the tendency to coerce the client may take the stronger forms of threats and compulsion against the client's expressed wishes (Szmukler & Appelbaum, 2008). *Threats* are considered more coercive than inducements because they threaten to take something away from the client. As with inducements, threats can involve tangibles (treasured possession) or intangibles (free time). *Compulsions* are the most problematic influence tactic because it completely removes client choice. Unilateral decisions to call a student's parents or to remand placement into an interim alternative educational setting fall into this category. As Hepworth and colleagues (2006) clarify, "the use of power becomes personal and punishing rather than appropriate to the circumstances and safety of children" (p. 545). For a visual portrayal of the different levels of professional influence, see Figure 1.3.

Self-Questions About Negative Overinvolvement

1. Do I feel like this student does not care enough about this ethical issue?
2. Do I find myself being argumentative or competitive with this student?
3. Am I bothered by this student due to our differences (backgrounds, faith, race)?
4. Do I think about involving other authority figures (parents, police, or parole officer)?
5. Do I consider using some type of coercion to make this student do the right thing?

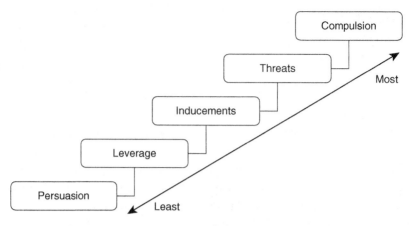

FIGURE 1.3 Hierarchy of Professional Influence.

Empathy and Positive Regard

We believe the solution to retaining the correct balance between these four positions involves both empathy and positive regard. *Empathy* can be defined as both a method of emotional understanding and the expression of that understanding. *Positive regard* can be defined as the consistent appraisal of others as deserving of our compassion and respect.

Empathy has been linked to ethical caregiving by a large number of authors (Coeckelbergh, 2007; Foltz, Kirby, & Paradise, 1989; Freedberg, 2009; Giesbrecht, 2008; Nadelson, 1993; Olsen, 1991). Empathy differs from sympathy because it not only involves feeling with the client but also involves a cognitive component to gain insight into those feelings (Black, 2004; Goldie, 1999; Raines, 1990). Empathy serves to balance overinvolvement and underinvolvement because it requires the ethical agent to reflect on mutually shared feelings in order to understand her own reactions to the client. These insights can then be tentatively communicated to the client to determine their accuracy (Hepworth et al., 2006; Raines, 1990; Vreeke & van der Mark, 2003). Empathy has two further benefits. First, the modeling of empathy fosters the students' own emotional development (Eisenberg, Wentzel, & Harris, 1998; Mussen & Eisenberg, 2001; Saarni, 2007). Second, children's use of empathy with peers has been demonstrated to improve prosocial and ethical behavior (Findlay, Girardi, & Coplan, 2006; Sprinkle, 2008; Thompson & Gullone, 2008; Volling, Kolak, & Kennedy, 2008). Moreover, this association between empathy and prosocial behavior in children has been found to apply cross-culturally (deKemp, Overbeek, deWied, Engels, & Scholte, 2007; McMahon, Wernsman, & Parnes, 2006; Sanchez-Queija, Olivia, & Parra, 2006; Sukemune, 1992).

A clinical vignette will provide an example of how empathy can be used to further the relationship:

> Just before 15-year-old Chet's regular appointment with his social worker, the practitioner received a phone call from his single mother, who explained that they had been in a fight the night before that had turned violent. Her boyfriend had come home and pushed Chet out of the house, knocking him over and causing him to scrape his knee. When Chet arrived, the practitioner asked how things were going at home. Chet ignored the social worker and tried to redirect the conversation, "How much money do you make at this job anyway?" The social worker smiled at his attempted distraction and replied, "Isn't it interesting that when I ask you a question you don't want to answer that you ask me a question I don't want to answer?" Chet smiled too and then guessed that his mother had called the practitioner, who confirmed his hunch. Chet and the social worker then talked about the conflict with his mother.

In the previous example, it would have been easy to miss the "parallel process" that occurred, but clients rarely change the topic without some connection to the previous subject. Following that conversational thread can be difficult at best. In this case, the social worker experienced a concordant identification and empathized with Chet's resistance while owning his own resistance at the same time. Chet then knew that the practitioner understood his hesitation and could talk about the issue at hand.

Positive regard is an essential quality of social-emotional nurturance that enables students to feel cared for (Doyle, 2003; Nabors & Prodente, 2002; Spear, 2002) and supported by school personnel (Metheny, McWhirter, & O'Neil, 2008). Respect given to students enables them to give respect to others in their environment. We often hear the complaint from teachers that youth are disrespectful (Friedman, 1995; Hastings & Bham, 2003), but this is simply a symptom of the lack of respect they feel from important others (Sava, 2002). Unfortunately, disrespect often creates a downward spiral where teachers become ever more punitive rather than using their feelings to increase understanding (Kawamura, Suzuki, & Iwai, 2004). Positive regard also facilitates relationship building with parents (Hoida, 2007; Moran & Diamond, 2008) and collaboration with other professionals in the school building (Darlington, Feeney, & Rixon, 2005). Combined with empathy, it serves to help pupil services professionals maintain a consistent attitude regardless of their feelings because it commits to a particular point of view. Positive regard is more of a decision than a sentimental feeling—it is cognitively controlled rather than subject to emotionality. It is this volitional aspect that allows professionals to treat students with dignity and respect. As the National Association of School Nurses (2002) *Code of Ethics* states, this should occur "regardless of race, gender, socio-economic status, culture, age, sexual orientation, disability or religion" (§1). In short, positive regard is a matter of will, not whim.

A clinical anecdote will illustrate how this principle of positive regard can be used to further the relationship.

> Eighteen-year-old Jill kept her sexual orientation in the closet. Sexually abused as a young girl by her drug-addicted mother's series of paramours, she was removed from her mother and put up for adoption. She was eventually adopted by an evangelical Christian family that truly loved her and enrolled her in a Christian school. Jill became a "born again" Christian and loved singing in the choir and reading her Bible, but she just could not shake her attraction to other girls. Her previous counselor had recommended she attend a public school, where she could quietly join a gay-lesbian support group without the knowledge of her adoptive parents. Jill respected her former therapist but felt that she would be "selling out" her faith if she attended a secular school. Her new counselor wondered whether Jill also expected him to "take sides" in this war, so he reflected that she was caught between two closets: one hiding her sexual orientation and the other hiding her Christian faith. Jill agreed. She knew her Christian friends probably would not understand her homosexuality and her gay friends probably would not understand her Christianity. She felt trapped and alone. The new counselor asked her if she knew that there was a denomination that was both evangelical Christian and welcoming to gays and lesbians. She was shocked that such a combination existed! He suggested that she look up the Metropolitan Community Church online and see what she thought. She jotted down the name and promised to do so, excited at the prospect that she could someday integrate these two important aspects of her identity.

The new counselor's positive regard for Jill's entire person meant that he could not ask her to choose between her religious faith and her

---

Ethical Decision Making in School Mental Health

sexual orientation. Just as Heisenberg had discovered that light was both a particle and a wave, it seemed that Jill was both a Christian and a lesbian. It did not make sense to force her into an either-or dilemma (Holmes, 2005). As Jill put it in her own words, she simply loved "Jesus and other girls." All of her experience (even with her former counselor), however, had told her that such a combination was anathema. Agosta (2003), however, has provided a list of 16 Christian gay-lesbian support groups within major denominations. Positive regard held out the possibility that both parts of her were acceptable, not just a contradiction in terms.

Professional Responsibilities

As mentioned earlier, an essential part of ethics is knowledge of one's professional responsibilities. Throughout this volume, we will refer to parts of the professional codes of ethics across all of the pupil services providers (see Box 2.3 in Chapter 2). This thematic approach, however, does not substitute for a thorough familiarity with your own professional code of ethics. We believe that professionals should maintain copies of their codes both at work and at home and be sure that they are working with the most current edition. In addition to an in-depth knowledge of your code, you should also be familiar with the federal and state laws governing your professional practice. In schools, the major federal laws include the Family Educational Rights and Privacy Act (FERPA), the Individuals with Disabilities Education Act (IDEA), the No Child Left Behind Act (NCLB), and the Rehabilitation Act. Practitioners should also remember that each state has specific laws and rules that govern educational services. We will have much more to say about the legal aspects of professional practice in Chapter 3.

Ethical Guidelines

- Be familiar with your profession's stated values and principles. The primary source is your profession's code of ethics.
- Be aware of where your personal and professional values may conflict.
- Know and use your sense of self in relation to each client.
- Be sensitive about the degree of professional influence you employ.
- Know your profession's code of ethics thoroughly.
- Be familiar with the federal and state laws that govern your profession's pupil services practice.

Exercises

1. Deontological Ethics

Use Box 1.2 as a group exercise. Ask each other if anyone would care to add unmentioned values/principles to the list. After pairs have discussed the questions, report out to the whole group. Apply the principles to a shared ethics problem. Discuss whether people are moved by the opinions of others.

2. Consequentialist Ethics

View part of the film *Lean on Me*. Have you ever met a charismatic figure like Principal Joe Clark? What is so appealing about this kind of person? What are the dangers of following such a charismatic leader? Groups can review the information in Box 1.3, and then debrief it together. Taking a strictly utilitarian point of view, what are the different teleological arguments that could be made on both sides of this issue?

3. Virtue Ethics

We used the example of Jane Buri as a virtuous person in Box 1.4. Chances are that you never heard of her before. Below is a list of 10 people commonly cited as examples of virtue. Which ones do you know best? Which ones do you not recognize? (We hope you will look them up on Wikipedia.) Which one would you choose as role model?

Jane Addams	Martin Luther King
Corazon Aquino	Aung San Suu Kyi
Cesar Chavez	Pope John Paul II
Dorothy Day	Mother Teresa
Mahatma Gandhi	Desmond Tutu

4. Ethics of Care

What do you consider your closest relationships? How does your closeness change your empathy for these persons? What expectations do these persons have of you that the general public does not share? How do you feel about these responsibilities? In your opinion, is caring more of an act or an attitude?

Ethical Decision Making in School Mental Health

5. Use of Self

Review the material in Box 1.5. Which professional did the right thing in your view? Was this based on Shakespeare's famous dictum that "all's well that ends well" or some other conclusion? How would you have handled the situation if you were the parent-consultant? Look at Figure 1.2. When have you experienced one of these positions? What are the implications of this for clinical consultation?

Internet Resources
Ethical Theory
> Deontological Ethics
> http://plato.stanford.edu/entries/ethics-deontological/
> Consequentialist Ethics
> http://plato.stanford.edu/entries/consequentialism/

Virtue Ethics

> Virtue Ethics–Current Debates
> http://science.jrank.org/pages/11566/Virtue-Ethics-Current-
>   Debates-about-Virtue-Ethics.html
> Virtue Ethics (not too) Simplified
> http://www.bu.edu/wcp/Papers/TEth/TEthCafa.htm
> VirtueEthics.Org
> http://www.virtueethics.org/
> Virtue Ethics–Stanford Encyclopedia of Philosophy
> http://plato.stanford.edu/entries/ethics-virtue/

Codes of Ethics

> American Counseling Association
> http://www.counseling.org/Resources/CodeOfEthics/TP/Home/
>   CT2.aspx
> American Psychological Association *Ethical Principles*
> http://www.apa.org/ethics
> American Nurses Association
> http://www.nursingworld.org/MainMenuCategories/
>   EthicsStandards/CodeofEthicsforNurses.aspx

American School Counselor Association *Ethical Standards*
http://www.schoolcounselor.org/content.asp?contentid=173
National Association of School Nurses
http://www.nasn.org/Default.aspx?tabid=512
National Association of School Psychologists *Principles for
Professional Ethics*
http://www.nasponline.org/standards/ProfessionalCond.pdf
National Association of Social Workers *Code of Ethics*
http://www.socialworkers.org/pubs/code/code.asp
School Social Work Association of America *Ethical Guidelines*
http://www.sswaa.org/index.asp?page=91

2

Analyzing the Predicament

Ethical predicaments are, by their very nature, challenging. They challenge our ethical predispositions, our understanding of our profession's code of ethics, our willingness to take on professional risk on behalf of our students, our ability to negotiate solutions with our students and other stakeholders, our understanding of the law and how it applies to minors, and our ability to implement different complex practice alternatives. Analyzing the quandary involves taking the time to ensure you fully understand the presenting problem and issues, identifying everyone who will be affected by your practice decision, and considering the ethical values and other professional responsibilities that are in conflict with each other.

Common sense dictates that we make better decisions when we are fully aware of all of the information that is relevant to the presenting problem. Many people have lamented in hindsight, "If I had only known that before, I would have made a different (and better) decision." By pausing to ensure you fully understand the presenting problem and issues when faced with an ethical quandary, you can help to avoid this lament in your professional practice.

This step (or a variation of it) is featured in the majority of ethical decision-making models reviewed for this book (Cottone & Claus, 2000; Mattison, 2000; McNamara, 2008; Nasser-McMillan & Post, 1998; Stone, 2005; Strom-Gottfried, 2008; Van Divner & Champ Morera, 2007). If you determine that your understanding is lacking, you should seek out more information to fill any gaps. This will likely often involve further conversations with your student but may include other sources as well. Not to do so may interfere with the successful management of the predicament, regardless of how diligent you are with the rest of the decision-making process.

Identify the Stakeholders

As pupil services professionals, our primary responsibility is to the student. There are, however, many other people that may be affected by your eventual professional practice decision to manage an ethical quandary. These people are important stakeholders whose rights and responsibilities should be considered (Cottone & Claus, 2000; Glosoff, 2002; Isaacs, 1999; Raines, 2009; Reamer, 2006; Van Divner & Champ Morera, 2007). Issacs (1999) and Glosoff (2002) note that school counselors need to consider their legal and ethical responsibilities to all stakeholders (i.e., students, parents, teachers, colleagues, other students, and administrators). Cottone and Claus (2000) cite a problem-solving approach that was used to teach psychologists to ask two questions about ethical predicaments. These questions included the following: Who needs to be considered in making the decision? What consideration is owed to whom, and why? This second question specifically implies that the mental health professional has responsibilities to more people than just the client. Reamer's (2006) ethical decision-making model recommends not only identifying who is likely to be affected by the decision but also the participants involved in each possible course of action. Van Divner and Champ Morera (2007) advise gathering input from those involved. This could aid in understanding the problem and issues discussed in the previous section. Raines (2009) defines stakeholders as concerned parties with a vested interest in the outcome and further clarifies that stakeholders should not be considered competing clients.

Consideration of other stakeholders' involvement in the management of an ethical quandary can be framed as part of our ethical responsibility to the student. Again, one of the six ethical principles of the NASW (2008) *Code of Ethics* recognizes the importance of human relationships:

> Social workers understand that relationships between and among people are an important vehicle for change. Social workers engage people as partners in the helping process. Social workers seek to strengthen relationships among people in a purposeful effort to promote, restore, maintain, and enhance the well-being of individuals, families, social groups, organizations, and communities. (p. 8)

Ethical Decision Making in School Mental Health

It is clear from this ethical principle that social workers' careful considerations extend far beyond the social worker–client relationship to all of the important individuals in the client's life. In the school setting, that includes all of the stakeholder groups discussed in the following sections.

Involvement of other stakeholders can enhance the delivery of pupil services. Reiner (2007) examined teachers' perceptions of school counselors. She notes the *ASCA National Model* of a developmental, comprehensive counseling program is believed to be dependent upon collaborative relationships with other stakeholders in the school-community. Conversely, refusal to cooperate with stakeholders can detract from pupil services delivery and, in extreme situations, harm the profession. Consider the following scenario described to one of the authors:

> A small school district hired a school social worker for the first time. The building principal wanted the school social worker to focus her services on families who were disengaged from the school. The students from these families were struggling in school and the district had hired the school social worker specifically to reach out to these families. The school social worker resisted this emphasis on her practice. The result was her contract was not renewed at the end of the school year and the school district chose not to hire another school social worker.

Since this was the building principal's only contact with a school social worker, he unfortunately generalized the school social worker's resistance to supervision to all school social workers. In addition to the school social worker losing her job, the school district's students are also adversely affected through lack of access to school social work services in the future.

Stakeholders have important responsibilities for the student (e.g., parenting, classroom instruction) just as pupil services professionals do (Prout, DeMartino, & Prout, 1999). These are discussed more in detail in each of the stakeholder sections below.

Parents, Guardians, and Families

First and foremost among other stakeholders are parents and other family members. Parents and legal guardians have a moral and legal responsibility to ensure the safety and welfare of their children (*Pierce v. Society of Sisters*, 1925). Glosoff (2002) states that while minor clients have the same ethical right to confidentiality as adults, parents have the legal right to control the

---

professional services their children receive and to be involved in planning those services. Prout, DeMartino, and Prout (1999) identify five rights and responsibilities of parents related to mental health services for their minor children:

1. To provide for the child's welfare
2. To access information related to the child's welfare
3. To seek treatment for the child
4. To be involved in decision making and goal setting for the child
5. To release confidential information about the child

Kocet (2005) notes the ACA (2005) *Code of Ethics* expects counselors to establish, to the extent appropriate, collaborative relationships with parents to best serve minor clients. Isaacs (1999) extends this responsibility to school counselors as well as community-based professional counselors.

State laws prohibit child neglect, which is generally defined as failure to provide adequate food, shelter, health care, clothing, or supervision to a dependent child. However, in order for parents to honor this responsibility, they must be aware of any possible threats to the child's welfare and safety. In addition, compulsory school attendance laws require parents to compel their school-aged children to attend school. State laws provide for a wide variety of consequences for truancy, some of which may be targeted to parents as well as students (Buser, 2009; Hatfield, 2009).

Whatever professional practice decision you choose to manage the ethical predicament, parents and other family members may have to deal with the repercussions, for better or worse. To the extent that we can appropriately involve parents and other family members, we can empower them to be partners in the helping process and improve the outcomes for our students. The ASCA (2004) *Ethical Standards* (§B) devote an entire section to the responsibilities of parents/guardians. It makes clear that school counselors are to honor both the rights and the responsibilities of families, including the establishment of a collaborative working relationship with parents. Similarly, the NASP (2000) *Principles for Professional Ethics* (§IIIC) include a subsection on parents, legal guardians, and appointed surrogates. School psychologists are expected to obtain informed consent from parents prior to the delivery of services (§IIIA4, §IIIC2) and are encouraged to promote the involvement of parents in designing services for their children (§IIIC3).

School Administrators

School administrators are another important category of stakeholder. Building principals are ultimately responsible for all of the activities in their respective schools. Like coaches of athletic teams, they may get more credit than they deserve when things go well, but they may also get more blame than they deserve when something bad happens. Not surprisingly, a review of articles related to the ethical decision making of building principals notes the rise in accountability over the past two decades, primarily related to two federal laws: the Individuals with Disabilities Education Improvement Act (IDEA) and No Child Left Behind (NCLB), the most recent version of the Elementary and Secondary Education Act (Fulenwider, 2007; Lashley, 2007; Strike, 2007).

Dechiara (2007) notes the topic of ethics in school administration is a relatively recent one in comparison to other professions, with the vast majority of the literature having been produced over the past 15–20 years. Lashway (2006) shares that the research literature is divided about how values impact educational leadership.

Denig and Quinn (2001) offer two complementary approaches to moral decision making for school administrators. The justice approach emphasizes universal moral principles of law and policy. The care approach stresses a concern for people. Regardless of which approach is used, better decisions are made when school administrators discuss their ethical decisions and moral perspectives with others.

Shapiro and Stefkovich (2005) go further and share two additional paradigms that school administrators may use to manage ethical predicaments: justice, critique, care, and the profession. Lashley (2007) cites their work in his article on an ethical framework to help building principals provide leadership in special education. Each of these four paradigms is guided by different considerations to help the administrator manage the ethical quandary. The justice paradigm considers laws, rights, and policies and their enforcement. If there are none that apply to the ethical predicament, the school administrator may consider if there should be. The critique paradigm addresses oppression into the decision-making process, considering who makes the applicable laws and policies, who benefits from them, and who has the power in the given situation. In addition, consideration is given to anyone who will be affected by the decision who has not yet had input. The care paradigm focuses on issues of loyalty and trust, including who will benefit, who may be harmed, and long-term impacts of the decision. The profession paradigm incorporates the considerations of the first three but also goes beyond to look at what the profession and community would expect in this situation (see Box 2.1). Furthermore, the diversity of the student body is recognized, as well as how the decision may impact them differentially.

Box 2.1 Counseling in a Fishbowl

Jamie was a first-year school counselor straight out of graduate school at the age of 24. Her first job was in a small rural school district in the Midwest. The school district served a large rural county made up of a few small towns. The district's only school building was in a town of 900 and served kids from kindergarten through 12th grade. Many of the staff had grown up in the county and most had lived there for at least a decade. The principal also served as the district superintendent. Jamie had an enthusiastic and engaging personality that quickly warmed the hearts of the area's long-term residents. She conducted whole classroom guidance programs with the elementary grades and provided career and college counseling for the secondary grades.

One day Jamie was asked to come into the nurse's office. The gym teacher had referred one of the children who complained that his legs hurt too much to participate in Physical Education. The district no longer had a school nurse and relied on the county health office for severe illnesses or injuries, but this case was different. The 5-year-old boy complained that his muscles hurt and he didn't want to put on his gym clothes. This nonsensical explanation raised the suspicions of the principal and was the reason he buzzed Jamie. Jamie bent down on her knees and asked how his muscles got hurt. The little boy began to cry and said that his Pa had whipped him for breaking eggs on the farm. Jamie asked if the boy could show the back of his legs to the principal. The boy bent over and dropped his pants to reveal several raw lash marks across his thighs. The principal told him to pull up his pants and asked Jamie to step outside.

The principal shook his head and asked Jamie if she knew whose kid that was. Jamie knew his last name, but she couldn't

---

Ethical Decision Making in School Mental Health

place the parents. "That's Louise's kid in there," the principal explained. Louise was the school secretary and had been the school secretary for 20 years. This little boy was the youngest of her seven children. Jamie looked shocked and said, "We have to report this, you know." The principal shook his head again and warned, "If we do that, the whole community will know and most of them will blame us." "What do you mean?" Jamie asked. "I mean," the principal continued, "that these are country folk—they believe that if you 'spare the rod' you'll spoil the child." Jamie was a Christian—United Methodist—and she recognized the allusion to the Old Testament book of Proverbs. She still didn't believe that the Bible condoned leaving lash marks on a 5-year-old child. She repeated her earlier stance: "But we're mandated reporters."

Questions for Discussion

1. Have you ever lived or worked in a small community where everyone knew everybody's business? What are the pros and cons of such communities?
2. Who are the stakeholders in this community? Think beyond the obvious ones. Who in the community (outside of the school) might be helpful in this situation?
3. What resources do the principal/superintendent and the counselor each have? Who has the most power in this situation?
4. What dangers exist for the counselor if she decides to go against her principal's wishes?
5. What would you do if you were in her shoes and faced with a similar situation?
6. Did the school counselor and the building principal have the right to ask the boy to drop his pants to examine him for injuries? What is the law in your state in this kind of situation?

The American Association of School Administrators (2007), the National Association of Secondary School Principals (2001), and the National Association of Elementary School Principals (1976) each have ethical statements that are almost identical. The standards address a variety of issues, most of which are also found in pupil services professions' ethical standards. These include concern for the well-being of students, integrity, due process and the law, conflict of interest, research, and continuing professional development. The AASA (2007) *Code of Ethics*, the most recently revised of the three, adds two additional statements related to accountability and commitment to serving others.

Teachers and Other Educators

Teachers and other educators are also important stakeholders. As pupil services professionals, our contact with students is minimal compared to the instructional time students spend in the classroom with teachers. The primary goal of our work as school-based, mental health professionals is to support the social, emotional, and behavioral needs of students so they can function better in the classroom and other educational settings. The outcomes we achieve with students directly affect their ability to perform in the classroom.

Reiner (2007) found that teachers are powerful stakeholders for school counselors, because they can significantly affect the impact of the school counseling program. She recommends school counselors do more to seek collaborative working relationships with teachers. Both the NASW (2008) *Code of Ethics* (§2.03) and the NASN (2002) *Code of Ethics* (§1) speak to interdisciplinary collaboration.

Kaigler (1997) found the primary factors that affected the ethical decision making of teachers were the teachers' moral development, situational factors, and individual factors. After providing continuing education to experienced teachers, Broidy and Jones (1998) concluded that teachers draw on four different kinds of moral authority to help make ethical decisions in their daily work: theological, philosophical and ideological, community based, and institutional (i.e., school district policies). Conflicts occurred when the teachers perceived competing courses of action indicated by two or more of these sources of moral authority.

Tirri (1999) cites a survey in which teachers reported they did not feel adequately prepared to deal with classroom-based ethical predicaments. Broidy and Jones (1998) found that many experienced teachers required

Ethical Decision Making in School Mental Health

specific direction to perceive any ethical aspects to a variety of classroom-based ethical predicaments. Kidder and Born (1998) discuss the struggle of classroom teachers to make ethical choices, where all of the alternatives are "right." Significantly, they counsel against "either-or" thinking and stress how generating additional, possible solutions to the quandary may bring about better resolution (see Box 2.2).

Box 2.2 Christine's Dilemma

In the fall of 2001, Christine Pelton had an ethical dilemma. She was a second-year biology teacher at Piper High School near Kansas City, Kansas. Christine was so concerned about classroom ethics, she asked both students and their parents to sign a contract. Rule seven read as follows: "Cheating and plagiarism will result in the failure of the assignment. It is expected that all work turned in is completely their own" (McKay, 2002). The problem began with a botany assignment called the "Leaf Project"; students were supposed to collect 20 different tree leaves and give oral and written reports. The assignment was worth 50% of the final grade. When she began to recognize complex and common phrases across papers, she began to suspect plagiarism. She scanned the students' papers and used the software at Turnitin.com, a Web-based plagiarism checker, to determine that 28 of her sophomore students had copied portions directly from the Internet. The school principal and district superintendent concurred with her conclusions. In accordance with the student handbook, she told the students that they would fail her course. The students, however, complained to their parents. They admitted that they had copied stuff from the Internet, but they denied that they had committed plagiarism. Three of the parents complained that their children didn't understand the definition of plagiarism (O'Reilly, 2002). When Christine wouldn't back down, the parents took the issue to the school board. At their December meeting, the school board met secretly in executive session and unilaterally decided to reduce the weight of the paper to 30% of the final grade, enabling the students to pass the course ("Cheating", 2002). Christine feels that the only honorable thing to do is to turn in her resignation.

Questions

1. Both Christine and the student handbook had consistent rules about plagiarism.
   a. Would you expect the average high school sophomore to understand this term?
   b. Would you expect the average high school sophomore to know how to correctly cite an Internet source?
2. What is the average weight of an assignment at the high school level? Was 50% too much emphasis on the completion of one project?
3. Meeting behind closed doors was a violation of Kansas' Open Meetings Act (Simpson, 2002). What recourse did Christine have to overturn their decision?
4. By the end of the school year, nine of Christine's 37 colleagues also resigned along with the principal and vice-principal (Jerome & Grout, 2002). Were there other ways to manage this ethical predicament?
5. Tenbusch (2002) describes seven strategies for preventing plagiarism (http://www2.scholastic.com/browse/article.jsp?id=462). What ideas can you offer?
6. What procedural rules would you advise for teachers who suspect plagiarism?
7. What punishment do you think is fair for first-time offending students?

The National Education Association's (1975) *Code of Ethics* includes two fundamental principles: commitment to the student and commitment to the profession. The 16 statements include many of the principles found in the pupil services professions' ethical standards (i.e., health and well-being of students, respect, nondiscrimination, conflict of interest, confidentiality, and integrity). However, it is noteworthy that all but one of these statements are written to describe what the educator should not do (e.g., not discriminate), rather than what the educator should aspire to in her professional teaching (e.g., protect the student from conditions that are harmful).

We would like to add a distinction between primary (K–5) and secondary teachers (6–12). In our professional experience, primary teachers generally know and interact with their students much more than secondary teachers do. Effective intervention for primary students, then, is usually improved by considering the importance of the teacher–student relationship. Secondary students are more likely to be known and interact with teachers who serve as extracurricular trainers (e.g., athletic coaches; band, choir, or drama directors). At this age, it is helpful to empower the student to choose which teacher should be part of the decision-making process.

Other Pupil Services Professionals

If other pupil services professionals are working with the student, they are stakeholders as well. Unlike the previous stakeholders, they are more likely to understand and identify the ethical quandary, because of their own professional training, their professional practice consistent with a professional code of ethics, and their first-hand knowledge of the student. Box 2.3 cross-references the primary ethical standards of the four pupil services professions. It is clear from this summary that the four professions have a great deal in common in how they guide the practice of their respective professions (e.g., advocacy, privacy and confidentiality, professional competence).

Box 2.3 Pupil Services Professions Ethical Standards Cross-Reference

Ethical Values, Priorities, or Principles	School Counselors	School Nurses	School Psychologists	School Social Workers
Primary obligation to student	A1, A2g	ANA 2.1	IVA1	1.01
Advocacy	Preamble	#12, ANA 8.1	I, IVA	EP #2
Equitable access to educational opportunities	Preamble	ANA 8.1		EP #2
Diversity and nondiscrimination	Preamble, E2	NASN 1, ANA 8.1	IIIA2, D3	EP #2, 4.02

Social justice and change	Preamble, E2c	ANA 8.2, 9.4	IIID2; IVB5	EP #2
Service		ANA 8.2		EP #1
Dignity and worth of the person	Preamble	NASN 1, #12: ANA 1.1, 1.3, 5.1, 5.3, 8.2	I; IIIA1, B1	EP #3
Importance of human relationships		ANA 5.3		EP #4
Integrity	Preamble	ANA 5.4, 9.3		EP #6
Nonmaleficence, i.e., "Do no harm"			I	
Moral virtues and values		ANA 6.1		

Ethical Responsibilities to Clients

Privacy and confidentiality	Preamble, A2	#12, ANA 3.1, 3.2	IIIA9, 11	1.07
Self-determination, direction, and development	Preamble	ANA 1.4		1.02
Informed consent/ assent	A2		IIIA4, B2	1.03
Respect for values	A1	ANA 1.2, 5.3, 6.1		EP #3
Knowledgeable of laws, regulations, and policies	A1; A2e, f	NASN 2	IIID5, E5; IVB1-2, D5	
Cultural competence	E2		IIIA3	1.05
Conflicts of interest/dual relationships	A4, F1f	ANA 2.1	IIA5; IIIA3, 5-7; D1	1.06

Clients who lack decision-making capacity		ANA 2.3, 5.3		1.14
Interruption of services				1.15
Termination of services				1.16
Group work	A6			1.07f, g
Student records	A8, A2f		IVE	1.07l, m, n; 1.08; 3.04
Evaluation and assessment	A9		IVC	
Student peer support program	A11			
Technology	A10		IVE	
Counseling plans	A3			
Harassment/sexual relationships		#12	IIIA6	1.09–1.12
Interventions			IVC	

Ethical Responsibilities to Parents and Families

Parents rights and responsibilities	B1	1	IIIC	
Parents and confidentiality	B2		IIIC	

Ethical Responsibilities to Professional Colleagues

Sharing information with other professionals	C2	ANA 3.2	IIIA10	
Respect	C1	ANA 1.5, 3.2	IIIE1, 2	2.01
Confidentiality		NASN 1, ANA 3.2	IIIA10	2.02
Interdisciplinary collaboration	Preamble	ANA 1.5, 2.3	IIIE4	2.03

Disputes involving colleagues		ANA 1.5	IIIA4	2.04
Consultation	A2b, A4a	ANA 1.5, 5.2	IIA1, B1	2.05
Referral for services	A5	ANA 5.2	IIIE4-6	2.06
Harassment/sexual relationships			IIIA6	2.07–2.08

Ethical Responsibilities to Others

Communicable disease	A2c			
Duty to warn	A2b, A7	ANA 3.2	IIIA9	1.07c
Ethical Responsibilities to School District/ Employers	D1	#12; ANA 6.2, 6.3	IIID	3.09
Ethical Responsibilities to Community/ Society	D2	ANA 7.1, 8.2	IIID	6.01–6.04

Ethical Responsibilities to Profession

Participation in professional association	F2a	ANA 9.2		5.01c
Share expertise with colleagues	F2b	ANA 7.1, 7.3	IIIF	5.01d
Mentor new professionals	F2c		IIIF	
Research		NASN 3; ANA 3.3, 7.1, 7.3	IVF	

Professionalism

Competence	E1	NASN 2, ANA 4.3, 5.2	I; IIA1-3	EP #6, 1.04, 4.01

Acceptance of responsibility for professional practice	E1a	ANA 4.1-4.3, 5.2	IIIA1	
Continuing education	E1c	ANA 5.2	IIA1, 4	EP #6
Ethical Violations				
Impairment of colleagues		#12; ANA 3.5, 3.6, 6.3	IIIE7	2.09
Incompetence of colleagues		ANA 3.5, 6.3	IIIA8, E7	2.10
Unethical conduct of colleagues	F1a, G	ANA 3.5	IIIE7	2.11

Notes: ASCA and NASP have developed stand-alone ethical standards separate from ACA and APA, respectively. Consequently, the ACA and APA ethical standards are not referenced in this cross-reference. The NASN Code of Ethics is designed to be used in conjunction with the ANA Code of Ethics for Nurses and the NASN/ANA Scope and Standards of Practice, Standard #12. The NASW Code of Ethics is the applicable ethical standard for school social workers (i.e., there is no code of ethics specific to school social work practice). In the School Social Workers column, "EP" stands for "ethical principle." There are six ethical principles in the NASW Code of Ethics, which form the foundation for the ethical standards.

Sources: American School Counselors Association (ASCA) Ethical Standards for School Counselors; National Association of School Nurses (NASN) Code of Ethics; NASN/ANA Scope and Standards of Practice (Standard #12); American Nurses Association (ANA) Code of Ethics for Nurses; National Association of School Psychologists (NASP) Principles for Professional Ethics; and National Association of Social Workers (NASW) Code of Ethics.

Used by permission from the Wisconsin Department of Public Instruction, 2010.

At the same time, members of these professions can learn from one another to improve professional services and better manage ethical predicaments that may arise. The ASCA (2004) *Ethical Standards* (§B) and the NASP (2000) *Principles for Professional Ethics* (§IIIC) include helpful guidelines for working with parents and families, while the NASW (2008) and NASN (2002) *Codes of Ethics* are silent in this area. The NASW (2008) *Code of Ethics* speaks to how to ethically manage interruptions in services to clients, a critical skill when working in schools because of the many vacations. The other associations have a lapse on this point. Only occasionally will other pupil services providers have different standards regarding a similar situation. Box 2.4 illustrates the conflicting guidance provided when determining whether to break confidentiality.

Box 2.4 Comparison of Four Codes of Ethics Regarding Breaking Confidentiality

ANA	NASP	ASCA	NASW
Duties of confidentiality, however, are not absolute and may need to be modified to *protect the patient, other innocent parties* and in circumstances of mandatory disclosure for public health reasons (§3.2, emphasis added).	Information is revealed only with the informed consent of the child, or the child's parent or legal guardian, except in those situations in which failure to release information would result in *clear danger to the child or others* (§III.A.9, emphasis added).	Keeps information confidential unless disclosure is required to prevent *clear and imminent danger to the student or others* or when legal requirements demand that confidential information be revealed (§A.2.b, emphasis added).	The general expectation that social workers will keep information confidential does not apply when disclosure is necessary to prevent *serious, foreseeable, and imminent harm to a client or other identifiable person* (§1.07(c), emphasis added).

ANA, American Nurses Association; ASCA, American School Counselors Association; NASP, National Association of School Psychologists; NASW, National Association of Social Workers.

Ethical Decision Making in School Mental Health

Another pupil services professional who has direct knowledge of the student and the ethical quandary is an ideal candidate to seek out for consultation. See Chapter 3 for more information on this step in the ethical decision-making process.

Professionals From Community-Based Systems

Many of the students that pupil services professionals work with may be involved in community-based systems, such as child welfare, juvenile justice, mental health, and so on. Service providers in other systems are also stakeholders. Ideally, parents have given permission or there is some statutory authorization that allows the school to communicate with these other systems in the best interests of the student. Occasionally, there may be a court order. Regardless, consideration should be given to how your professional management of the ethical predicament will impact these community-based professionals and their ability to meet the needs of the student.

Other Students and Members of the Community

Like all of us, students are social creatures. Indeed, for many adolescent students, social interaction is the single most important reason they report they attend school. As such, the problems they experience are often intimately involved with other students (e.g., a pregnancy or sexually transmitted infection). As school-based mental health professionals, there is an expectation that we will be concerned with the well-being of all of the students in the school, even if we do not have direct contact with them. Our student may be a victim or a perpetrator (e.g., a bully) and may be in a victim–perpetrator relationship with other students. Our student may also be involved in social relationships with people who are not members of the school community (e.g., an adult "peer"). These latter individuals are stakeholders, as well, but the pupil services professional's responsibility to them is generally much less than the stakeholders listed earlier. A notable exception to this would be if the student is threatening serious harm to someone he knows in the community. The importance of involving the student and other stakeholders in courses of action will be discussed more in Chapter 4.

Organizational Power

Different stakeholders can bring different types of pressure to bear on the school practitioner struggling to make the right decision about an ethical problem. Even small schoolchildren are aware of the power structure of a school (Buchanan-Barrow & Barrett, 1996). Outside consultants also quickly recognize that there is a power hierarchy in schools. As Prilleltensky, Peirson, and Nelson (1997) stated, "The school consists of various groups with vastly different amounts of power. Administrators, teachers, parents, staff, custodians, and students differ greatly in their degree of control over school life" (p. 168). Here we define power as the ability to influence the behavior of other people.

Blase (1990) clarified the type of power strategies school principals can employ with subordinate staff. Control tactics included coercive punishment and rewards regarding both tangible resources (equipment, curricular materials, space, and funds) and intangible resources (case load, assigned duties, rule flexibility, and professional support). These strategies had a host of negative effects on staff, including lower morale, constrained decision making, increased frustration, and limited resources. Eventually school staff members who are subjected to this kind of power and control tactics feel bitter, defeated, uncertain, and/or resigned. Erlen and Frost (1991) have delineated the effects of powerlessness on the capacity of nurses to make ethical decisions. The nurses felt angry, frustrated, and eventually exhausted. They concluded that "power is necessary to effectively fulfill one's role" (p. 404). Ultimately, Lee (1997) concludes that powerlessness only serves to maintain the status quo.

It is easy to feel powerless when working under a domineering despot, but not all sources of power come from having a position of influence. French and Raven (1968) described five different sources of power. The first base is *legitimate* power. This power comes from one's position within the organizational hierarchy. District superintendents, directors of special education, and building principals all possess legitimate power. The second base is *reward* power. This power comes from a person's ability to reward others with valued resources. As mentioned earlier, these resources can be tangible (e.g., a raise) or intangible (e.g., respect). The third base is *coercive* power. This power comes from a person's ability to punish others by removing valued assets (e.g., loss of a job or professional development opportunities). Both reward and coercive power often derive from legitimate power, but not always. The fourth base is *expert* power. This power comes from a person's specialized knowledge or skill. For instance, school psychologists are valued for their ability to administer and interpret psychometric tests. School counselors possess specialized knowledge about career and college entrance requirements. School social workers are sought out for their knowledge of community resources or family situations. School nurses are valued for their health care

Ethical Decision Making in School Mental Health

expertise. The fifth base is *referent* power. This power comes from one's attractive personality characteristics or interpersonal skills (e.g., conflict mediation). It is sometimes summarized as charisma, but it can be as simple as friendship. Referent power is a great equalizer because it does not depend on the level of education or years of experience. It potentially belongs to anyone in the school system. Benfari and colleagues (1986) added three more sources of power. Their sixth base is *information* power. This power comes from having access to information that is not public. With the advent of evidence-based practice, for example, the person who knows how to locate scientifically based interventions holds a distinct advantage (Raines, 2008). Their seventh base is *affiliation* power. This power comes from one's associations. For example, the school secretary often controls access to the school principal. She can determine who gets in, when they get in, and how long the appointment will last. Their eighth base is *group* power. This power comes from assembling a unit of people with like-minded interests. The NASW (2008) *Code* specifically allows social workers to participate in collective bargaining: "Social workers may engage in organized action, including the formation of and participation in labor unions, to improve services to clients and working conditions" (§3.10).

Buchanan and Badham (1999) make four caveats about these bases of power. First, they are dependent upon the perceptions of others. In the final analysis, all power is relational—if people believe you have power, then you possess power. Second, the same person may utilize different sources of power at different times. Indeed, the wise use of power requires that it be used with discretion. Third, the bases of power are interrelated. The use of coercion, for example, tends to deplete one's referent power. Finally, most of the bases can have either positive or negative effects on their recipients. The use of reward power, for example, is generally considered positive, but not if the recipient believes that they are already entitled to the reward (e.g., a cost-of-living raise or professional respect).

Benfari and associates (1986) observe that referent power has the most potential but is the least used. Covey (1989) identifies seven ways to increase one's effectiveness in an organization. The first method is to *be proactive*. Take the initiative to know your administrator by asking about his or her toughest ethical decisions. This will provide clues about the administrator's ranking of ethical principles. The ASCA (2004) *Code* recommends that a professional "establishes and maintains professional relationships with faculty, staff and administration to facilitate an optimum counseling program" (§C.1.a).

The second method is to *begin with the end in mind*. Every school (or district) develops its own mission statement. It is helpful for school-based practitioners to identify how their skill set contributes to the overall mission of the school. As the NASP (2000) *Principles* state, "School psychologists attempt to become integral members of the client service systems to which they are assigned. They establish clear roles for themselves within that system." (§IV.B.3). The third method is to *put first things first*. It is easy to get trapped in the tyranny of the urgent. For example, schools traditionally have spent too much time on student compliance and discipline without realizing that this is a product of good faculty–student relationships (Winett & Winkler, 1972). If practitioners can help schools focus on building good relationships with students and their families, compliance will come naturally. The fourth method is to *think win-win*. Referent power is built on reciprocal relationships. It helps to frame an ethical solution in terms of mutual benefit. For example, the NASP (2000) *Principles* state, "School psychologists attempt to resolve situations in which there are divided or conflicting interests in a manner that is mutually beneficial and protects the rights of all parties involved" (§III.A.4). The fifth method is to *seek first to understand, then to be understood*. Reflective listening is a rare skill because most people are thinking about how they want to reply while others are talking. By demonstrating an empathic understanding of the other person's viewpoint, the other person is freed to listen to a different point of view. The sixth method is to *synergistically work toward a solution*. It is important to value different perspectives, build on divergent strengths, and collaborate on the best solution to complex problems. For example, the ASCA (2004) *Ethical Standards* say a professional "collaborates with agencies, organizations and individuals in the community in the best interest of students" (§D.2.a). The final method is to "*sharpen the saw*." Engage in self-reflection and self-care. This may include activities, such as the creative arts, reading of a book, or physical exercise. Ethically, this ensures against professional impairment. As the NASW (2008) *Code* states,

> Social workers should not allow their own personal problems, psychosocial distress, legal problems, substance abuse, or mental health difficulties to interfere with their professional judgment and performance or to jeopardize the best interests of people for whom they have a professional responsibility. (§4.05)

Link (1991) posits that when practitioners are employed by host settings such as schools, "they become 'guests' of another house" (p. 278). Negative aspects of working as a mental health practitioner in schools include the following: less autonomy over the use of time, more involvement in student discipline and coercion, more susceptibility to school-related stress, supervision by an educational administrator, being perceived as aligned with the school, less involvement in the community, and less value placed on students' psychosocial needs. She found that practitioners used three types of accommodation in the host setting. First, *co-opted* practitioners were fully absorbed by the school system. They did not advocate their professional values, but chose to serve the status quo. They sacrificed their professional autonomy and acquiesced to assigned duties such as crisis intervention, student discipline, and truancy prevention. Second, *creative* practitioners held their professional values, such as advocacy for vulnerable students and mediation between the school and community resources. However, these professionals often felt marginalized and alienated unless they had regular support from like-minded professionals. Finally, *negotiated* practitioners tried to reach a compromise between their professional identity and the school's job description. They often sought consultation from fellow professionals but also collaborated with the educational staff. They tried to find "middle ground" between professional values and institutional values. In the end, school-based practitioners must conscientiously decide how much they can compromise their professional values in a host setting. As the APA (2002) *Ethical Principles* state,

> In applying the Ethics Code to their professional work, psychologists may consider other materials and guidelines that have been adopted or endorsed by scientific and professional psychological organizations and *the dictates of their own conscience*, as well as consult with others within the field. (p. 2, emphasis added)

Identifying the Primary Client

One of the causes of ethical problems is having multiple clients (Loewenberg, Dolgoff, & Harrington, 2000). The NASW (2008) *Code of Ethics* states that the term "'clients' is used inclusively to refer to individuals, families, groups, organizations, and communities" (p. 1). NASP makes a similar claim: "Throughout the *Principles for Professional Ethics*, it is assumed that, depending on the role and setting of the school psychologist, the client could include children, parents, teachers and other school personnel, other professionals, trainees, or supervisees" (p. 15). There is no doubt that any of these *can be* a client, but this inclusiveness only serves to muddy the ethical waters. The ASCA (2004) barely uses the term "client" at all—it is only found once in their *Ethical Standards*. The standards, however, do offer this statement as the very first duty:

> A. 1. The professional school counselor:
>   a. Has a primary obligation to the student, who is to be treated with respect as a unique individual.

Unfortunately, the indefinite article "a" in front of primary does not clarify who is owed "the" primary obligation.

Solutions

Hus (2001) concludes that school counselors must learn to split hairs: "Without clear-cut guidelines for determining who is actually the client, it seems appropriate to suggest that *ethically* the student is the client but that *legally* the parent is the client" (p. 17, emphasis in the original).

The NASW Commission on Education (1991) suggested that school-based professionals have ethical obligations to multiple clients in every situation. Kopels and Lindsey (2006), however, object that this complicated position creates an irresolvable problem for school-based practitioners and propose the following solution:

> When social workers view students, school administrators, teachers, parents, and the community equally as clients, then it becomes almost impossible to sort out who is entitled to information about a student. When school social workers do not view the student as their *only client*, then the worker is forced to juggle the competing interests of all these other stakeholders. (p. 75, emphasis added)

This certainly makes the situation clear cut, but we think that if the NASW Commission errs on the side of too much complexity, Kopels and Lindsey err on the side of too much simplicity.

We posit that there is a middle path between "everyone is a client" and "the student is the only client." Our solution is to view the student as the primary client and other stakeholders as secondary or even tertiary clients. There are three reasons for doing this. First and foremost, students are the most vulnerable group in the school. We talked about eight different bases of power earlier, and students hold none of these. One might argue that students could organize, but the authorities might call it rioting! Second, the essence of being a "client" is that the person knows that he or she has entered into a fiduciary relationship with a professional. This relationship may be voluntary or involuntary, but the student is aware that this special relationship exists. Loewenberg and associates (2000) make a helpful distinction between clients and three other types of participants in professional work. There are *supplicants*—those who request our help. Teachers often fit into this category when they refer a student for services, but they should not be considered clients because they have no intention of entering into a fiduciary relationship. (Remember that fiduciary relationships always involve some form of dependency.) There are *targets*—those whose behavior we hope to modify. Administrators often fit into this category, but they should not be considered clients because they usually hold the upper hand. There are *beneficiaries*—those who benefit from our work with the client. Parents and school systems often fit into this category, but they are not always considered clients. Finally, schools are the only social institution that is supposed to be child centered. When school-based practitioners offer their aid to administrators, teachers, colleagues, or parents, it is for instrumental reasons. For example, we often help parents to help their children. The teleological goal of such interactions is to help the students. Of all the professional associations, we think that NASP comes to the best solution. The NASP (2000) *Principles* support this conclusion in two places: "School psychologists typically serve multiple clients including children, parents, and systems. When the school psychologist is confronted with conflicts between client groups, *the primary client is considered to be the child*" (§IV.A.1, emphasis added) and "If conflicts of interest between clients are present, the school psychologist supports conclusions that are in the best interest of *the child*" (§IV.A.2, emphasis added).

Exceptions

There are at least two general exceptions to the view that the student is the primary client. First, there are *parent guidance* situations in which the parent is the client and the child is the unwitting target. Many behavioral management interventions fall into this category. The student is not the client because he has not entered into a fiduciary relationship with the practitioner. Second, there are *teacher consultations* in which the teacher is the temporary client and a particular child or the entire class of children are the unwitting targets. Again the students are not clients because they have not entered into a fiduciary relationship with the service provider. If either parent guidance or teacher consultation, however, serves as an adjunctive intervention to student-centered treatment, then the student remains the primary client and the parent or teacher is the secondary client. If both parent guidance and teacher consultation are adjunctive interventions, then the student is the primary client, the parent is the secondary client, and the teacher is the tertiary client because teacher consultation is the most time limited.

Identifying the Values in Conflict

The heart of an ethical quandary is the tension between different ethical values and other important responsibilities (e.g., the rights and responsibilities of parents and families or legal requirements), all of which we hold to be important. Use of an ethical decision-making model can help us to identify the relevant ethical values and other responsibilities and how they may be in conflict with each other. This step is critical prior to considering different, possible courses of action, which we will discuss in Chapter 4.

Schaffer, Cameron, and Tatley (2000) note how ethical problems arise when important health and safety considerations are in conflict with one or more of the following priorities: school district administrators' directives, school board policies, or budget and staffing decisions that adversely impact a school nurse's ability to provide appropriate nursing care. Parallels certainly apply to school counselors, school psychologists, and school social workers as well. Different loyalties can lead to ethical conflicts.

Common Competing Ethical Values

There are some fundamental ethical standards that are common to the pupil services professions (see Box 2.3). We understand privacy and confidentiality to be the cornerstone to an effective, helping relationship between the pupil services professional and the student. We hold the information shared by the student in confidence, unless the student gives permission to share it or there are compelling professional reasons to share information without consent (e.g., someone may be hurt if a disclosure is not made).

Self-determination is the student's right to determine personal courses of action. We understand that part of the student's growth toward adulthood is making choices about what she will (or will not) do. Next to families, schools play the most critical role in the development of autonomy prior to adulthood.

Ethical Decision Making in School Mental Health

We also have a fundamental interest in the health and well-being of our students. We want them to be healthy and successful in their school and personal lives. Our goal is for them to grow to be contributing members of our society, whatever they choose to do with their lives.

Other Important Responsibilities

As described earlier in the section on stakeholders, parents and families have a moral and legal responsibility to ensure the safety and well-being of their children (Stone, 2005). Fulfilling that responsibility requires knowledge of any threats to the child's safety or well-being. The default assumption in our society is that parents have the right to be informed of proposed services for their minor children and to approve (or not approve) those services. There are notable exceptions (e.g., medical emergencies during which the parent is not available and the health of the child is in immediate danger). Additionally, there are specific and narrow circumstances in which minors, often of a minimum age, may access services without parental knowledge or consent (e.g., medical treatment for a sexually transmitted infection). However, absent statutory exceptions, parents and guardians are assumed to have the right to be made aware of and give prior informed consent to services their children receive.

There are a myriad of state and federal laws that pupil services professionals should know and understand as part of their professional practice. These laws may require or prohibit specific actions in given situations. Conversely, they may allow (but not require) specific actions in particular circumstances. Related to the former, in some cases, noncompliance can ultimately result in legal prosecution and/or loss of professional licensure (e.g., failure to report suspected child maltreatment or unauthorized disclosure of private health care information).

Pupil services professionals typically sign a contract of employment with the school district or other educational agency by which they are employed. A standard expectation of the contract is that the educator will become knowledgeable of and comply with all of the school district's policies and procedures. By signing the contract, the educator accepts and agrees to this responsibility (Prout, DeMartino & Prout, 1999).

Identify the Relevant Values in Tension

It is important to identify the relevant values and other competing responsibilities in any given ethical predicament. Once that is done, the conflicts between these important considerations can be analyzed. Consider the following scenario:

> A 15-year-old student is seeing a school psychologist for counseling in the school and a community-based mental health professional for therapy. The student is engaged in high-risk behaviors, such as substance abuse, and is noncompliant with her parents. The mother has signed a release form for the school psychologist and therapist to exchange information and coordinate their work. However, the student objects to the disclosure and the therapist is honoring that objection by not communicating with the school psychologist. The school psychologist and the mother believe the student is manipulating the therapist with false claims of anxiety related to school attendance in order to avoid some classes (e.g., physical education) or school in general.

McNamara (2008) offers three questions to help identify the basis of the conflict:

1. *Are the interests of the parties conflicted?* In the scenario just described, the student does not want to attend school, while the school psychologist and mother want her in school. Presumably, the community-based therapist wants the student to attend school as well, but with accommodations for the student's presented anxiety about school attendance. McNamara then recommends two follow-up questions:
   - *How might each party's interests be affected by my action?* The focus of this ethical quandary is the student's poor school attendance, presumably for unjustifiable reasons, and how to manage it in light of her refusal to share information among the professionals working with her. The school psychologist should consider how each party will be affected by the student's continued truancy, as well as how each would be affected by a course of action that would work toward regular school attendance.
   - *What is my responsibility to each party?* While the school psychologist's primary responsibility is to the student, this does not necessarily mean that the ethical standards of privacy and self-determination will be given the most weight in this situation. Clearly, long-term absence from

school is not in the student's best interests. She risks not completing high school and endangers her academic future. The ethical standard of our interest in the student's health and well-being would likely carry more weight. Furthermore, the mother has a legal responsibility to compel her daughter to attend school. Similarly, the school psychologist's contractual relationship with the school district would expect her to work toward the student's regular school attendance. The school psychologist's responsibility to the community-based therapist, consistent with her primary responsibility to the student, is to help ensure the therapeutic relationship is working in the best interests of the student.

2. *Are there competing ethical standards?* There are several relevant considerations in this situation, including the student's right to confidentiality and self-determination. Clearly, the parent is actively and appropriately seeking to involve her daughter in services that are in the daughter's best interests. She wants to be a partner in the intervention, which is the ideal and her right. Assuming the school psychologist and mother are correct that the student is simply trying to avoid school with false claims of anxiety, the student is absent from school without a valid excuse (i.e., truant), which would violate both the law and the school district's policy. In this case, the student's rights to privacy and self-determination are in conflict with the parent's wishes, the law, and the school district policy that the student should attend school on a regular basis.

3. *Are the ethical standards unclear in this case?* If the relevant ethical standards and other important responsibilities are not clear, it is likely that more information still needs to be gathered to fully understand the predicament. Earlier in this chapter, we offered that in most cases the student would be the primary source of information. In this scenario, however, further discussions with the mother may be very helpful. The community-based therapist also likely has important information.

Ethical Orientation to Treatment

Many problems can be avoided if practitioners provide clients with an ethical orientation to treatment. The ASCA (2004) *Ethical Standards* state that the counselor "informs students of the purposes, goals, techniques and rules of procedure under which they may receive counseling *at or before the time when the counseling relationship is entered* (§A.2.a). The NASP (2000) *Principles* also state that "school psychologists inform children and other clients of the limits of confidentiality *at the outset of establishing a professional relationship*" (§III.A.11, emphasis added). The NASW (2008) *Code of Ethics* concurs, "Social workers should review with clients circumstances where confidential information may be requested and where disclosure of confidential information may be legally required. This discussion should occur *as soon as possible in the social worker–client relationship*" (§1.07e, emphasis added). Generally, the more mature the client, the more in-depth this orientation should be. With small children, it is best to follow the KISS rule: keep it short and simple. For example, it can be helpful to orient young children to treatment by telling them something similar to the following:

> There are two special rules in this office. The first rule is that everyone is safe. The second rule is that everything you tell me is just between us. Sometimes these rules don't get along and, when that happens, Rule #1 wins here. I would rather have everyone be safe than to keep a secret.

It helps to have students paraphrase this explanation back to the practitioner to ensure that their comprehension is adequate.

This kind of explanation has at least three advantages. First, it addresses school-aged children in language they can understand. Students are accustomed to rules. They know that there are rules for the classroom, rules for the lunchroom, and rules for games on the playground. This brief set of rules lets them know that there are also special rules that apply to the professional office. This is in accord with the NASW (2008) *Code of Ethics* when it states, "In instances when clients are not literate or have difficulty understanding the primary language used in the practice setting, social workers should take steps to ensure clients' comprehension" (§1.03b). The NASP (2000) *Principles* agree, "The explanation should take into account language and cultural differences, cognitive capabilities, developmental level, and age so that it may be understood by the child, parent, or guardian" (§III.A.3). It may be especially useful to recruit parents to help young children understand the concept of confidentiality (Krivda, 2005). The ASCA (2004) *Ethical Standards* also agree, "The meaning and limits of confidentiality are defined in developmentally appropriate terms to students" (§A.2.a). Second, it lets children know in simple language that the school-based practitioner has a clear set of priorities. Finally, if the occasion arises that the professional has to violate the student's confidentiality, the student can be reminded of this original orientation. It is also important to rehearse this orientation with young children on a regular basis (e.g., the beginning of each semester or after a holiday break). This is also in keeping with the NASW (2008) *Code*, "Social workers should review with clients circumstances where confidential information may be requested and where disclosure of confidential information may be legally required... *as needed throughout the course of the relationship*" (§1.07e, emphasis added).

Informed Consent

Schools have a long history of taking informed consent for granted. A common, but mistaken practice is for schools to use *passive consent*. For example, a school note may read that all children in the sixth grade will discuss puberty in science class unless parents write a note stating that they do not want their child to participate. Passive consent, however, is an oxymoron that places schools at risk for being sued if something goes wrong. The federal Protection of Pupil Rights Amendment requires school districts to allow children to opt out of any activity that would involve gathering information from students about sensitive topics, including "mental or psychological problems" (34 CFR Part 98). Furthermore, in light of the 1973 federal court case *Merriken v. Cressman*, it would be dangerous to assume that passive consent would ever be sufficient for the screening or assessment of mental health problems (Fisher, 2004; Jacob & Hartshorne, 2007).

Informed consent must possess three qualities: capacity, information, and voluntariness. *Capacity* is the ability to comprehend the information and appreciate the consequences of a decision. Capacity is always decision specific; in other words, it only applies to a specific choice offered at a specific time (Schacter, Kleinman, & Harvey, 2005). *Information* refers to the adequacy of one's knowledge. What must a decision-maker know? The Joint Commission on Accreditation of Healthcare Organizations (2007) provides the following list of six essential points to be covered:

- The nature of the proposed services, medications, interventions, or procedures

- Potential benefits, risks, or side effects, including potential problems that might occur during recuperation
- The likelihood of achieving goals
- Reasonable alternatives
- The relevant risks, benefits, and side effects related to alternatives, including the possible results of not receiving services
- When indicated, any limitations on the confidentiality of information learned from or about the patient (p. 7)

Voluntariness is the freedom from coercion, constraint, or compulsion. A person must be free to choose either to participate or not to participate without any negative repercussions such as the loss of previously earned privileges.

In the United States, it is assumed that adults have the capacity to consent unless proven otherwise. For children, however, the opposite is true. It is assumed that minors only have the capacity to consent under three circumstances: specific health issues, mature minors, and emancipated minors. *Specific health issues* that allow adolescents to legally authorize certain services are usually defined by state law. These concerns may include abortion, alcohol and drug treatment, contraception, medical emergencies, pregnancy, psychiatric problems, or sexually transmitted diseases. The reason that each of these is given a special dispensation under the law is that all of these issues share the unfortunate trait that some minors would rather forego treatment than disclose these problems to their parents (Kuther, 2003). As a result, state legislatures have enacted laws that allow minors to access treatment and services in these areas without parental consent or knowledge. Typically, this access is balanced with a requirement that the professional the minor is seeing for services report a situation in which the minor has been or may be harmed. *Mature minors* are adolescents who may be treated as if they were adults for a specific situation beyond what is provided by statute. Based on the 1967 federal case, *Smith v. Seibly*, the mature minor doctrine requires clinicians to carefully assess a student's capacity to understand the benefits and risks of a specific decision. Strom-Gottfried (2008) recommends that practitioners carefully document the criteria and circumstances around such consent. *Emancipated minors* include those adolescents who are financially independent, living independently of their parents, married, serving in the military, or already parents. They may not be considered adults in all situations (e.g., drinking age). These situations are typically determined by state law or by court decree.

Assent

The concept of assent is not synonymous with consent. It has been generally construed to refer to minors' ability to participate in treatment decisions. In other words, it is never assumed that they have complete autonomy, such as the right to refuse treatment. Assent simply means that practitioners should treat children as agentic human beings (Conroy & Harcourt, 2009). This should be done with developmental sensitivity. For example, in school-based counseling a child may be given some limited choices about the day, time, or modality used (e.g., individual or group counseling). An adolescent, however, may be given the larger choice of whether to receive treatment within or outside of the school. The primary benefit of obtaining assent is the engagement of the child in the therapeutic relationship. Assent should always be accompanied by parental permission when working with minor children.

Masty and Fisher (2008) recommend that pediatric clinicians consider the contextual "fit" when obtaining informed assent from children. They recommend that practitioners think about four aspects of the situation. First, they should assess the child's current intellectual capacity and his emotional readiness to contribute to treatment decisions. It should not be assumed that either the child's cognitive ability or emotional maturity is age appropriate. Determination should be based on an assessment of the individual student, not his same-age peers. Second, they should consider the parents' understanding of the child's needs. Parental anxiety often serves as a barrier to their discernment. Parents may be desperate for any help when previous attempts have failed and needlessly coerce the child's cooperation. Third, they should determine the family history of shared decision making. Some families do not seek out children's opinions, even on matters that directly affect them, and this leaves children ill prepared to make important decisions. While we would like to believe that all parents support their child's best interests, there are some parents who prefer to make the child the "identified patient" to avert attention from their own inadequacies (e.g., abuse, neglect, or marital discord). Finally, clinicians should maintain a balance between parental responsibility and the child's developmentally appropriate autonomy. Too much focus on parental responsibility may undermine the child's cooperation, and too much focus on the child may discount parental expertise.

Informed Dissent

Of course, it is always possible for students to give informed dissent to any of the options provided to them. This presents a significant problem for the service provider. Generally, the right to refuse treatment requires a higher level of capacity than the right to consent (Alkhatib, Regan, & Jackson, 2008). This is because the student is presumably in conflict with both parents (who are assumed to be acting in their child's best interests) and professionals (who are assumed to have greater expertise) (Stirrat & Gill, 2005). Disagreement alone, however, is an insufficient reason to override a student's veto of services. Professionals must also weigh the level of risk such a refusal entails for the student's welfare against the prognosis for success when treatment proceeds against the student's wishes (Pescosolido, Fettes, Martin, Monahan, & McLeod, 2007; Stewart & Tan, 2007). As Evans (2008) puts it, "A child who understands, agrees with, and consents to a treatment plan and its goals is more likely to collaborate, engage with therapy, and learn generalizable skills" (p. 183). Generally, pupil dissent is due to worries that the risks (e.g., embarrassment or loss of self-esteem) will outweigh the benefits (Wolthers, 2006). An in-depth discussion of risks and rewards as well as the willingness to compromise may overcome the adolescent's refusal. If the student insists on being an involuntary client, practitioners should work toward engagement prior to working on therapeutic goals.

There are three situations when an adolescent's wishes should be constrained. First, belligerent refusal may be a symptom of the problem such as in attention-deficit/hyperactivity disorder (ADHD), oppositional defiant disorder, or an eating disorder (Masty & Fisher, 2008; Schacter, Kleinman, & Harvey, 2005). Second, students' addictions (e.g., compulsion to gamble or abuse drugs and alcohol) may be stronger than their volitional control (Glaser & Cohen, 2005; Wagner & Austin, 2008). The best way to engage these students would be to use Prochaska and DiClemente's (2005) stages of change model. Finally, students who are clearly a danger to self or others should be compelled to seek treatment (see Box 2.5). School-based practitioners should be forewarned that there is no evidence for the effectiveness of "no-suicide" or "no-harm" contracts (Busch, Fawcett, & Jacobs, 2003; Edwards & Harries, 2007; Rudd, Mandrusiak, & Joiner, 2006). Clients will sign almost anything under duress but ultimately go their own way (McMyler & Pryjmachuk, 2008). Such agreements may actually place teens in greater danger because their caregivers may mistakenly believe that the danger is over and subsequently let down their guard.

Box 2.5 Minors and Informed Dissent

Danny Hauser, from Sleepy Eye, Minnesota, was 12 years old when his doctors diagnosed him with Hodgkin's lymphoma in January of 2009. His doctors told the family that the cancer was 90% curable and recommended a standard treatment of chemotherapy and radiation. Upon getting sick after the first round of chemotherapy in February, Danny and his parents balked and chose to fight the disease with herbal remedies and vitamins. Based on Danny's continuing symptoms, the doctors thought that the tumor had continued to grow in April. After his parents repeatedly refused chest X-rays to confirm the doctor's suspicions, the hospital finally reported them to child protective services. Accordingly, the county attorney filed petition alleging medical neglect and endangerment by Danny's parents. For his part, Danny claimed to be a medicine man in the Nemenhah Native American religion and argued that the government should not be able to interfere with his "spiritual path" (Lerner, 2009). The doctors, however, warned that Danny would probably die within 5 years without the recommended treatment. In May, the judge allowed Danny to remain in the custody of his parents as long as they cooperated with medical assessment and treatment. If the delay in treatment had already worsened his prognosis, however, the judge agreed to reconsider the decision (Wolfe & Lerner, 2009). A day after submitting to an X-ray, however, Danny and his mother disappeared. Doctors reported that the X-ray showed that the tumor had clearly worsened and had given his mother a referral to an oncologist. His father testified that he and his wife were originally going to propose a regimen of low-dose chemotherapy with adjunctive herbal treatments and appeal the decision if the court did not agree. He guessed that the mother may have left the country. The judge found the mother in contempt of court, ordered Danny to be placed in a foster home when found, and remanded treatment with a pediatric oncologist (Wolfe, 2009a). The judge also issued an arrest warrant upgrading the charge to a felony so that authorities in other states, the FBI, or Interpol could arrest and detain Danny's mother (Ross & Walsh, 2009). After a week on the run, Danny and his mother were spotted in southern California, presumably on their way to Mexico. When the mother learned of the arrest warrant and dangers in Mexico, she contacted a defense attorney and voluntarily returned home on a charter flight. She later explained that she fled because Danny had threatened to run away rather than comply with treatment (Crosby, Lonetree, Brown, & Ross, 2009; Gupta et al., 2009). Danny was immediately taken for a medical examination by child protective services where the doctors determined that the tumor had grown so much it was compressing his airway. The judge returned Danny to the custody of his parents on the strict condition that they comply with medical treatment. Alternative remedies could be used only as a complement, not a substitute, for routine treatment (Ross & Crosby, 2009). A month after resuming chemotherapy, X-rays confirmed that Danny's medical condition improved (Wolfe, 2009b). In September, Danny completed his chemotherapy and was scheduled to begin radiation treatment in October. His parents, however, credit the herbal remedies with weakening the tumor before the chemotherapy was restarted (Moore, 2009).

Questions

1. What do you think about Danny and his parents being forced to comply with medical care? Would it have been different if his life was not at stake?
2. The doctors gave Danny a 90% chance of recovery. What if his chances were only 50% or 10%? Would you then be more likely to support alternative remedies?
3. Danny was 13 years old by the time he showed up in court. At what age should adolescents be able to make their own medical decisions?
4. In two other cases, Noah Maxin and Abraham Cherrix,* judges allowed a doctor to oversee alternative remedies instead of chemotherapy (Gupta et al., 2009). Do you think this is fair compromise?

5. What if the recommended treatment had not worked? Would you advocate for nontraditional remedies or experimental treatments?

---

*Noah Maxin later died, but Abraham Cherrix is now a healthy adult.

Ethical Guidelines

- Check to make sure you have all the information you need about a particular situation before coming to any conclusions about it.
- Identify where your values may be in conflict with the client's values.
- Identify all the people that are likely to be affected by any ethical decision.
- Carefully consider parental rights and responsibilities when making a decision involving their child.
- Carefully consider how teachers and administrators can or should be involved in the ethical decision-making process. If other pupil services providers are involved with the child, treat them as ethical equals in the decision-making process and compare professional ethical guidance about the situation.
- Collaborate with community-based professionals using a two-way release of information so that school-based and community-based practitioners are not manipulated into working against each other.
- Analyze all stakeholders' power bases within the school system, especially their ability to coerce the pupil services provider. Improve your own referent power by monitoring your interpersonal effectiveness in the school system.
- Be clear about the identity of the primary client in each ethical predicament. Make a distinction between clients, supplicants, targets, and beneficiaries in each situation. Think about whose interests are in competition or conflict.

- Mull over the different ethical standards that seem to be in conflict. Make sure you understand them correctly. Reflect on why the ethical standards seem unclear.
- Contemplate collecting more information before making any decision. Identify which values/principles conflict in the current predicament. Prioritize which value/principle should be highest in the current situation.
- Consider the ethical orientation provided to students. Make sure they understood the initial information and were reminded at suitable intervals about possible ethical issues. Consider the student's ability regarding capacity, information, and voluntariness. Think about which level of consent or assent was appropriate to this situation.
- Determine whether the issue is primarily ethical, legal or both.

Exercises

1. Stakeholders

Review a recent ethical decision that was made at your school. Which of the stakeholders mentioned earlier were affected by the decision? Which ones were satisfied by the outcome? Which ones were dissatisfied with the outcome? What could have been done differently to bring more people "on board" with the decision?

2. Organizational Power

Think about an organization or school with which you are familiar. What power bases were evident? Who controlled each of these resources? What kind of power did you have in the situation? How could you have improved your influence?

3. Primary Client

Think of a situation in which you had allegiances to more than one client? How did you establish who was the primary client in the situation?

Ethical Decision Making in School Mental Health

How does the distinction between clients, supplicants, targets, and beneficiaries help clarify your ethical thinking?

4. Identifying the Values in Conflict

Review the ethical values in Box 1.2 in Chapter 1. Which ones did you identify in the aforementioned situation? How did you prioritize these values as you grappled with your predicament? In hindsight, did you order the values appropriately?

5. Ethical Orientation

How do you usually introduce ethical responsibilities to a child? Did you like the example used in the text or did you come up with a better one? (We hope you'll send it to us!) What kinds of choices do you allow children to have when using Assent? How does practice in a school setting delimit these choices?

Internet Resources

American Association of School Administrators' *Code of Ethics*
http://www.aasa.org/content.aspx?id=1390
Changing Minds
http://changingminds.org/
National Association of Education's *Code of Ethics*
http://www.nea.org/home/30442.htm
National Association of Elementary School Principals' *Statement of Ethics*
http://www.naesp.org/resources/1/Pdfs/code_of_ethics.pdf
National Association of Secondary School Principals' *Ethics for School Administrators*
http://www.principals.org/s_nassp/sec.asp?TrackID=&SID=1&D
ID=47104&CID=33&VID=2&RTID=0&CIDQS=&Taxonomy=
False&specialSearch=False
Power Defined
http://www.geocities.com/athens/forum/1650/htmlpower.html

Protection of Pupil Rights Amendment
http://www2.ed.gov/policy/gen/guid/fpco/ppra/index.html
Stages of Change Model
http://www.addictioninfo.org/articles/11/1/Stages-of-Change-
  Model/Page1.html

3

Seeking Consultation

We define consultation as the act of conferring with other professionals in order to deepen or broaden our understanding of the issues. In Barnett and Johnson's (2008a) 10 ethical decision-making steps, obtaining consultation occurs twice because they view it as an essential part of making a wise decision. Some Codes of Ethics explicitly expect this. For example, the Introduction to the NASP (2000) *Principles* states, "To obtain additional assistance in applying these principles to a particular setting, a school psychologist should consult with experienced school psychologists and seek advice from the National Association of School Psychologists or the state school psychology association." (p. 15). The ASCA (2005) *Ethical Standards* recommend consultation 10 times, especially when in doubt about an ethical issue. Stone (2008) concludes that "consultation, if at all possible, is one step that you should never skip" (p. 19). Finally, the Introduction of the NASW (2008) *Code of Ethics* specifies:

> For additional guidance social workers should consult the relevant literature on professional ethics and ethical decision making and seek appropriate consultation when faced with ethical dilemmas. This may involve consultation with an agency-based or social work organization's ethics committee, a regulatory body, knowledgeable colleagues, supervisors, or legal counsel. (p. 6)

It even appears as an NASW (2008) ethical standard: "Social workers should seek the advice and counsel of colleagues whenever such consultation is in the best interests of clients" (§2.05(a)). Here we will address ethical consultation, clinical consultation, and legal consultation.

Ethical Consultation

There are at least 10 reasons for professionals to seek out ethical consultation. Bowers and Pipes (2000) identified seven advantages. First, consultation can stimulate the practitioner's own thinking process so that he or she can generate new ideas or options about resolving the ethical predicament. Second, clinicians receive feedback about their current thinking and the quality of their ideas. Third, the consultant may generate new options that the professional would not normally consider. Fourth, the consultant may point out personal factors and conflicts that were not apparent to the practitioner. We will discuss this in more depth in the section "Clinical Consultation." Fifth, the consultation process may provide reassurance that the professional is making her best effort and even going the "extra mile" for the client. Sixth, the consultation process may provide the clinician with greater confidence in the outcome. For example, Duke's (2004) research found that professionals who used consultation reported higher levels of satisfaction, certainty, justification, and conceptualization of ethical predicaments. He concluded that the primary benefit of ethical consultation was one of emotional support. Seventh, consultation may reduce the professional's legal liability. Reamer (2005b) and Shaw and Lane (2008) concur that consultation provides a procedural standard of care to protect the practitioner from malpractice claims. Doverspike (2008) adds an eighth advantage when he observes that consultation is also one of the best ways to prevent ethical problems. For example, the consultant may advise the professional to initiate or modify his or her ethical orientation to treatment. Bowers and Pipes (2000) point out a ninth reason: some clinicians seek consultation after implementing a decision to determine how to mitigate unintended consequences. Koocher and Keith-Spiegel (2008), however, warn that after-the fact consultations can backfire if the consultant is subpoenaed in a malpractice suit. Finally, Dalen (2006) mentions the "meta-learning" effect. As practitioners work through an ethical conundrum with a consultant, they become more competent at managing future predicaments and discussing these with colleagues.

Walsh-Bowers, Rossiter, and Prilleltensky (1996) found that social workers were least likely to go to an administrative supervisor for ethical consultation because it often resulted in summative criticism on their performance reviews. They found it safest to consult with their immediate colleagues. Womontree (2004) found similar feelings among psychologists. Freud and Krug's (2002) experience on an ethics committee suggested that ethical decision making happened best in professional peer teams where different perspectives were valued. Tarvydas, Leahy, and Saunders (2004) found that counselors considered a professional association ethics committee to be the most helpful interpersonal source for resolving ethical predicaments. Pinnock and Crosthwaite (2005) recommended that the most difficult ethical predicaments require the assistance of a multidisciplinary team. We agree and recommend that school-based practitioners consider consultation with the other pupil services providers in their school district. An important caveat is that consultation is never a substitute for a thorough review of the appropriate professional codes of ethics (Bush, Grote, Johnson-Greene, & Macartney-Filgate, 2008; Rossiter, 1996).

There are several conditions under which ethical consultation occurs best. First, as Holland and Kilpatrick (1991) noted, it is best to have structured opportunities for ethical consultation. A regularly scheduled occasion to address ethical problems decreases professional isolation, and this is a significant problem among professionals working in host institutions such as schools. Second, as Bush and associates (2008) observe, ethical consultation occurs best in the context of an ongoing relationship. They posit that nothing "can replace the kind of very specific and free-ranging oral discussion you can have with a perceptive colleague who knows your practice well" (p. 327). Stone (2005) agrees that having routine consultations also helps to reduce the anxiety related to complex ethical predicaments. Third, the ideal consultant should be a mature colleague willing to nurture practitioners to reach their own ethical maturity. The professional associations often have an ethics committee or experienced board members willing to consult about ethical issues. Many school districts designate a "lead" practitioner who is considered the "first among equals." Lacking formal authority, they often possess considerable expertise and referent power. Disparities in formal power, however, can subvert the democratic nature of the consulting process and reduce the ability of both participants to converse as moral equals (Walsh-Bowers, Rossiter, & Prilleltensky, 1996).

An important caveat to the consultation process is that consultants can seldom give a definitive answer. This is because they are always working with limited information and only one person's perspective on the problem (Shaw & Lane, 2008). Furthermore, any advice proffered should be considered "nonbinding" (Reamer, 2006). This is due to the fact that consulting relationships are voluntary nonhierarchical associations, so the consultee remains free to accept or reject any suggestions proposed by the consultant (Jacob & Hartshorne, 2007). Freud and Krug (2002) report that clinicians may be disappointed to find out that there is more than one "right" answer:

> Our ethics call line committee is made up of experienced social work practitioners and educators, but we do not have superior ethical knowledge or wisdom. Our consultative position rests on the privilege of a group discussion regarding the interpretation of the code. The group's iterative process affords us an opportunity to take a second look at our first opinion. We usually surface not one, but several ethically justifiable courses of action. (p. 481)

Bush and colleagues (2008) also warn professionals that making "a reasonable attempt to consult others and think through the problem, may be a more realistic goal than expecting to always find a course of action that ultimately would be judged as 'correct' by a majority of one's colleagues" (p. 329). Dalen (2006) concludes that asking the right questions is a more important skill for ethics consultants than giving right answers. This accords with the ACA (2005) *Code of Ethics* when it states that the ultimate goal of "the consulting relationship is one in which consultee adaptability and growth toward self-direction are consistently encouraged and cultivated" (§D.2.c).

Seeking consultation has three ethical responsibilities for the consultee. First, they should protect the client's confidentiality during consultation. The APA (2002) *Ethical Principles* address the need for continued confidentiality as follows:

> When consulting with colleagues, (1) psychologists do not disclose confidential information that reasonably could lead to the identification of a client/patient, research participant, or other person or organization with whom they have a confidential relationship unless they have obtained the prior consent of the person or organization or the disclosure cannot be avoided, and (2) they disclose information only to the extent necessary to achieve the purposes of the consultation. (§4.06)

The NASW (2008) *Code of Ethics* agrees that "Social workers should not disclose identifying information when discussing clients with consultants unless the client has consented to disclosure of confidential information or there is a compelling need for such disclosure" (§1.07(q)) and "When consulting with colleagues about clients, social workers should disclose the least amount of information necessary to achieve the purposes of the consultation" (§2.05(c)). For example, Raines (2009) discusses the case of a single young male school social worker who was worried about counseling a sexually enticing adolescent girl. As the consultant, he never had to know the identity of the teen to provide ethical guidance. A second ethical responsibility of the consultee is to check the credentials of the consultant. According to the NASW (2008) *Code of Ethics*, "Social workers should keep themselves informed about colleagues' areas of expertise and competencies. Social workers should seek consultation only from colleagues who have demonstrated knowledge, expertise, and competence related to the subject of the consultation" (§2.05(b)). Finally, the consultee is required to think critically about the quality of the advice rendered. There are times when an ethical consultant provides misleading or inappropriate advice. Koocher and Keith-Spiegel (2008) provide unfortunate examples of bad guidance, such as "trust your gut." They offer this bottom line: "If you doubt a confidant's advice, seek a second opinion" (p. 22).

Clinical Consultation

Clinical consultation can serve at least five purposes. First, since many school districts do not provide clinical supervision of pupil services providers, it makes sense for these professionals to engage a regular consultant for this purpose. For example, one of us recently worked as a clinical consultant to help two masters-level practitioners obtain their clinical licenses. Over several months, it became obvious that one of the consultees tended to rush the clinical process with her clients. Rather than respect their resistance, she wanted to run roughshod over it. The ongoing nature of the relationship enabled the clarification of this repetitive tendency. She was encouraged to become familiar with Prochaska and DiClemente's (2005) stages of change model and this reduced future occurrences. Second, school-based practitioners see many students who have comorbid academic and emotional problems. While pupil service providers are primarily present to reduce the adverse effects of clients' problems on their ability to benefit from an education, they frequently encounter clinical problems that demand the advice of someone with special expertise (Reamer, 2006). This expertise may be related to autism, child abuse, drug or alcohol addictions, domestic violence, eating disorders, psychotropic medications, or sexual assault. In metropolitan areas, there are likely to be clinical specialists in all of these areas. Professionals working in small towns and rural areas, however, may have to rely on

---

telephone or e-mail consultation to address their concerns (Dalen, 2006; Womontree, 2004). The generalist preparation of school-based providers may simply not be sufficient to handle all of the clinical difficulties that come their way. Third, there are times when our interventions with students are ineffective. This may be due to relying too much on our own clinical wisdom or outdated clinical theories. In these cases, the practitioner should locate an expert who is familiar with the current clinical research on the problem. For example, a few years ago one of the authors attended a continuing education workshop during which the presenter spoke about the "clinical triad" of fire-setting, enuresis, and cruelty to animals to identify the students most at risk for emotional disturbances. Since this Freudian-based theory reached its hey-day in the 1940s (Yarnell, 1940), the presenter was asked about current research on the topic (e.g., Slavkin, 2004). When she couldn't name any, the workshop participants began to doubt the veracity of her claims. Fourth, professionals should recognize the emotional toll that ethical predicaments take on themselves. This distress is most acute after an "adverse incident," where the professional faces a job dismissal, lawsuit, or possible revocation of her professional license or certification (Koocher & Keith-Spiegel, 2008). For example, the practitioner who is currently counseling a student whose family has initiated a due process complaint against the school district may require clinical consultation to assess her own ability to maintain clinical objectivity (Thomas, 2005). At these times clinical consultation can be part of the self-care that one needs to cope with difficult circumstances. As tempting as it may be to isolate oneself during an embarrassing professional incident, it only places us at greater risk for clinical mistakes. Finally, professionals may want help managing the clinical concerns surrounding the ethical quandary. These concerns include developmental considerations, cultural sensitivity, therapeutic empathy, and appropriate self-disclosure of feelings about the ethical conflict. We will have much more to say about all of these in Chapter 5.

Legal Consultation

Reamer (2006) identifies some occasions when a practitioner will want to seek out legal advice. He states that professionals:

> may want to seek legal advice when they need to decide whether
> to disclose confidential information to a third party against a
> client's wishes, comply with a subpoena that requests privileged

information, terminate services to a client who has threatened to file a lawsuit ... or rely on a deceased client's relative for informed consent purposes in a matter pertaining to the former client. (p. 12)

When considering the legal ramifications of an ethical issue, practitioners should locate a legal consultant that is knowledgeable about the U.S. Constitution, federal statutes, state statutes, administrative rules, case law, and local policies (Prasse, 2008).

Constitutional Law

The U.S. Constitution is the foundation for all other laws in the nation. While education is not a right guaranteed under the Constitution (*San Antonio Independent School District v. Rodriguez*, 1973), this does not mean that the Constitution does not affect education or mental health services in schools. The 10th Amendment to the Constitution specifically delegates any powers not given to the federal government to the individual states. Education is one of these powers. In this section, we will address three common issues where states (including State Education Agencies) get into legal conflicts with the U.S. Constitution. For a list of U.S. Supreme Court cases affecting school mental health, see the Appendix.

The 14th Amendment prohibits any state from taking away citizens' privileges without due process. It was one of the Reconstruction amendments passed in the wake of the Civil War and reads as follows:

No state shall make or enforce any law which shall abridge the privileges or immunities of citizens of the United States; nor shall any state deprive any person of life, liberty, or property, without *due process* of law; nor deny to any person within its jurisdiction the *equal protection* of the law (emphasis added).

The italicized terms have been the subject of much controversy. Known respectively as the due process and equal protection clauses, they require all states to apply the Bill of Rights to matters of education (Latham, Latham, & Mandlawitz, 2008).

Due Process

The due process clause has primarily been invoked when schools violate student privileges under three Amendments in the Bill of Rights, specifically the 1st, 4th, and 8th Amendments (Kopels, 2007). Let's examine each of these briefly.

The 1st Amendment provides three constitutionally guaranteed freedoms to all citizens (including students):

> Congress shall make no law (1) respecting the establishment of religion or prohibiting the free exercise thereof; (2) or abridging the freedom of speech, or the press; (3) or the right of the people peaceably to assemble, and to petition the government for a redress of grievances (numbers added).

The first right of religious freedom actually entails two separate clauses. First, schools cannot promote one religion to the exclusion of others. This is the reason that school-sponsored prayers are unconstitutional (*Engle v. Vitale*, 1962). For example, in *Lemon v. Kurtzman* (1971), the U.S. Supreme Court created three questions to determine when the establishment clause was violated (Anderson, 2000). Did the policy have a secular purpose? Was its primary effect to neither advance nor inhibit religion? Did it avoid excessive entanglement with religion? Second, schools cannot restrict students from practicing their religion. This is the reason why student-led public prayers are constitutional as long as there is no coercion of other students to participate (*Jones v. Clear Creek Independent School District*, 1992). For other school-related religious issues, see Box 3.1. The second right protects both freedom of expression and newspapers. *Tinker v. Des Moines Independent School District* (1969) was a landmark case regarding students' right to free expression. The U.S. Supreme Court provided three guidelines (Kopels, 2007). It asserted that students were protected under the 1st Amendment just like adults. It also stated that symbolic expression (e.g., armbands or buttons) was protected like verbal expression. It cautioned, however, that no right to free speech is absolute (e.g., hate speech, obscenities, or sexual innuendos). In other words, student freedom of expression has to be balanced with the school's right to expect socially appropriate behavior (*Bethel School District 403 v. Fraser*, 1986). *Hazelwood School District v. Kuhlmeier* (1988) addressed the right of schools to censor material in a student newspaper. Because the student newspaper was actually sponsored by the school, the court upheld school administrators' rights to editorially restrict certain stories. Other common freedom of expression issues concern student appearance and dress (Kopels, 2007).

The 4th Amendment protects all citizens (including students) from unreasonable search and seizure:

> The right of the people to be secure in their persons, houses, papers, and effects, against unreasonable searches and seizures,

shall not be violated, and no warrants shall issue, but upon probable cause, supported by oath or affirmation, and particularly describing the place to be searched, and the persons or things to be seized.

Box 3.1 Ten Religious Issues in Public Education

Religious Issues	Possible Solutions
1. What accommodations can schools make regarding dietary restrictions (e.g., pork)?	1. Label all foods with restricted ingredients and provide alternate menu options for everyone (e.g., vegetarians).
2. What accommodations can schools make regarding pious modesty (e.g., rules against communal showers or shorts)?	2. Make some private bathroom facilities available to all students and allow the use of sweat suits in physical education.
3. What accommodations can schools make to allow religious clubs or groups to meet on campus?	3. Religious groups may gather before or after school according to the same rules as other community groups.
4. What are schools allowed to do to recognize religious holidays?	4. Schools can teach students *about* religious holidays as long as it is nonpreferential.
5. What can schools allow when students want to express their faith in their student assignments?	5. Student expressions of personal beliefs should be judged by academic standards (e.g., substance and relevance).
6. What can schools allow regarding student distribution of religious literature, such as evangelistic pamphlets?	6. Schools can regulate distribution by the same rules as any other student literature (e.g., birthday invitations).
7. How should schools handle student absences for the religious observance of their holidays?	7. Subject to state laws, schools can excuse students as for family reasons (e.g., weddings or funerals).

---

8. What accommodations can schools make regarding the wearing of religious ornaments or clothing (e.g., hijab)?	8. Students can express their beliefs according to the same rules as other faiths (e.g., crosses or yarmulkes).
9. How can schools allow students to attend religious education classes during school hours?	9. Subject to state laws, schools may give students "release time" to attend off-campus activities.
10. How can schools accommodate students who need to pray during school hours (e.g., Muslims)?	10. Schools can designate an empty room during the lunch hour for voluntary gatherings with adult supervision.

Sources: American Bar Association (1998); Demac (1997); Haynes (1998).

The landmark case for schools in this regard is *New Jersey v. TLO* (1985). According to the court, a school's search is reasonable if it meets two criteria. First, the search must be justified by reasonable suspicion that the student has violated the law or school rules. This suspicion might include having some evidence about the particular situation (e.g., smelling smoke or observing odd behavior), student background information (e.g., history of office disciplinary referrals, suspensions, or arrests), or a reliable witness (e.g., school staff member or student in good standing). Second, the scope of the search must be reasonably related to the type of suspicion (Kopels, 2007). Searches of a student's private belongings (e.g., book bags or purses) require a higher degree of probable cause and greater degree of risk than searches of (school-owned) desks or lockers. For example, missing money in a classroom does not constitute grounds for a mass strip search. Such instances generally lack an eyewitness and there is no immediate danger if the money is not found (Essex, 2003). Strip searches require an even higher degree of probable cause and risk than a search of a student's property (*Doe v. Renfrow*, 1981; *Safford Unified School District v. Redding*, 2009). Suspicions of weapons possession or distribution of illegal drugs may be enough to warrant an invasive search of a specific individual (Kopels, 2007). See Box 3.2 for a recent Supreme Court case on this topic.

Box 3.2 Safford United School District #1 v. Redding

Savana Rdding's Story

I attended Safford Middle School for sixth, seventh, and part of eighth grade. I was an honors student and had never been in trouble. On October 8, 2003, I was in class when the vice principal, Mr. Wilson, came in and told me to collect my things and come to the office. I noticed that my planner was open on his desk and contained items that were not mine, such as knives, a cigarette, and a lighter. They belonged to my friend Marissa who had borrowed my planner to hide stuff from her parents. I admitted to Mr. Wilson that the planner was mine, but not the other things. Mr. Wilson then pointed to four white pills and a blue one. He had found them in Marissa's belongings and was told that I was passing out pills at school. I denied this and he asked to search my stuff. I said okay. They didn't find anything in my backpack, so I was taken to the nurse's office, where two female staff asked me to remove my shirt and pants. They still didn't find anything, so they asked me to stretch out my bra and panties and shake them, exposing my breasts and pubic area. No pills were found. I was embarrassed and scared and about to cry. I was never allowed to call my mother.

School District's Story

About a week before confronting Miss Redding, one of our students had told the school principal that some kids were bringing prescription drugs and weapons to school. On the day of the search, the same student gave Mr. Wilson a pill he said came from Marissa. Marissa was then called to the office and asked to turn out her pockets and the day planner. When pills fell out, Marissa said they belonged to Savana Redding. A strip search of Marissa in the nurse's office produced no other pills. The school nurse identified the white pills as 400 mg Ibuprofen and the blue pill as Naproxen. Mr. Wilson was sure that Savana and Marissa were both part of a group that had consumed alcohol and cigarettes during a school dance in the girls' bathroom 6 weeks earlier. With this history and the other students' allegations, he felt he had reasonable cause to search her belongings. The school started with the least intrusive search. We tried to contact Savana's mother, Mrs. Redding, without success. The school conducted the strip search in the privacy of the nurse's office and supplied two female staff members to supervise the procedure. No pills were ever found.

Questions

1. Do you think the school had reasonable cause to conduct a search of Savana's belongings?
2. Did the school take Savana's history into account when they suspected her?
3. Did the seriousness of risk to other students warrant the scope of the search?
4. Did the school take proper precautions to protect Savana's privacy?
5. Who could the school have consulted in this situation?
6. If you were one of the Supreme Court justices, how would you decide this case?
7. Look up the final verdict on the Internet. Did you agree with the justices?

Finally, the 8th Amendment guarantees protection for citizens (including students) against unusually harsh punishments: "Excessive bail shall not be required, nor excessive fines imposed, nor cruel and unusual punishments inflicted." This right has ethical implications for school-administered corporal punishment (Darden, 2009; McCarthy, 2005; Spengler, 2003) and zero-tolerance policies. In the first *corporal punishment* case, *Baker v. Owen* (1975), the U.S. Supreme Court denied that "paddling" in school was a form of cruel and unusual punishment as long as pupils were warned ahead of time about which infractions led to paddling and lesser remedies were tried first (Kopels, 2007). Two years later, the Supreme Court ruled that the 8th Amendment only applied to prisoners, not school children (*Ingraham v. Wright*, 1977)! Since this time, however, six federal appeals courts have affirmed that the 14th and 8th Amendments do apply to students and that extreme forms of corporal punishment (e.g., choking or hitting a student in the head) are not permissible (Sendor, 2001). While paddling does result in immediate short-term compliance of the pupil (Owen, 2005), it does not lead to long-term self-control that is ostensibly the goal of student discipline measures (Society for Adolescent Medicine, 2003). Dupper and Dingus (2008) recommend three strategies that school-based practitioners can use to decrease the use of corporal punishment in the 21 states where it is still legal. First, professionals can educate the public about the deleterious effects of corporal punishment (Hyman & Perone, 1998). Second, professionals can advocate for the use of positive behavioral interventions and supports (Sugai & Horner, 2007). Third, for people who justify paddling on religious grounds, pupil services providers can work with clergy to find theological reasons to utilize positive child development techniques. *Zero-tolerance policies* grew out of an explosion of school violence in the 1990s, culminating in the Columbine massacre in 1999. They now cover a variety of offenses, including alcohol and drugs, gang paraphernalia, physical fights, sexual harassment, and vulgar speech (Kopels, 2007). Raines (2006) points out that the 2004 reauthorization of the Individuals with Disabilities Education Act recommended (but did not require) schools consider student discipline on a "case by case" basis (see Box 4.3 in the next chapter). This was a direct result of the excesses of zero-tolerance policies that led to immediate expulsions for students who brought Midol or a nail file to school.

It is important to remember that a key role that all pupil services providers can play is that of mediator between the family and school when it comes to due process issues. Samuels (2008) reports on research that 80% of due process hearings can be avoided if the lines of communication between parents and school administrators are repaired. We believe that practitioners can and should help create an atmosphere where restorative justice rather than retributive justice is the norm.

Equal Protection

The equal protection clause is invoked whenever schools apply rules differentially for different groups of students. The landmark case in this regard is *Brown v. Board of Education* (1954) because it established education as a fundamental right that demands equal protection for students regardless of their race. Raines (1996b) pointed out that this logic was later extended to children with disabilities when the Education of All Handicapped Children's Act (later renamed the Individuals with Disabilities Education Act, IDEA) was passed in 1975 (P.L. 94-142). Equal protection applies when schools intentionally discriminate among categories of students. There are some occasions when schools unknowingly discriminate and are only guilty if they continue to discriminate after knowing the facts. For example, school districts have routinely referred minority children to special education in greater numbers than white children (National Research Council, 2002). This is the reason that No Child Left Behind (P.L. 107-110) aimed to close the achievement gap and the reauthorized IDEA (P.L. 108-446) required states to monitor disproportional minority representation in special education (Raines, 2006). Another example is minority disproportionality when it comes to student discipline. Darden (2009), for example, points out that 36% of corporal punishment recipients are African American when they represent only about 17% of the student population. He concludes that "the problem with corporal punishment is that the end does not necessarily justify the means" (p. 40).

Federal Statutes

There are many federal statutes that have ethical implications for pupil services providers. Here we will only briefly mention the most important by their earliest passage, although readers should stay current with each law's most recent reauthorization.

Elementary and Secondary Education Act

The Elementary and Secondary Education Act (ESEA) (P.L. 89-10) was originally passed in 1965 as part of President Johnson's War on Poverty program. It was reauthorized in January of 2002 as the No Child Left Behind Act. The most relevant part in the law concerning ethics was Title I, which funds school programs for low-income students (Cohen, Moffitt, & Goldin, 2007; Hunter, 2000).

Rehabilitation Act of 1973

This wide-ranging law disallowed discrimination in three areas: employment by the federal government, employment by federal contractors, and activities (including education) that receive federal grants. The most important part of this legislation for schools is Section 504, which requires that grantees (including school districts) provide accommodations to individuals with impairments that "substantially limit a major life activity," such as learning, to a "substantial" extent. Unlike the later Education of All Handicapped Children Act (see later discussion), these impairments did not have to an adverse effect on the child's ability to learn, so no extra funds for schools that made these accommodations were authorized.

In 2008, the Americans with Disabilities Act Amendments changed some of the eligibility criteria for Section 504. Specifically, it broadened the concept of "major life activity" to include cognitive problems such as concentration, reading, and thinking as well as somatic problems such as eating, incontinence, and sleeping. It also expanded the definition of "substantial" to include short-term episodic conditions such as anaphylactic reactions to food allergies or asthma attacks (Zirkel, 2009a, 2009b). Since all of these can affect children, it is important for school-based practitioners to stay current with these changes.

Family Educational Rights and Privacy Act

Also known as the Buckley Amendment, the Family Educational Rights and Privacy Act (FERPA) of 1974 was designed to provide parents and students of majority age access to the educational records as well as the opportunity to correct errors in those records. It also guarantees that grades, behavioral records, and school work are kept confidential in federally funded schools and shared only with school officials with "legitimate educational interests." FERPA has been amended nine times, most recently to accord with the passage of the U.S. Patriot Act of 2001 (P.L. 107-56).

Education of All Handicapped Children Act

Since its 1990 reauthorization, this 1975 law has been known as the Individuals with Disabilities Education Act (IDEA). It procures a free appropriate public education for all children whose disability adversely affected their ability to benefit from an education. IDEA is funded by sharing the extra cost of special education with the states. It also regulates the discipline of students with disabilities so that they cannot be punished for behavior that is a manifestation of their disability. This protection, however, is balanced by recognition of a school's need for order, so it allows for immediate remand into an interim alternative educational setting for 45 school days if the infraction involves weapons, drugs, or serious bodily injury (Raines, 2006).

Protection of Pupil Rights Amendment

Also known as the Hatch Amendment, the Protection of Pupil Rights Amendment (PPRA) of 1978 was meant to protect students and their parents in federally assisted programs from any testing designed to determine political affiliations, mental problems, sexual behavior, self-incriminating behavior, critical judgments of family relationships, privileged relationships, or income without parental consent.

Health Insurance Portability and Accountability Act

The Health Insurance Portability and Accountability Act (HIPAA) was enacted in 1996 to help provide health insurance coverage for workers when they lose or change jobs as well as establish national standards for the protection of health care records. For more information on how HIPAA relates to FERPA, see the section on "Administrative Regulations."

State Statutes

The relationship between federal laws and state laws is complicated. Certain federal laws (e.g., HIPAA) specifically require citizens to be familiar with state laws in their interpretation. Some state laws are meant only to supplement current federal laws (Latham, Latham, & Mandlawitz, 2008). States may and sometimes do enact laws that provide a higher level of protection and privacy for their citizens, including students, than is provided for in federal law. For instance, Wisconsin prohibits strip searches of students by school district employees or any agent of the school district (s. 118.32, Wis. Stat.). The state laws with which school-based mental health professionals should be familiar include statutes governing access to mental health therapy, reproductive and sexual health services, and substance abuse treatment. These are likely to give adolescents access to confidential health care without parental consent at different ages, so it behooves practitioners to know what age applies in the state where they practice.

Administrative Regulations

Administrative rules and regulations clarify statutes in two ways. First, the regulations may define terms which are undefined in the original law. Second, the rules may explain exactly how a specific program should be administered. Here we provide two examples from FERPA. At the end of the Bush administration, the U.S. Department of Education (2008) significantly expanded the federal definition of "school officials" to include "contractors, consultants, volunteers, and other outside service providers used by a school district… to perform institutional services and functions" (§99.31(a)(1)(i)(B) Outsourcing). The regulations failed, however, to establish a uniform set of criteria for "legitimate educational interests," opting to require school districts to specify these criteria in their annual FERPA notification to parents and students. Therefore, we encourage pupil services providers to be active on district committees that define such criteria.

Sometimes two federal agencies issue joint guidance where federal statutes may contain conflicting requirements about student confidentiality. Recently the U.S. Department of Health and Human Services and U.S. Department of Education (2008) published a joint statement on student health records. It was designed to address 10 common questions about the intersection of FERPA and HIPAA. For example, many school-based mental health professionals have wondered about their records when treating Medicaid-eligible youth for conditions covered under IDEA. The joint federal guidance provides the following contingency-based approach:

> If a public high school employs a health care provider that bills Medicaid electronically for services provided to a student under the IDEA, the school is a HIPAA-covered entity and would be subject to the HIPAA requirements concerning transactions. However, if the school's provider maintains health information only in what are education records under FERPA, the school is not required to comply with the HIPAA Privacy Rule. (p. 4)

Since some pupil services providers may also hold clinical licensure, this guidance is extremely useful in clarifying what has been for many a confusing issue. The reader will find the electronic link to this government publication at the end of this chapter.

Case Law

Case law consists of official verdicts in state and federal courts. These opinions may be binding (as in U.S. Supreme Court rulings) or simply influential (as in state Supreme Court or federal appeals courts), although these are binding for citizens of the respective states. For an illustration about the pathways that lower court cases take to the U.S. Supreme Court (Bouchoux, 2008), see Figure 3.1. As we have demonstrated in much of the previous discussion, case law can assist the ethical professional in thinking clearly about the nuances of state or federal laws. Here we will refer to two examples with direct implications for professional ethics. See the Appendix for other examples of education-related case law and the ethical issues involved.

Readers should be aware that the U.S. Supreme Court grants *certiori* (certification) to fewer than 5% of the approximately 5,000 annual cases petitioning it for a review. This means, of course, that 95% of the time, the Supreme Court lets the ruling of a lower court stand. The most likely clue

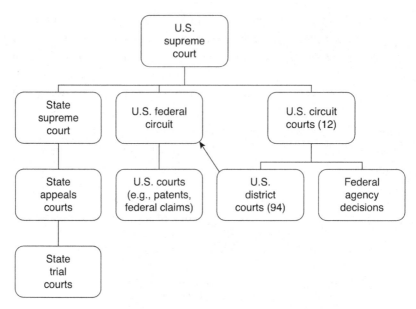

FIGURE 3.1 Pathways to the U.S. Supreme Court.

that a case will be heard is when the U.S. Courts of Appeals are divided or in direct conflict over a legal issue (Perry, 2005). There are 12 regional circuit courts with vastly different geographical boundaries. The smallest is the District of Columbia circuit and the largest is the ninth circuit, which covers nine states and small territories, such as Guam. Moreover, some of the circuits are not contiguous; Puerto Rico, for example, is lumped together with Maine, Massachusetts, New Hampshire, and Rhode Island. To find out which Court of Appeals decides cases affecting your state or territory, see Box 3.3.

Tarasoff v. Regents of the University of California

This case provides significant guidance regarding what therapists should do when counseling a potentially violent client. The plaintiffs in the case were the parents of Tatiana Tarasoff who had been murdered by her former boyfriend who had been in counseling with a psychologist employed by the University of California (Kopels & Kagle, 1993). In 1974, the California Supreme Court gave its first opinion that therapists had a *duty to warn* the intended victim. After appeals by several professional associations, the same court gave a second opinion that therapists had a more general *duty to protect* potential victims, issuing the famous dictum that "the protective privilege ends where the public peril begins" (*Tarasoff v. Board of Regents of the University*

Box 3.3 U.S. Court of Appeals Regional Circuit by State or Territory

State/Territory (Abbreviation)	U.S. Circuit Court
Alabama (AL)	11
Alaska (AK)	9
American Samoa (AS)	9
Arizona (AZ)	9
Arkansas (AR)	8
California (CA)	9
Colorado (CO)	10
Connecticut (CT)	2
Delaware (DE)	3
District of Columbia (DC)	DC
Florida (FL)	11
Georgia (GA)	11
Guam (GU)	9
Hawai'i (HI)	9
Idaho (ID)	9
Illinois (IL)	7
Indiana (IN)	7
Iowa (IA)	8
Kansas (KS)	10
Kentucky (KY)	6
Louisiana (LA)	5
Maine (ME)	1
Mariana Islands (MP)	9
Maryland (MD)	4
Massachusetts (MA)	1
Michigan (MI)	6
Minnesota (MN)	8
Mississippi (MS)	5
Missouri (MO)	8
Montana (MT)	9
Nebraska (NE)	8

Nevada (NV)	9
New Hampshire (NH)	1
New Jersey (NJ)	3
New Mexico (NM)	10
New York (NY)	2
North Carolina (NC)	4
North Dakota (ND)	8
Ohio (OH)	6
Oklahoma (OK)	10
Oregon (OR)	9
Pennsylvania (PA)	3
Puerto Rico (PR)	1
Rhode Island (RI)	1
South Carolina (SC)	4
South Dakota (SD)	8
Tennessee (TN)	6
Texas (TX)	5
Utah (UT)	10
Vermont (VT)	2
Virginia (VA)	4
Virgin Islands (VI)	3
Washington (WA)	9
West Virginia (WV)	4
Wisconsin (WI)	7
Wyoming (WY)	10

Source: http://www.uscourts.gov/

of California, 1976, p. 347). This duty to protect could be satisfied in several ways, including warning the victim, informing others who can alert the victim, or taking other reasonably necessary steps such as commitment of the potential assailant (Raines, 2004). While Tarasoff was not binding on other states, it was influential. Currently, 21 states (plus the District of Columbia and Puerto Rico) have passed statutes that contain a duty to warn or protect;

Ethical Decision Making in School Mental Health

9 states have case law supporting these responsibilities, 13 states allow a breach of confidentiality for these reasons, and only 7 states remain undecided about the issue. Clearly, practitioners need to know what their state statutes and case law say about this issue. Unfortunately, Pabian, Welfel, and Beebe (2009) found over three-quarters of their large sample of psychologists were misinformed about the legal requirements of their respective states regarding this duty. Kopels and Lindsey (2006) report that a similar confusion exists among school social workers who wrongly assume that the "duty to protect" justifies breaches of confidentiality in such phenomena as adolescent pregnancy, unsafe sex, or drug use. Unfortunately, there are many conflicting legal opinions about whether there is even a responsibility to breach confidentiality (see Box 3.4), with some states (e.g., Texas) giving professionals only the discretion to break confidences but refusing to shield those who do so from being sued. Thus, we recommend that practitioners become aware of the case law in their own state. For conflicting ethical opinions on this issue, see Box 2.4 in Chapter 2.

Box 3.4 Examples of Case Law and the Duty to Protect

Case	Conclusion
Bardoni et al. v. Kim, 390 N.W.2d 218 (Mich. Ct. App. 1986)	Therapists do not have a duty to protect in the absence of an identifiable victim.
Bellah v. Greenson, 81 Cal. App. 3d 614, 141 Cal. Rptr. 92 (Ca, 1977)	Therapists do not have a duty to warn in the case of a suicide because there is no threat to others, nor are they liable for personal or property damages.
Boynton v. Burglass (1991), 590 So. 2d 446 (Fla. Ct. App. 4th)	Therapists have permission to protect a third party, not a duty. Predicting dangerousness is an inexact science.
Brady v. Hopper, 570 F. Supp. 1333 (D. Colo. 1983)	Therapists have a duty to protect only when there are specific threats to an identifiable victim.

Cairl v. State, 323 N.W.2d 20 (Minn. 1982)	Therapists do not have a duty to protect in the absence of an identifiable victim, especially if the victim was well aware of the perpetrator's history.
Davis v. Lhim, 335 N.W.2d 481 (Mich. Ct. App. 1983)	Therapists have a duty to protect even in the absence of an identifiable victim.
Doyle v. U.S., 530 F. Supp. 1278 (D.C. Cal. 1982)	Therapists do not have a duty to protect in the absence of an identifiable victim.
Emerich v. Philadelphia Center for Human Development, 720 A.2d 1032 (Pa. 1998)	Therapists do not have a duty to protect in the absence of an identifiable victim.
Estates of Morgan v. Family Counseling Center, 77 Ohio St. 3d 284, 673 N.E.2d 1311 (Ohio 1997)	Therapists should use their professional judgment to "consider all alternatives" in protecting others.
Evans v. United States, 883 F. Supp. 124 (S.D. Miss. 1995)	Client-therapist confidentiality precludes a duty to warn others.
Garner v. Gwinnett County 1999 U.S. Dist. LEXIS 6370 (N.D. Ga. 1999)	Client-therapist confidentiality precludes a duty to protect others on the basis of violent fantasies.
Hamman v. County of Maricopa, 161 Ariz. 58, 775 P.2d 1122 (Ariz. 1989)	Therapists have a duty to protect nonidentifiable victims within the "zone of danger."
Hasenei v. United States, 541 F. Supp. 999 (D. Md. 1982)	Therapists' duty to control the conduct of an outpatient arises only if the situation involves the ability for such control and voluntary outpatient relationships usually lack such ability.

Hedlund v. Superior Court of Orange County,34 Cal. 3d 695; 669 P.2d 41 (Cal. 1983)	Therapists have a duty to protect and an affirmative duty to determine a client's dangerousness to protect innocent fourth parties.
In re commitment M.G.,751 A.2d 1101 (N.J. Super. Ct. App.Div. 2000)	Therapist has a duty to protect and an affirmative duty to review a client's medical records and assess the client's sexual fantasies.
Jablonski by Pahls v. United States,712 F. 2d 391 (9th Cir. 1983)	Therapist has a duty to protect and an affirmative duty to review of previous records about violent behavior even if there is no specific threat against an identifiable victim.
Leedy v. Harnett, 510 F. Supp. 1125 (M. D. Pa. 1981)	Therapists do not have a duty to protect in the absence of an identifiable victim.
Lipari v. Sears, Roebuck & Co.,479 F. Supp. 185 (D.Neb. 1980)	Therapists have a duty to initiate hospital confinement of a client even when there is no specific threat against identifiable victims.
Mahomes-Vinson v. U.S.751 F. Supp. 913 (D. Kan. 1990)	Therapists' duty to control the conduct of a voluntary client arises only if the situation involves the ability for such control and voluntary client relationships usually lack such ability.
Mavroudis v. Superior Court of San Mateo County, 102 Cal. App. 3d 594 (1980)	Therapists do not have duty to protect unless there is an imminent threat against an identifiable victim.

McIntosh v. Milano, 168 N.J. Supr. 466, 403 A.2d 500 (N.J. Supr.Ct. 1979).	Therapists have a duty to take reasonably necessary actions to protect potential victims.
Peck v. Counseling Service of Addison County, 499 A.2d 422 (Vt. 1985)	Therapists should seek supervision or consultation to demonstrate compliance with professional standards
Peterson v. State, 100 Wash. 2d 421, 671 P.2d 230 (Wash. 1983)	Therapists have a duty to initiate hospital confinement of a client even when victims are not identifiable.
Pettus v. Cole,49 Cal. App. 4th 402 (1996)	Nonspecific violent fantasies may serve as a psychological "safety valve," permitting the vicarious, but harmless discharge of angry feelings.
Robinson v. Mount Logan Clinic, LLC,182 P.3d 333 (Utah 2008)	There is no legal duty to protect unless there is a "clearly identified or reasonably identifiable victim," but there is a common law duty to exercise "reasonable care."
Schuster v. Altenberg, 144 Wis. 2d 223, 424 N.W.2d 159 (Wis. 1988)	Therapists have a duty to initiate hospital confinement of a client even when victims are the general public and not identifiable.
Shaw v. Glickman, 415 A.2d 625 (Md. Ct. Spec. App. 1980)	Client–therapist confidentiality precludes a duty to warn others, especially if the violence is due to risky behavior on the part of the victim.
Tarasoff v. Regents of the University of California, 13 Cal. 3d 117, 529 P.2d 533, 118 Cal. Rptr. 129 (1974). (Tarasoff I)	Therapists have a duty to warn a "readily identifiable victim."

Tarasoff v. Regents of the University of California, 17 Cal. 3d 425, 551 P.2d 334, 131 Cal Rptr. 14 (1976). (Tarasoff II)	Therapists have a duty to protect a "readily identifiable victim." "The protective privilege ends where the public peril begins."
Thapar v. Zezulka,994 S.W. 2d 635 (Texas, 1999)	Therapists do not have a duty to warn or protect others; they do have discretion to do so, but risk civil liability even when violating confidentiality in good faith.
Thompson v. County of Alameda, 167 Cal.Rptr. 70 (1980).	Therapists do not have a duty to protect when there are nonspecific threats to unidentifiable victims.
White v. U.S.,780 F.2d 97 (D.C. Cir. 1986)	Therapists do not have a duty to protect when they judge that threats against an identifiable victim are only violent fantasies even if there is a history of violent behavior.

Sources: Barbee, Combs, Ekleberry, & Villalobos (2007); Gellerman & Suddath (2005); Kopels & Kagel (1993); Lundgren & Ciccone (2009); Quattrocchi & Schopp (2005); Simone & Fulero (2005).

Jaffee v. Redmond

This 1996 U.S. Supreme Court decision established privilege in psychotherapist–client relationships by recognizing that mental health is a public good that should be protected by law (Raines, 2004). The case involved an Illinois clinical social worker whose client, Mary Lu Redmond, had killed an armed man in the line of duty and was then sued by the decedent's relatives. The social worker had refused to comply with a lower court subpoena mandating her to relinquish notes about her client's state of mind after the shooting. The Supreme Court reasoned that "effective psychotherapy... depends upon an atmosphere of confidence and trust in which the patient is willing to make a frank and complete disclosure of facts, emotions, memories, and fears" (p. 10). This opinion is binding on all lower federal courts (Knapp & VandeCreek, 1997). Clearly this is good news to pupil services providers who also hold clinical licensure. It remains to be determined, however, if courts will uphold privilege if the client is considered a danger to self or others or whether therapists will be forced to testify against these clients (Applebaum, 2008). For more guidance about responding to subpoenas, see Box 3.5.

Box 3.5 Responding to a Subpoena

A subpoena is a legal document that requests someone to testify and/or produce documents requested by the court. Subpoena literally means "under penalty," but this should not be interpreted to mandate automatic compliance. Subpoenas differ from court orders, which are legal documents compelling someone to testify and/or produce documents. Knee-jerk submission to a subpoena would be unethical! The ASCA (2004) *Ethical Standards* state that a professional "requests of the court that disclosure not be required when the release of confidential information may potentially harm a student or the counseling relationship" (§A.2.d). Likewise the APA Committee on Professional Practice and Standards (2003) states that "receipt of a subpoena in a situation in which the client has not explicitly waived privilege may still require the psychologist to assert privilege on behalf of the client" (p. 598). There are two types of subpoenas. A *subpoena duces tecum* is a legal request to produce specific records. It is important to realize that court clerks routinely sign blank subpoena forms that are filled in by attorneys who might abuse their power. Some states require that subpoenas must be hand-delivered to the recipient to be legally valid. Practitioners should review the subpoena carefully and retain an attorney (sometimes provided by a malpractice insurer). Then they should contact their clients and provide them with copies. Clients do not have to agree to the release of information to the court. The NASW (1999) *Code of Ethics* addresses what happens if the client refuses to comply:

> When a court of law or other legally authorized body orders social workers to disclose confidential or privi-

---

Ethical Decision Making in School Mental Health

leged information without a client's consent and such disclosure could cause harm to the client, social workers should request that the court withdraw the order or limit the order as narrowly as possible or maintain the records under seal, unavailable for public inspection. (§1.07(j))

Clinicians should always obtain a signed release to talk to and give copies of the requested records to the client's attorney. In the absence of a client attorney, the court clerk can be consulted or, preferably, professionals may talk to their own attorneys. In the absence of a signed release of information, practitioners should petition the court to quash the subpoena or restrict it as narrowly as possible on the basis of privilege. If the court upholds the subpoena, clinicians should ask that the documents remain "under seal" and be reviewed *in camera* (in chambers) only. A *subpoena ad testificandum* is a legal document requesting that a person testify at a deposition or trial. If the place or time is inconvenient, practitioners may contact the attorneys to arrange a different location or date.

Complete failure to appear or produce documents, however, may result in being charged with contempt of court. This may be threatened by an attorney, but only a judge can decide what constitutes contempt. A ruling against the practitioner can lead to fines or imprisonment, but these punishments do not release the professional from the requirement to act ethically. A better course is to file a formal objection to the subpoena and appeal the court's verdict if necessary.

Sources: Kagle & Kopels (2008); Polowy, Morgan, & Gilberton (2005).

Relation Between Ethics and Laws

It is important to distinguish ethical and legal obligations. While professionals probably hope that the two sets of duties are usually congruent with each other, this is unfortunately not always the case. Several years ago, Raines (2004) developed a typology of how ethics and laws might interrelate (see Fig. 3.2). Ethical conundrums can then be placed into four categories. First, some predicaments are neither ethical nor legal issues. Professional self-disclosures fit

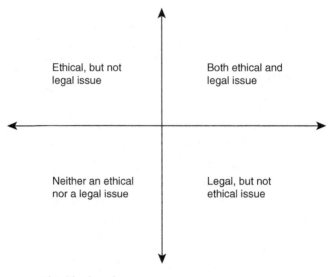

FIGURE 3.2 Ethical-legal typology.

Ethical, but not legal issue

Both ethical and legal issue

Neither an ethical nor a legal issue

Legal, but not ethical issue

into this group. Some practitioners feel that this increases the client's sense of being understood in the therapeutic encounter (Raines, 1996a), while others argue that it is an unnecessary distraction (Strean, 1997). In this sense, they do not belong in this book because they are clinical predicaments, not ethical ones. Second, some quandaries are ethical issues, but not legal ones. Ethical orientation to the treatment relationship is one such issue. It is strongly supported in the codes of ethics, but it is less clear in the law. In *Jaffee v. Redmond* (1996), the U.S. Supreme Court only assumed that professionals would provide some type of orientation, but it deliberately left the exceptions to confidentiality vague—to be determined later. Third, some controversies are both ethical and legal issues. The issue of exceptions to confidentiality is one such quandary. As we pointed out in Box 2.4, the major codes of ethics for school-based mental health providers conflict on which criteria should be used. As we noted in the section on *Tarasoff* earlier, less than half of the states have legislated the application of *Tarasoff* guidelines. Fourth, there are some issues that are primarily legal issues, but not ethical ones. The decision about whether to obtain malpractice insurance may fit into this category. While we think that malpractice insurance is a financially wise decision for practitioners working in a litigious environment, it is not an ethical requirement in any of the codes of ethics. It is, however, a legal requirement for school-based providers who wish to bill Medicaid for their services (Angeles, Tierney, & Osher, 2006).

Civil Disobedience

Civil disobedience has a long history in America—dating back to the Boston Tea Party in 1773. Over time, the concept has been refined by the likes of Thoreau (1849/1960), Tolstoy (1894/1951); Mahatma Gandhi (1948), and Martin Luther King (1958). Pope and Bajt (1988) define *civil disobedience* as "an act involving open and public violation of the law while volunteering to accept the legal penalties" (p. 828). There are some occasions when an ethical practitioner has no choice but to disobey a legal statute. As Rawls (1971) posited, "We are not required to acquiesce in the crushing of fundamental liberties by democratic majorities which have shown themselves blind to the principles of justice upon which justification of the Constitution depends" (p. 352). Several associations and authors recognize that sometimes practitioners are caught between their professional ethics and laws (APA, 2008; Raines, 2004; Reamer, 2005a; Robinson & Reeser, 2000). The NASP (2000) *Principles*, for example, state: "At times, the Ethics may require a higher standard of behavior than the prevailing policies and pertinent laws. Under such conditions, members should adhere to the Ethics" (Introduction).

Here we would like to address how an ethical professional might break an unjust law in civil disobedience and propose four guidelines for this very difficult situation. First, no professional should act alone, but in concert with others. Civil disobedience, if it must happen, occurs best in consultation with other professionals. One needs only to remember the civil rights marches under Martin Luther King to recognize the power of a large multitude. The NASW (2008) *Code of Ethics* specifically suggests:

> Instances may arise when social workers' ethical obligations conflict with agency policies or relevant laws or regulations. When such conflicts occur, social workers must make a responsible effort to resolve the conflict in a manner that is consistent with the values, principles, and standards expressed in this Code. If a reasonable resolution of the conflict does not appear possible, *social workers should seek proper consultation before making a decision.* (Preamble, emphasis added)

Soper (2002) argues that there are two kinds of people willing to commit civil disobedience. Some do so because they believe that their obligation to obey the law is superseded by a higher duty. Others do so because they do not believe in an obligation to obey any law except their own conscience. Thus, it is especially important to consult one's professional association before breaking a law and inquire if they would be willing to file an *amicus curiae* (friend of the court) brief if an arrest occurs. The NASW, for example, filed such a brief in *Jaffee v. Redmond* ("Supreme Court," 1996). If the professional association is unwilling to do so, then it is wise to reconsider whether civil disobedience is the only option. Second, prior to disobeying a law, practitioners should actively advocate for changes in the law. The ASCA (2004) *Ethical Standards* states that a true professional:

> Adheres to ethical standards of the profession, other official policy statements, such as ASCA's position statements, role statement and the ASCA National Model, and relevant statutes established by federal, state and local governments, and *when these are in conflict works responsibly for change.* (§F.1.d, emphasis added)

NASP (2000) concurs: "If regulations conflict with ethical guidelines, school psychologists seek to resolve such conflict through positive, respected, and legal channels, including *advocacy efforts involving public policy*" (§III.D.5, emphasis added). Third, a practitioner should only engage in civil disobedience after exhausting all other legal recourses. These recourses include enacting the rights under the 1st Amendment to peaceable assembly and petition for a redress of grievances. Civil disobedience should only occur as a last resort. Finally, the ethical professional should not attempt to elude law enforcement or resist arrest. As all of these associations make clear, it is generally assumed that ethical practitioners will submit to the rule of law rather than support anarchy. It is also assumed that when questioned by officials about their illegal actions and the motivations behind them, ethical professionals will answer honestly. Ethical standards for both school psychologists and school counselors expect these professionals to accept personal responsibility for their actions (ASCA, 2004, §E1c; NASP, 2000, §IIIA1).

Ethical Guidelines

- Seek consultation for all ethical predicaments prior to taking action if possible. Identify a respected colleague or professional ethics committee to consult about ethical issues. Locate a consultant who is expert at keeping current with the latest clinical research about relevant practice issues. Check the credentials of ethical consultants. See if they have conducted agency- or association-sponsored presentations or authored peer-reviewed publications.

- Routinely seek clinical consultation if clinical supervision is unavailable in your work setting. Recognize the limits of your clinical competence. Seek clinical expertise for issues beyond the scope of your training.

- Identify a legal consultant who is familiar with all the sources of law-related advice. Inquire about Constitutional, federal or state statutes, case law, or regulations that have a bearing on the issue. Disclose the least amount of information necessary to achieve the purpose of the consultation. Avoid the use of names or other identifying information.

- Do not expect one definitive ethical answer. Do expect that options will be broadened and reasons deepened as a result of consultation. Use critical thinking when obtaining ethical advice. Do not blindly accept their word just because they are regarded as authorities or experts.

- Do not comply with a subpoena in knee-jerk fashion; speak to an attorney and take appropriate precautions to protect your client.

- Be extremely careful about civil disobedience. Seek out the advice and support of a professional association before engaging in unlawful behavior.

- Be sure to seek emotional support during adverse incidents involving potential job loss, lawsuits, or revocation of certification or licensure.

Exercises

1. Professional Association Ethics Committees

Using the Internet, find out which professional associations sponsor an ethics committee to determine ethical guidelines or to investigate questionable conduct among its members. Does the association publish information apart from its Code of Ethics? How would you contact the association ethics committee for guidance around an ethical quandary not covered by the Code? How do association members get recruited to join such committees?

2. Residential Treatment

Look up and read the following story by David Royko in the *Chicago Tribune* archives: (http://archives/chicagotribune.com/2007/jun/10/ magazine/chi-mxa0610magautismjun10). What difference does Ben's father being a psychologist make in the story? Where did the family turn for help in managing Ben? Why did they feel like they had to hire an attorney? If Ben was your child or a child in your school, how would you locate an expert in this area of practice? Which avenue might work best: word of mouth, the Internet, professional associations, or scholarly publications? Ben's twin brother seemed to be treated as if he were a surrogate proxy. Do you agree with this process? Did you agree with the family's and school's decision about residential treatment? What might have convinced you otherwise?

3. Legal Resources

Think about a legal question that has nagged you. What legal resources exist in your community, state, or national association to provide guidance on this issue? What questions could you frame in light of the legal consultation section above?

Internet Resources

Legal Information

> AltLaw
> http://www.altlaw.org/
> American Bar Association
> http://www.abanet.org
> Center for Law & Education
> http://www.cleweb.org
> Federal District Court filings
> http://dockets/justia.com

Find Law
http://www.findlaw.com
Hieros Gamos
http://www.hg.org/edu.html
Legal Archiver
http://www.legalarchiver.org
Legal Information Institute, Cornell University
http://www.law.cornell.edu/
LexisOne Community
http://www.lexisone.com/caselaw/freecaselaw
Open Jurist
http://openjurist.org/
Oral Argument Recordings Supreme Court
http://www.oyez.org
Public Library of Law
http://www.plol.org
U.S. Supreme Court
http://www.supremecourtus.gov/

Religion and Public Schools

Parent's Guide to Religion in the Public Schools
http://www.freedomforum.org/publications/first/
religioninpublicschools/parentsguidereligion.pdf
Prayer in Public Schools
http://www.ed.gov/policy/gen/guid/religionandschools/prayer_
guidance.html
Religion in the Public Schools: Joint Statement
http://www.aclu.org/religion/schools/16146leg19950412.html
Religion in the Public Schools
http://www.adl.org/religion_ps/religion_ps_2004/

Conflict Between Ethics and Laws

Comparison of Different Associations
http://www.apa.org/ethics/standard-102/associations.pdf

4

Identifying Courses of Action

After you have addressed your own reaction to the predicament, fully analyzed the ethical quandary, and obtained consultation about the issues involved, the next step in this decision-making process is to identify courses of action. Considering the different alternatives to managing the ethical predicament is broadly supported in the literature (Cottone & Claus, 2000; Koocher & Keith-Spiegel, 2008; Mattison, 2006; McNamara, 2008; Pope & Vasquez, 2007; Reamer, 2006; Stone, 2005; Strom-Gottfried, 2008; Van Divner & Champ Morera, 2007).

Initial presentation of ethical predicaments may initially predispose a practitioner to either-or thinking (Kidder & Born, 1998). Consider the following:

> A school social worker has been facilitating a support group for middle school students whose families are experiencing or have recently experienced a divorce. About 6 weeks after the group has been meeting, one of the student's fathers comes to school and demands to know what his daughter has been saying in the group. He says his wife is making up lies about him in order to keep him from sharing custody of their two children. The school social worker begins to tell the father that it is critical the students feel that what they talk about is not shared outside the group, but the father says his right to know as a parent outweighs any right to confidentiality of his minor daughter. He believes he is in a desperate fight to maintain his relationship with his daughter.

The school social worker's initial response in this confrontation may be to frame it as an ethical dilemma with only two possible (and opposite) responses: (1) respect the student's right to confidentiality and refuse the father's request, or (2) give greater weight to the parent's right to be fully informed of his child's activities and the importance of maintaining the parent–child relationship through and following the divorce. Campbell (2003) argues against taking extreme positions (i.e., full or no disclosure) in these kinds of circumstances, in that it compromises either the importance of parents' influence or the autonomy of the student. Either of the alternatives above has adverse consequences for the student, stakeholders, and the school social worker. These consequences will be discussed in detail in the next section.

We believe that successful management of ethical predicaments can be enhanced dramatically when the practitioner takes time and uses consultation to identify all reasonable courses of action. The term *dilemma* comes from the Greek meaning "two assumptions." When practitioners assume that there are only two choices in an ethical quandary, they inadvertently foreclose on other possible alternatives. This is why we have deliberately avoided this term unless we are referring to either-or thinking or quoting another source. Loewenberg, Dolgoff, and Harrington (2000) recommend seeking to minimize the conflicts among the competing values, interests, and responsibilities to help manage an ethical quandary. What can be done to reduce the tension among personal values, societal values, professional values, and ethics? What can be done to reduce the tension between protecting the client's rights and interests and the rights and interests of stakeholders? Responses to these questions may help to generate additional courses of action beyond "either-or" alternatives (see Box 4.1).

For any given ethical predicament, there are likely a variety of different courses of action. For instance, in the father's scenario above, there are at least two additional courses of action that should be considered. The father's ultimate goal is to maintain a custodial relationship with his daughter. If the daughter has not said anything derogatory about the father in the group counseling sessions, he may be satisfied simply to be reassured of that. If the daughter has shared concerns about her father, the school social worker could volunteer to meet with the father and his daughter to help facilitate a discussion where the daughter could control what confidential information is shared. This respects her right to confidentiality and responds to the father's desire to learn more about what his daughter feels about him and their relationship.

Box 4.1 Showdown at the IEP Meeting

Jamal was a 6-year-old African boy referred to the individualized education program (IEP) team for cognitive delays. He was being raised by his maternal grandmother, who gained custody after his mentally ill mother tried to drown her children in a bathtub. When she arrives at the IEP team meeting, she is accompanied by her pastor from the African Methodist Episcopal church, a vocal advocate of equal rights for African American students. As the team members give their reports, the school psychologist reported that Jamal's WISC-IV scores put him at the high end of the mentally retarded range (Full scale score = 68). Jamal's verbal score was within the normal range (75), but his performance score was quite low (61). The school social worker administered the Vineland Adaptive Behavior Scale and found that Jamal was functioning in the borderline range with significant strengths as well as weaknesses. The school psychologist concluded that Jamal was clearly mentally retarded and needed to be in a special education classroom for most of the school day. Jamal's grandmother objected to this term and said that while she knew that Jamal could be a "little slow" sometimes, he got along fine with normal children and she didn't want him "segregated" in a special class. The social worker tried to explain that the special class would help Jamal catch up to his peers and that he would still be able to enjoy their company at lunch or in P.E. class. At this point, the pastor stood up and railed against the school: "I'm tired and weary of young Black boys getting shunted off to an inferior education! You know good and well that minority students are given this label more often than the White kids!" The principal tried to calm him down with the observation that most of the kids in the special class are White, not minorities. The pastor, however, would not be deterred and said, "I'm talking about disproportionate representation! The whole school has got more White kids than minorities, what does that prove?" The school psychologist also tried to allay his concerns with the suggestion that Jamal try the special class for a year and then they could meet again. The pastor, however, challenged them to name a single Black child who has been shunted

     Ethical Decision Making in School Mental Health

off to that class who ever returned to his regular class on a full-time basis. At this point, the rest of the IEP team was stymied—no one could think of a case where a student had returned to regular education from the special education class. Finally, the school social worker offered a compromise: "Why don't we consider Jamal as having a learning disability? We could offer him tutoring in the Resource Room and keep him in his regular classroom for most of the school day." The principal crossed her arms and said, "We talked about this in our pre-meeting. Jamal clearly needs the special class." The grandmother became suspicious and said, "What's a pre-meeting?" The principal suddenly realized that she had said more than she wished. "It's just a meeting before the real meeting to make sure we're all on the same page." The pastor interrupted, "All on the same page—you mean a united front! I thought parents and guardians were supposed to be part of the team. This is an outrage!"

Questions

1. What ethical issues do you see in this case? Do people of different races see this issue differently?
2. How much emphasis should be placed on testing to determine educational placement?
3. What label would you put on Jamal's difficulties? Does it make a difference if he has mental retardation versus a specific learning disability? Are there any other options?
4. The National Research Council (2002) found that minority disproportionate representation has been a problem in special education for 20 years. What steps can schools take to avoid this?
5. Special education is supposed to balance two sometimes conflicting ideals: the least restrictive environment and the most appropriate education (Raines, 1996b). Which value do you think is most important for Jamal?
6. If the IEP team members could have thought of a case who did return to regular education, would it

have been ethical to disclose the identity of the
child?

7. Have you ever been part of a school that had
"pre-meetings" before the IEP? What are the pros
and cons of such gatherings? Is it legal to determine
the recommendations beforehand?

Consider the Consequences

It is important to consider the possible consequences to each course of action
that is identified, including all stakeholders (Koocher & Keith-Spiegel, 2008;
Loewenberg, Dolgoff & Harrington, 2000; McNamara, 2008; Pope &
Vasquez, 2007; Reamer, 2006; Stone, 2005). In the scenario shared earlier,
the father's daughter is the primary client, but the other students in the small
group are clients as well. The other stakeholders include the daughter's
parents, the school administration and (possibly) the school board, other
students in the school who may benefit from individual and small group
counseling in the future (and their families), and other pupil services professionals in the school district. The consequences to the school social worker
should be considered as well. Velasquez and colleagues (2006) state that
"Virtue ethics asks of any action, 'What kind of person will I become if I do
this?' or 'Is this action consistent with my acting at my best?'" Let's examine
the potential consequences of these different courses of action.

Alternative 1: Refuse to Disclose Any Information

As emotional as the father is, if the school social worker refused to comply
with his demand for information about what his daughter has said in the
group, this response would most likely exacerbate, rather than mediate, the
situation. The father's next contact may be the building principal, some other
school administrator, or even the school board. The father could also contact
other parents to support his outrage at the school social worker's refusal to
cooperate. The school administrators and school board could choose to
examine the school district's policies regarding the rights of students to confidentiality in comparison to their parents' rights to be informed of any school
activities their children participate in, possibly reducing students' current
rights to confidentiality in individual and group counseling activities.

Confidentiality is a cornerstone of a successful relationship between a pupil services professional and a student (ASCA, 2004, §A2; ANA, 2001, §3.1, 3.2; NASP, 2000, §IIIA9-10; NASW, 2008, §1.07). This change would not only adversely affect the school social worker's practice but the professional practice of other pupil services providers as well. Counseling opportunities could be reduced in the school to the detriment of students and their families who may value these services that enhance their children's ability to learn and be successful. The school administration and school board may adopt a less favorable opinion of the importance of school social work services and pupil services. Furthermore, the father could be correct that his wife is trying to obtain sole custody of the children. It is all too common for children to be used as weapons in bitter divorces (Kurtz & Derevensky, 1993). If the father has been a good parent to his daughter, then the loss of this relationship is not in the best interests of the student. A divorce formally severs the relationship of the parents, but the parents continue to have responsibilities to their children. These responsibilities are harder to fulfill if the parent–child relationship is not healthy.

Alternative 2: Disclose Confidential Information

If the school social worker chooses to disclose what the student has shared in the group, the student may feel betrayed by the school social worker and she may share this perceived betrayal with her peers in the group and in the school. The school social worker may lose her reputation among students as a "safe" person to talk to. This negative perception may be projected onto other pupil services professionals in the school, resulting in students being less willing to come forward for help (Helms, 2003). Students' involvement in unhealthy risk-taking behaviors may have more serious consequences without the support of pupil services professionals to help students navigate these challenges, resulting in increased student absenteeism and reduced focus on school activities and performance. In addition, the daughter may become angry with her father for the intrusion into what she thought was a confidential part of her life, perhaps turning the father's fear of the loss of his relationship with his daughter into a self-fulfilling prophecy.

Alternative 3: Focus on and Address the Father's Primary Concern

Some alternative solutions may have the elegance of simplicity. If it is true that the father's real and only concern is to maintain a custodial relationship with his daughter and the daughter has not shared anything negative about the father in the group, then the father may be reassured (and grateful) if the school social worker simply shares that information with him. This responds to the father's demand and respects his daughter's right to confidentiality. That is, the school social worker did not share any information divulged by the student in the group sessions. Furthermore, it gives the social worker an opportunity to provide parent guidance about child custody issues (Mullis & Otwell, 1998). The integrity of the school's counseling services are maintained and available for all students in the school.

Alternative 4: Meet With the Student and the Father

If the daughter has shared some concerns about her father in the small group, the last alternative involves the school social worker responding to the father by offering to meet with him and his daughter. This alternative includes consequences that go beyond simply managing this ethical predicament to enhance the development of the student and the relationships involved. The father feels his concerns have been heard and he has little reason to take his plea to the school administration. The student has her right to confidentiality maintained and by allowing her to control what confidential information she divulges to her father, her development into an autonomous person is supported. The school social worker can facilitate the discussion between the father and his daughter to enhance their relationship (Frieman, 1994). For instance, they might begin to discuss how their relationship will change but still be maintained following the divorce. The father has the opportunity to tell his daughter how much their relationship means to him, which she may not perceive, especially if the mother is sharing negative perceptions of the father with her daughter. And once again in this course of action, the integrity of the school's counseling services are maintained and available for all students in the school. To use a figure of speech, this alternative allows the school social worker to take the "lemons" presented to her in the father's initial demand for information and to make "lemonade" for her student and the other stakeholders involved.

Evaluate the Alternatives

After you have generated all of the reasonable alternatives to manage the ethical quandary and identified the possible consequences of all of these alternatives to the student and stakeholders, you should evaluate these alternatives in preparation for selecting and implementing the best available course of action, which will be addressed in Chapter 6 (Lowenberg et al, 2000;

Ethical Decision Making in School Mental Health

McNamara, 2008; Pope & Vasquez, 2007; Reamer, 2006; Stone, 2005; Van Divner & Champ Morera, 2007).

Moral Principles

An important way to evaluate these different courses of action is to consider their congruence (or lack thereof) with commonly accepted moral principles (McNamara, 2008; Stone, 2005). Stone identifies the moral principles of autonomy, beneficence, nonmaleficence, justice, and loyalty, while McNamara prioritizes the moral principles of respect for the dignity of persons, responsible caring, integrity of relationships, and responsibility to society. We also obtain important guidance from our professions' ethical standards. In Chapter 1, we listed the five general principles of the American Psychological Association (APA) and the six core principles of the National Association of Social Workers (NASW). The American Nurses Association's (2001) *Code of Ethics* lists a wide range of moral virtues and values, including wisdom, honesty, courage, compassion, and patience as attributes of a good nurse (§6.1). These moral principles are articulated in different ways (i.e., values, virtues, priorities, or principles) in the ethical standards for pupil services professionals. Box 2.3 in Chapter 2 demonstrates the congruence among these professions' stated values.

These moral principles lead us to ask these kinds of questions to evaluate each of the possible alternatives to manage the ethical quandary:

1. Is this alternative fair to the student and the other stakeholders?
2. Does this alternative help the student and the other stakeholders?
3. Does this alternative avoid harm to the student and the other stakeholders?
4. Does this alternative maintain my integrity as a professional with a fiduciary responsibility for my client(s)?
5. Does this alternative respect the autonomy of the student and other stakeholders?
6. Is this alternative consistent with my responsibility to the community and society?

Reviewing the responses to these questions for each course of action can help to prioritize which alternatives may more successfully manage the ethical predicament. The more positive responses to these questions, the more likely that the course of action will be successful.

In the earlier scenario involving the father's demand for information, if we were to ask these questions of the first two alternatives, the answers would predominantly be no. However, with the latter two alternatives, the responses would be yes, or at worse, neutral.

Responsibilities to Stakeholders

While we have acknowledged that a pupil services professional's primary responsibility is to the student, that responsibility should not be used to ignore other important responsibilities that the pupil services professional has to the other stakeholders who will be affected by whatever action is taken to manage the ethical predicament.

Parents/Family

If the school social worker in our earlier scenario was to consider the complementary ethical standards of school counselors and school psychologists, she would find the expectation to engage parents as partners in the delivery of services to students (ASCA, 2004, §B; NASP, 2000, §IIIA3). One of the ethical principles in the NASW's (2008) *Code of Ethics* acknowledges the power of human relationships in the change process. Clearly, the parent–child relationship is critical in the development of minor children. Alternatives 2–4 above recognize the rights of the father in this situation, but only Alternatives 3 and 4 successfully manage the ethical quandary.

School/Employer

Presumably, the school social worker has been assigned by the school administration to facilitate the group for students whose families are experiencing divorce. The school values the counseling services provided by the school social worker and other pupil services professionals because these services support students to be more successful in school. The school social worker's responsibility to the school is to provide this service in a professional manner in the best interests of the students. Conduct that would cause the counseling program to be criticized and perhaps less trusted by students and/or families (i.e., Alternatives 1 and 2) potentially diminishes the value of this program to the school. Alternatives 3 and 4 support and even enhance the value of the counseling program to the school.

Ethical Decision Making in School Mental Health

Colleagues

Pupil services professionals have an ethical responsibility to engage in respectful relationships with other educators (ASCA, 2004, §C; ANA, 2001, §1.5, 3.2; NASN, 2002, §1; NASP, 2000, §IIIA4, IIIF1; NASW, 2008, §2.01). Part of a respectful relationship is considering one's responsibilities to professional colleagues. Alternatives 1 and 2 potentially diminish the ability of other pupil services professionals to deliver counseling services to students in the school. Furthermore, the lack of social-emotional support for students may adversely affect their ability to be successful in the classroom—high priorities for both teachers and administrators. Alternatives 3 and 4 honor the school social worker's responsibilities to fellow educators.

Community-Based Professionals

Had the student in this scenario been seeing a community-based professional for therapy, the school social worker's response to the father's demands in Alternative 1 could adversely affect the therapeutic relationship. The father may decide that counseling is not in his best interests as a parent (Taylor & Adelman, 1989/2003). He could withdraw his daughter from therapy or make a similar demand on the therapist for confidential information. Conversely, in Alternative 2, the school social worker's disclosure of confidential information may lead the father to believe that his daughter's therapist should also share confidential information. Alternatives 3 and 4 honor the school social worker's responsibilities to the community-based therapist.

Responsibilities to Other Students

In this scenario, the father's daughter is not the only student. All of the other students in the group have the same status as students. Furthermore, any student in the school is a potential client in the future. The ethical standards for school counselors make a clear statement that they have a responsibility to every student in the school (ASCA, §A1b, 2004). Alternative 1, while maintaining the confidentiality of the student, potentially endangers the availability of counseling services in the future to these and other students in the school. Alternative 2 sets the precedent that students do not have the right to confidentiality, which could make students less likely to come forward for or to cooperate with supportive services. Alternatives 3 and 4 maintain (1) the precedent of students' ethical right to confidentiality and (2) the integrity of the school counseling program.

McNamara (2008) offers a helpful series of questions to reflect on when identifying and considering alternative courses of action:

1. What are the probable consequences, both beneficial and adverse, to the client, stakeholders, and the practitioner?
2. Can the adverse consequences be minimized or eliminated? If so, how?
3. Consider the moral principles involved. Which action enables respect for the dignity of people, responsible caring, integrity of relationships, and responsibility to society?
4. If I were sought out for consultation by a colleague, is this a course of action I would recommend?
5. Would I be comfortable with my colleagues knowing I have done this?

These questions can help to evaluate different courses of action and their impact on the student, stakeholders, and the practitioner.

Moral Development

Ever since Kohlberg (1969) first identified his stages of moral development, clinicians have wondered how to enable children to reach ethical maturity. Kohlberg, however, was less interested in whether children made the "right" decision than the reasoning behind their decisions. Gilligan (1982) argued that Kohlberg was overly rational in his approach and posits that women are more relational in their moral deliberations (see Box 4.2).

Kochanska and Aksan (2006) suggest that moral development has three dimensions. First, *moral reasoning* (ala Kohlberg and Gilligan) is concerned with understanding how people make decisions. It tends to focus on the justifications for specific predicaments. Second, *moral emotions* address feelings such as shame, guilt, and sympathy. This also enables the development of empathy (understanding the feelings of others). Third, *moral conduct* is the behavioral aspect of moral development. Here children learn the difference between prosocial and antisocial actions. They also engage in either committed compliance when they eagerly comply with expectations or situational compliance when they comply only while closely supervised (Kochanska, Coy, & Murray, 2001).

The research on child development demonstrates that even young children can make important distinctions. By age 3, children ascribe greater

Ethical Decision Making in School Mental Health

Box 4.2 Kohlberg and Gilligan's Stages of Moral Reasoning

Kohlberg's Stages

Pre-Conventional Morality
  Stage 1: Obedience and
  Punishment
  Stage 2: Self-Interest and
  Exchange
Conventional Morality
  Stage 3: Interpersonal
  Conformity
  Stage 4: Maintenance of Social
  Order
Post-Conventional Morality
  Stage 5: Social Contract Rights
  Stage 6: Universal Principles

Gilligan's Stages

Pre-Conventional
  Personal survival
  Transition from
    Selfishness to
    Responsibility to others
Conventional
  Self-sacrifice for others
  Transition from Goodness to
  Truth that she is also a
  person
Post-Conventional:
  Nonviolence

fault to a person who does something wrong on purpose than to someone who does it by accident. Preschoolers are capable of making distinctions between moral imperatives (e.g., stealing), social customs (e.g., manners), and matters of personal choice (e.g., clothing preferences) (Berk, 2004). Experts agree that the primary influence at this age is social experience through the parent–child relationship (Royal & Baker, 2005; Termini & Golden, 2007; Walker, 1999). Children note that adults give care to victims and criticism to bullies. Children grow the most when adults engage them in moral discussion, encourage empathy for others, and stimulate their reflection on the reasons behind the rules. They grow the least when adults simply insist on compliance without giving explanations (Laible, Eye, & Carlo, 2008).

There is empirical evidence that a parallel process occurs between teachers and students (DeVries, Hildebrandt, & Zan, 2000; Thornberg, 2006). The Child Development Project is a program that aims to promote academic, social-emotional, and ethical growth of students (Munoz & Vanderhaar, 2006). It is built on four principles: (1) establish caring and supportive relationships between students, teachers, and parents; (2) give routine opportunities for student collaboration; (3) provide regular chances for students to engage in democratic decision making; and (4) encourage students to reflect on and discuss their core values and ideals (Lewis, Watson, & Schnaps, 2003). Long-term effects in students were positively related to their experience of caring from their elementary teachers (Watson, 2006). Teachers, of course, vary greatly in their beliefs about their ability to effect moral development in the classroom. Generally, elementary teachers, teachers who received staff development on character education, and teachers who earned their undergraduate degrees from religiously affiliated universities were most likely to feel effective in improving students' morality (Milson, 2003; Milson & Mehlig, 2002).

Such findings have strong implications for systemic discipline policies in schools and, as the reader will learn later in this chapter, our argument for a collaborative decision-making approach between the pupil services professional and the student. The explicit moral formation programs are too often isolated into character education classes and segregated from the rest of the curriculum. This is especially likely when they are taught by pupil services providers and not teachers. In Hoagwood and colleagues' (2007) research, however, the programs that helped build both academic and social-emotional competencies were integrative. They concluded: "The majority of the interventions that were effective in both domains were time-intensive as well as complex, with multiple targets (e.g., students, parents, and teachers) and across multiple contexts (school and home)" (p. 89). The implicit moral formation occurs "subtly in teacher–student interactions and school policies" (Obidah, Jackson-Minot, Monroe, & Williams, 2004, p. 112). Even more confusing to students is that the explicit instruction and implicit interactions send mixed messages. Character education programs emphasize reflection and dialogue, while classroom and school discipline policies emphasize compliance and top-down dictates.

Noddings (2005) argues that education should be based on care, and it possesses four components. First, *modeling* by adults is required for students to learn how to care for others. This includes caring for colleagues as well as students. Second, *dialogue* allows participants to build relationships and arrive at better decisions. Genuine dialogue occurs when neither party knows ahead of time what the conclusion will be. Third, *practice* gives students the opportunity to improve in caring as they reflect upon their experience (Leming, 2001). Fourth, *confirmation* is the act of affirming and encouraging students to be their best selves. Zero-tolerance policies put both concerned teachers and caring pupil services providers in unwanted ethical predicaments (see Box 4.3). Obidah and associates conclude that schools must reject

Box 4.3 Student With a Gun

Obidah and colleagues (2004) use the example of a teacher who works in an inner-city school. She is about to start her morning lesson when some students suddenly blurt out that they saw a dead body on the way to school that morning. Flustered, she decides to face the issue head-on and ask the students to write about their feelings. She reasons that violent deaths are regular occurrences in large urban school districts (Schaper, 2009). One student seems particularly anguished about the incident but declines to talk about his feelings in front of his classmates. After class, she reaches out to this young adolescent to discover what seems to be bothering him. She learns that his parents are going through a divorce and his father is feeling suicidal. His father asked the boy to remove his 9-mm handgun from the home. Confused and scared the boy brings the firearm to school in his backpack because he does not know where else to turn. He tearfully explains his worries about his father to his teacher and voluntarily offers her the gun. She gingerly takes the gun and locks it in her desk drawer. The student breathes a huge sigh of relief and thanks her for her help. She expresses empathy with his concern about his father and requests that he stop by after school to talk. Previously she had been a strong advocate of the school's zero-tolerance policy, but now she has her doubts. This is a promising and sensitive student with no history of disciplinary problems. Kopels (2007) provides several examples of zero-tolerance policies run amuck because they were overly broad, expelling kids for minor offenses such as wearing gang paraphernalia, smoking tobacco, making verbal threats, or giving away Midol. The new IDEA recommends, but does not require, that schools consider "circumstances" when administering discipline (Raines, 2006). This example, however, involves a regular education student with a loaded firearm—a dangerous weapon clearly covered under the Gun-Free Schools Act of 1994 that requires schools to expel the student for at least 1 year with only the district superintendent empowered to change the requirement on a case-by-case basis (Hanks, 2004).

Questions

1. If the teacher came to you for consultation about her dilemma, what you advise?
2. What further information would you like to have in this case?
3. What would you do for this student? For his father?
4. Think of the public school you know best. How would they handle this incident?
5. Listen to the 5-minute NPR broadcast about Chicago school violence at http://www.npr.org/templates/story/story.php?storyId=104566915
   What should schools do to address this epidemic of violence?

zero-tolerance policies in favor of disciplinary procedures that balance justice and care. Automated school punishments seldom leave room for student intentions and do not allow dialogue and reflection to enter into the equation, making it difficult for children to reach moral maturity.

School-based practitioners are sometimes caught between trying to fulfill their obligations to the school and their fiduciary responsibility to students. The NASW (2008) *Code of Ethics* illustrates both sides of this coin. On one hand, social workers "generally should adhere to commitments made to employers and employing organizations" (§3.09(a)), but in the same section they are also expected to "work to improve employing agencies' policies and procedures" (§3.09(b)) and "not allow an employing organization's policies, procedures, regulations, or administrative orders to interfere with their ethical practice of social work" (§3.09(d)). The ASCA (2004) *Ethical Standards* also note that part of a professional's responsibility to the school is to assist schools in developing "educational procedures and programs to meet students' developmental needs" (§D.1.g(2)). Likewise school psychologists are expected to:

> maintain professional relationships with children, parents, and the school community. Consequently, parents and children are to be fully informed about all relevant aspects of school psychological services in advance. The explanation should take into account language and cultural differences, cognitive capabilities, *developmental level, and age...* (NASP, 2000, §III.A.3, emphasis added)

If pupil services providers are involved in determining the appropriate discipline of students, then part of their responsibility is to explain how the child's developmental level and age should have a bearing on that aspect of the school policy. We recognize that some practitioners would prefer to isolate themselves from the school's disciplinary procedures, but this means sacrificing their obligation to advocate for students. In conclusion, school-based clinicians cannot claim divestiture of school policies that they do not like, but must remain invested in trying to make those procedures developmentally appropriate.

Collaborative Decision Making

All of the ethical decision-making models we were able to find start from the premise of a single ethical agent. That is, the mental health professional, while wisely and prudently seeking out consultation from appropriate professionals and considering responsibilities to the client and stakeholders, ultimately makes the decision of what course of action to take individually. Some might argue that a single ethical agent is necessary for a mental health professional to fully take responsibility for the course of action that is chosen, as is expected within the ethical standards for school counselors, school nurses, and school psychologists (ASCA, 2004, §E1a; §ANA, 2001, §4.1-4.3, 5.2; NASP, 2000, §IIIA1). Pope and Vasquez (2007) and Van Divner and Champ Morera (2007) both include acceptance of responsibility for the course of action in their respective decision-making models, with Pope and Vasquez adding the responsibility for any consequences that result from that course of action. Their qualifiers that the mental health professional take "sole" or "personal" responsibility for the decision reinforces the belief that there should be a single ethical agent (i.e., the mental health professional) who is ultimately responsible for how the ethical quandary is managed.

Self-determination and autonomy of the client are critical ethical standards, but if emphasized at the expense of the best interests of the client, they can allow the professional to abdicate his responsibility to the client (Staller & Kirk, 1997). When working with mature, adult clients, the emphasis on the client taking responsibility for personal courses of action is understandable. For many clients, this is actually a necessary part of their growth and recovery (Dickey, Kiefner & Beidler, 2002). However, school-based mental health professionals work primarily with minor students who are still learning to make positive choices in their lives. Young adults can also make decisions that are not in their best interests. A balance is necessary between helping

---

students make choices and keeping them from actions that may put them in dangerous circumstances.

In this book, we make the case for a collaborative decision-making model with students consistent with their development and ability. Taking responsibility for one's actions is clearly consistent with practicing with integrity, but we do not believe that necessarily requires a single ethical agent making a decision alone. Let's look first at the ethical reasons for a collaborative decision-making model with the student.

The Preamble of the NASW's (2008) *Code of Ethics* states, "Social workers seek to enhance the capacity of people to address their own needs" (p. 5). The *Code* goes on to clarify this statement through an explanation of the ethical principle regarding the dignity and worth of persons: "Social workers promote clients' socially responsible self-determination. Social workers seek to enhance clients' capacity and opportunity to change and to address their own needs" (NASW, 2008, pp. 5–6). Both the NASW's (2008) *Code of Ethics* (§1.02) and the ANA's (2001) *Code of Ethics* (§1.4) include specific references to client self-determination. Similarly, the ASCA (2004) *Ethical Standards* include statements in the Preamble that support the student's right to "move toward self-direction and self-development" (p. 1). Finally, the NASW's (2008) *Code of Ethics* explanation about the importance of human relationships specifically states, "Social workers engage people as partners in the helping process" (p. 6). We believe that a true partnership with the student necessarily involves shared decision making consistent with the student's development and understanding.

Jacob (2008) builds on the principle of autonomy in NASP's (2000) *Principles for Professional Ethics* (§IIIB2) to state "school psychologists permit and encourage student involvement in intervention decisions ... to the maximum extent appropriate to the student and the situation" (p. 1924). Pitcairn and Phillips (2005) share that engagement of an older, mature adolescent in the decision-making process reinforces the student's autonomy, strengthens the helping relationship, and empowers the student to have choices.

Students attend school to learn. While most people may associate that learning taking place in the classroom with teachers as the instructors, there are other settings where students learn and other educators who teach them as well. Pupil services professionals, while not having the classroom instructional expertise of teachers, are still educators. Small group and individual counseling provide students with learning opportunities that supplement their learning in the classroom. An ethical predicament is not simply a situation a pupil services professional must manage; it is also an opportunity for learning and growth of the student. By engaging the student in a partnership to consider and evaluate the alternative courses of action, the practitioner is teaching good decision-making skills that will help the student grow to become an autonomous adult. The student is guided to look beyond the present and how his choices will affect his future. The student is helped to understand how her actions affect not just herself but others in her life.

Taylor and Adelman (1989) suggest enabling students to disclose confidential information. These steps engage the student as a partner, preserve the student's right to confidentiality and self-determination, and teach the student valuable skills for navigating challenging life situations.

1. *Enhancing motivational readiness for sharing.* Are there any advantages to the student sharing the information? Are there any costs, either in the present or future, to not sharing information?
2. *Enabling students to share information.* How can the student be empowered to share the information? What support does the student need?
3. *Minimizing negative consequences of disclosure.* What can be done to minimize any costs related to disclosure?

Student as Partner

Consider the following case example and the collaborative approach taken by the school counselor to manage this ethical predicament.

A school counselor is seeing a 17-year-old student and learns the student is sexually active with multiple partners. The student refuses to seek out health care services or to use any kind of protection to avoid pregnancy and sexually transmitted infections (STIs). The high school is experiencing an outbreak of STIs among its students, specifically Chlamydia and herpes. While neither of these STIs is life threatening, Chlamydia is associated with pelvic inflammatory disorder that can lead to female sterility if left untreated. Herpes is a lifelong infection that can be treated but never cured. Furthermore, these STIs may be asymptomatic, especially in females. Despite the presentation of this information by the school counselor, the student is not dissuaded and states the intention to continue to be sexually active. Additionally, the student refuses to share the names of any sexual partners, but comments by the student lead the school counselor to believe they are students at the high school. Finally, the school counselor's conversations with other educators in the school indicate many students have a casual approach to sex (i.e., multiple partners, inconsistent use of protection from pregnancy and STIs, casual "hook-ups" or "friends with benefits"). See Box 4.4 as you consider this scenario.

Ethical Tensions and Competing Responsibilities

The school counselor is presented with a variety of ethical tensions and competing responsibilities in this scenario. On the one hand, the student has the right to confidentiality and self-determination, which the school counselor

---

Box 4.4 Quick Check for Personal Bias

We devoted Chapter 1 to help prevent practitioners from having their personal views and ethical preferences inappropriately affect their ethical decisions. One of the authors has used the ethical quandary about the sexually active student with multiple partners in Chapter 4 in trainings on ethics and professional boundaries for school social workers and other pupil services professionals. The gender of the student was purposely left neutral. The author has found that some training participants have unknowingly imposed a gender on the student (i.e., assuming the student is female or male). Typically, when participants do this, they have usually also imposed a gender-based motivation for the sexual activity on the student. Specifically, a male student is often assumed to be a perpetrator, while a female student is often assumed to be a victim. In this scenario, the school counselor may well find out through interactions with the student that the student has been victimized or has victimized other students, but that should be an objective determination, rather than a gender-based assumption. Did you assume a gender of the student in this scenario? Did you assume the student was a victim or perpetrator? If so, you may want to take another look at Chapter 1 and the exercises it offers.

---

wants to respect and preserve. The student is almost of adult age and the legal right to manage his or her own affairs. That being said, the student's current position is not in his or her best interests and the school counselor is concerned about the student's health and well-being.

On the other hand, the school counselor has important responsibilities to all of the other students in the high school as well. The ASCA (2004) *Ethical Standards* clearly state that school counselors are to be "concerned with ... every student" (§A1b). Depending upon the STI infection rate, this scenario describes an actual or potential public health emergency. Because these infections may be asymptomatic, the infection rate could potentially be much higher than is presently known. The ASCA (2004) *Ethical Standards* include a provision for disclosure of confidential information for communicable diseases (§A2c). However, that guidance applies only when the communicable disease may be fatal (e.g., AIDS) and the potentially infected other party is identifiable. Neither is the case in this scenario. Chlamydia and herpes are not life threatening, but they do have potential and serious lifelong consequences. In addition, the school counselor does not know the identities of the sexual partners.

The school counselor also has responsibilities to the school/employer, the families, and the greater community. No doubt the school administration is genuinely concerned about the outbreak of STIs in the high school and wants its employees to do everything they can to help address this health crisis. The parents of the students in the high school want their children to be safe and free from infection. The public health department will also see this situation as important and may already be directly involved.

When engaging a student as a partner in managing an ethical quandary, these ethical tensions and competing responsibilities can be shared with the student in a developmentally appropriate manner. The school counselor can share that she considers the student's right to confidentiality and self-determination to be very important. She can also share her concern for the student's health and well-being and for all of the students in the high school, as well as her competing responsibilities to the school, the families, and the community. By sharing these ethical tensions and competing responsibilities, the student may begin to empathize with the school counselor's predicament.

Generate Courses of Action

In this scenario, the student is asserting his or her right to confidentiality and self-determination. In a partnership between the school counselor and student, we believe that the school counselor may assert her refusal to accept the student's current position (i.e., continued, unprotected sex with multiple partners and nondisclosure to affected parties). The school counselor can simply state that she cannot support the student's current position and they need to work together to find a course of action that they can both agree to. This approach respects the student's right to self-determination but also allows the school counselor to help the student move toward a course of action that is in the student's best interests. This offer of collaboration with the student must be sincere and not simply a guise for coercion of the student into a course of action (e.g., change your behavior or I will notify your parents).

There are several potential courses of action open to the school counselor and the student. These courses of action are not mutually exclusive and can be used in conjunction with each other to best address the ethical tensions and competing responsibilities.

1. *Notify the parents.* The student may immediately reject this alternative, but it is important for the student to understand that the school counselor has responsibilities to the student's parents. The student could be given the option of determining which parent is contacted first.

2. *Notify another responsible adult in the family.* Does the student have a responsible adult sibling, aunt or uncle, or grandparent that the student trusts? This alternative is a variation of 1, in that the school counselor is involving the family in helping the student move toward more sexually responsible behavior. The student may be able to identify someone, who while not legally responsible for the student, has a sincere personal interest in the student's health and well-being.

3. *Refer the student to the school nurse.* Communicable disease is an area of expertise of the school nurse and this person is likely to be more familiar with the public health system than the school counselor. Additionally, the student may have additional legal rights to confidentiality by seeing a licensed, health care professional regarding family planning services (*Carey v. Population Services International*, 1977; *Planned Parenthood of Central Missouri v. Danforth*, 1976).

4. *Refer the student to the public health department.* Public health departments have specific procedures for managing

outbreaks of communicable disease, including confidential notification of partners and access to health care services. In addition, public health officials have experience dealing with individuals who are reticent to share information about their sexual behavior, including the names of sexual partners.

5. *Refer the student for health care services.* Clearly, it is in this student's best interests to be tested for sexually transmitted infections. While the student has refused to access health care services to date, the student may not be aware of his or her right to obtain confidential health care services. Continued discussion with the student on this issue is critical. If the student continues to refuse, any of the other steps may help to move him or her in this direction.

6. *Treat this problem as an opportunity for universal precautions.* In conjunction with the school administration and school board, alert all parents to the current rate of sexually transmitted infections. Encourage all parents to speak with their children about sexual activity and emphasize the importance of routine medical care and check-ups. Provide information about low-cost medical care for all income-eligible families.

Regardless of the course(s) of action selected in collaboration with the student, the school counselor has ethical responsibilities to the other students in the high school. If no systemic response has yet been begun to address the outbreak of STIs in the high school, the school counselor can partner with the school nurse and/or the public health department to raise students' awareness about STIs and their consequences, responsible sexual behavior, the current outbreak of STIs in the high school, and minors' rights to confidential treatment for STIs. In addition, the public health department can help to proactively contact students who may be infected, rather than waiting for students to come forward for testing and treatment.

Student Readiness

Pupil services professionals may interact with students as young as 3 years and as old as 22 years when considering the rights of students with disabilities to a free appropriate public education. That dramatic age range represents almost the complete continuum of child to adult development.

In addition to age and maturation, a student's ability to participate in collaborative decision making is also affected by cognitive development and mental health, which may be impaired in some students. A willful preschooler who insists on riding her tricycle into the street cannot be afforded self-determination. The adults in her life must take control of her dangerous behavior and ensure her safety until she understands the potential consequences of her conduct and agrees to ride her tricycle in a safe manner. On the other end of the scale may be a high school student who is very mature for his age and is struggling with an important life decision for the very reason that he is fully cognizant of the short- and long-term consequences for him and others in his life. His adult-level awareness is what makes the decision difficult. In these two extreme cases, the decision of whether to involve the student in collaborative decision making is easy. The challenge for pupil services professionals becomes greater as the age, maturity, and capacity of students change over time.

The rights and abilities of students to participate in collaborative decision making and the rights of parents to be informed of and consent to services for their children is an iterative and interactive process that evolves over students' progression from elementary school to middle school to high school. In general, the younger the student, the more important the involvement of the parent (Prout, DeMartino, & Prout, 1999) and other adults is to protect the child's well-being (Pitcairn & Phillips, 2005). Campbell (2003) cites studies of cognitive development that suggest students under the age of 14 years do not have the capacity to consider long-term outcomes of decisions.

Advocates for Youth (1998) offers three criteria to help determine if a student is capable of assenting to services and participate in decision making:

1. Consent is given with information (i.e., the student knows the risks and alternatives).
2. Consent is given with competence (i.e., the student is not too immature, cognitively impaired, or mentally ill).
3. Consent is given voluntarily (i.e., the student has not been coerced or misled).

If the pupil services professional is unable to answer "yes" to all three conditions, this should lead to the conclusion that the involvement of the parent or some other responsible adult in the student's life is necessary.

Isaacs (1999) surveyed school counselors to investigate factors that affected their professional choices regarding confidentiality. Not surprisingly, school counselors working with younger students were more likely to disclose confidential information from students than school counselors working with older students. However, the school level at which the school counselor worked was found to actually have more influence on decision making than the student's age. That is, a school counselor working in a middle school was less likely to disclose confidential information from a 12-year-old student than a school counselor working with a same-age student in an elementary school. Similarly, a school counselor working in a high school was less likely to disclose confidential information from a 14-year-old student than a school counselor working with a same-age student in a middle school.

Some states have laws that give minors specific rights, including access to confidential health services without parental knowledge and/or consent, at certain ages (e.g., 12 or 14 years old). These areas include alcohol and other drug treatment, mental health assessment and treatment, and family planning services (Dibble, 2007). While not applicable in the school setting, pupil services professionals can use these legal parameters to help guide their decisions about student readiness for collaborative decision making.

The pupil services professional needs to take care not to overwhelm a student with information or decisions that are beyond the child's ability to comprehend and manage (Jacob, 2008). If students are too young, immature, cognitively delayed, or suffering from a mental illness that impairs their judgment, the pupil services professional should look to other adults in their lives who can participate in the collaborative decision making. The default adult should always be the parent (*Pierce v. Society of Sisters*, 1925; *Wisconsin v. Yoder*, 1972). As we have discussed previously, parents have both a moral and legal responsibility to provide for and protect their minor children. Earlier in this chapter, we shared the alternative strategy of involving another adult member of the student's family (e.g., mature sibling, aunt, uncle, or grandparent) who is willing to take responsibility for the child. In some cases, another educator in the school may be genuinely concerned about the child and willing to participate in collaborative decision making, including carrying out the selected course of action. For instance, a classroom teacher may feel invested in the well-being of a child in her classroom and may welcome the opportunity to help manage the ethical quandary. The student can help to select what adult, other than the pupil services professional, will participate in the collaborative decision making.

Ethical Guidelines

1. Understand your primary (teleological) goal in each situation. What are the potential costs and benefits of each option in light of this ultimate goal?
2. Avoid polarized or "either-or" thinking that actually creates an ethical dilemma. Generate at least three possible courses of action to potentially manage the situation.
3. Take time to think about what can be done to reduce the tension between the relevant ethical values and the competing responsibilities.
4. Project the outcomes, both positive and negative, to each possible course of action. Be sure to project the consequences for not just the student, but to all of the stakeholders as well.
5. Evaluate the possible courses of action, considering the projected consequences to the student and other stakeholders, and the moral principles that are fundamental to your profession (e.g., autonomy, beneficence, nonmaleficence, justice, integrity, responsibility to society).
6. Embrace the ethical predicament as an opportunity for the student to learn valuable life skills. Engage the student, and perhaps other stakeholders, as a partner in the decision-making process. Consider the student's age, developmental maturity, cognitive functioning, and mental health when determining whether and how to partner with the student or other stakeholders.

Exercises

1. Classroom Instruction

What kind of instruction on character education or other forms of social-emotional development does your school provide? Has your school adopted the ASCA National Model for comprehensive school counseling? If so, how is the classroom instruction portion of the program being taught and by whom? Consider the research of Hoagwood and colleagues (2007) that found the most effective programs were integrated, rather than being taught separately from other instruction. Discuss the local implementation of your school's social-emotional instruction and determine whether change is warranted to improve efficacy.

2. Multiple Courses of Action

Review the two scenarios presented in this chapter. Can you generate additional courses of action other than what the authors have suggested? Do any of these additional courses of action do a better job of mediating the ethical tensions and competing responsibilities?

3. Minors' Rights to Confidential Services

Research what rights minors have to confidential services in your state from community-based mental health, alcohol and other drug, family planning, legal, sexual assault, and domestic violence services. Share your research with your fellow students or the pupil services colleagues in your school.

Internet Resources

ASCA National Model for comprehensive school counseling
http://www.ascanationalmodel.org/
Character Counts
http://charactercounts.org
Character Education Partnership
http://www.character.org
Collaborative for Academic, Social, and Emotional Learning
http://www.casel.org/links.php
Emotional Intelligence
http://www.6seconds.org
George Lucas Educational Foundation
http://www.GLEE.org
National Center for Innovation & Education—Hope Foundation
http://www.communitiesofhope.com
National Professional Resources, Inc.
http://nprinc.com

5

Managing Clinical Concerns

Managing the clinical concerns is perhaps less of a "step" in ethical decision making than a continuing concern. We place it here only as a reminder to practitioners about the importance of the therapeutic relationship throughout this process (Jobes & O'Connor, 2009; Kooyman & Barret, 2009; Norcross, 2002).

Most professional codes of ethics require that ethical practitioners should be clinically competent. This competence, however, is never conceived as a lasting achievement, but an ideal that one is constantly striving toward. The ASCA (2004) *Ethical Standards* require that the professional counselor "strives through personal initiative to maintain professional competence including technological literacy and to keep abreast of professional information. Professional and personal growth are ongoing throughout the counselor's career" (§E.1.c). The NASP (2000) *Principles* state, "School psychologists engage in continuing professional development. They remain current regarding developments in research, training, and professional practices that benefit children, families, and schools" (§II.A.4). The ANA (2001) *Code of Ethics* states, "Continual professional growth, particularly in knowledge and skill, requires a commitment to lifelong learning. Such learning includes, but is not limited to, continuing education, networking with professional colleagues, self-study, professional reading, certification, and advanced degrees" (§5.2). Finally, the NASW (2008) *Code of Ethics* requires that:

> Social workers should strive to become and remain proficient in professional practice and the performance of professional functions. Social workers should critically examine and keep current with emerging knowledge relevant to social work. Social workers

should routinely review the professional literature and participate in continuing education relevant to social work practice and social work ethics. (§4.01(b))

There is no shame in admitting that we do not know how to handle a difficult situation. As many good professors tell their students, "There is no such thing as a dumb question." We are all lifelong learners when it comes to excellence in clinical practice. In this chapter, we will explore three related issues: threat assessments, developmental readiness, and cultural sensitivity.

Threat Assessments

There are two kinds of threat assessment that every pupil services provider should be prepared to conduct. The first is threats against the self; the second is threats against others. In both situations, our goals should be to keep students safe and to help students grow through the crisis. While the first goal is evident, the second may be overlooked or fail to be recognized in the midst of addressing a crisis. Both types of threat assessment should involve express parental permission for the evaluation, if at all possible, before the assessment begins (Koocher, 2006).

Suicidal Threats

Roberts (2006) points out that suicides are the third leading cause of death for adolescents and can even be attempted by children as young as 7 years old. He and others have identified over 20 different warning signs (see Box 5.1). We make a distinction between risk factors and warning signs. *Risk factors* are group characteristics statistically correlated with greater risk (e.g., males under 25 years of age), whereas *warning signs* are individual signals that students' level of dangerousness is escalating (Rudd et al., 2006). The problem with lists of warning signs, however, is that professionals are tempted to take an additive approach and conclude that the student exhibiting the greatest number of symptoms is the student most at risk. This approach fails, however, to consider that the intensity of a single sign may be sufficient cause for alarm, such as the student with an eating disorder who has lost half of her body weight (Gentile, Manna, Ciceri, & Rodeschini, 2008; Pompili, Girardi, Ruberto, & Tatarelli, 2006; Ruuska, Kaltiala-Heino, Rantanen, & Koivisto, 2005). It is also helpful for practitioners to record these warning signs in their clinical notes in case they are later called to account for their conclusions.

Box 5.1 Warning Signs for Suicide

- Direct or indirect threats ("The world would be better off without me")
- Access to means (e.g., guns, narcotics)
- Prior suicide attempts
- Intense emotional pain
- Extreme sense of hopelessness and helplessness
- Social isolation (often self-induced)
- Prolonged feelings of emptiness, worthlessness, and/ or depression
- Sudden improvement in mood after prolonged depression
- Mental confusion (irrational thinking)
- Prior family history of suicide
- Past psychiatric history
- Alcohol or substance abuse
- Anger, aggression, or irritability (esp. in children)
- Childhood history of physical or sexual abuse
- Running away from home
- Sleep or eating disturbances
- Loss of positive motivation (e.g., decline in grades)
- Loss of interest in pleasurable activities (anhedonia)
- Poor personal hygiene or lack of concern about appearance
- Excessive focus on death and dying
- Daring or risk-taking behavior
- Lack of interest in planning for the future (lacking goals)
- Making final arrangements (e.g., giving away prized possessions)

Sources: Brock, Sandoval, & Hart (2006); Poland & Lieberman (2002); Roberts (2006).

Ethical Decision Making in School Mental Health

In addition to these warning signs, school-based practitioners should be familiar with standardized scales for assessing depression in youth. There are two major reasons to employ research-based instruments in suicide risk assessment. First, empirical research has concluded that clinician-only based assessments are often biased and haphazard (Jensen & Weisz, 2002; Lewczyk, Garland, Hurlburt, Gearity, & Hough, 2003). Including standardized instruments in clinical assessment protocols improves objectivity and establishes a baseline by which to measure future change (Doss, 2005). Second, students from some cultural groups are unlikely to admit to suicidal ideation verbally. They will, however, indicate these thoughts on a written instrument (Eskin, 2003; Morrison & Downey, 2000). In fact, low self-disclosure may be a warning sign for suicidal behavior (Horesh, Zalsman, & Apter, 2004).

There are eight validated scales that can be used to measure depression in children and youth. *Youth Self-Report* by Achenbach and Rescorla (2001) includes an affective problem subscale that possesses high diagnostic reliability and validity (Aebi, Metzke, & Steinhausen, 2009; van Lang, Ferdinand, Oldehinkel, Ormel, & Verhulst, 2005). The *Reynolds Adolescent Depression Scale* (2nd ed.; Reynolds, 2002) and the *Reynolds Child Depression Scale* (1989) are also useful in assessing depressive symptomatology in children and youth. The adolescent version has a short form that has been demonstrated to have good reliability and validity (Milfont et al., 2008). The *Children's Depression Rating Scale, Revised* (Poznanski & Mokros, 1995) is another reliable and valid measure of depression for school-aged children (Frazier et al., 2007). The *Children's Depression Inventory* (Kovacs, 1992) is an internationally used multi-informant (child and parent) scale that can be used with children ages 8–18 years (Timbremont, Braet, & Dreessen, 2004). It also has a short form with just 10 questions. The *Brief Multidimensional Students' Life Satisfaction Scale* (Huebner, 1994) is a strengths-based instrument that measures contentment in five domains: family, friends, school, living environment, and self. It has been validated with middle-school through college students (Funk, Huebner, & Valois, 2006; Huebner, Suldo, Valois, & Drane, 2006). While the *Beck Depression Inventory-II* (Beck, Steer, & Brown, 1996) is appropriate to use with older adolescents, ages 14–19 years (Osman, Barrios, Gutierrez, Williams, & Bailey, 2008; VanVoorhis & Blumentritt, 2007), the *Beck Depression Inventory for Youth* (Beck, Beck, & Jolly, 2001) is more appropriate for younger students, ages 9–13 years (Stapleton, Sander, & Stark, 2007).

There are five validated scales that aim to predict future suicidal behavior for youth. The *Suicide Ideation Questionnaire* has a high school form (Reynolds, 1987) that can be used with adolescents (Abdel-Khalek & Lester, 2007). The *Suicide Probability Scale* (Cull & Gill, 1988) was designed for adults, but it has been tested with students ages 12–17 years (Huth-Bocks, Kerr, Ivey, Kramer, & King, 2007). The *Child Suicide Potential* scale's (Pfeffer, Coute, Plutchik, & Jerett, 1979) inter-rater reliability is good, but its test-retest reliability is low (Ofek, Weizman, & Apter, 1998). The *Multi-Attitude Suicide Tendency Scale* (Orbach, Milstein, Har-Even, Apter, Tiano, & Elizur, 1991) is a brief 30-item instrument to measure suicidal tendencies in adolescents. It has four sub-scales: attraction to life, repulsion by life, attraction to death, and repulsion by death. Its four factor structure has been confirmed for White and Asian students (Osman, Barrios, Grittmann, & Osman, 1993; Wong, 2004), but not for African American students (Gutierrez, Osman, Kopper, & Barrios, 2004). Finally, the *Columbia TeenScreen* program is a multistage screening procedure for high school students (Brown, & Grumet, 2009; Shaffer et al., 2004). Brock, Sandoval, and Hart (2006) warn, however, that many screening measures frequently produce false positives so practitioners should balance such instruments with a clinical interview. Again, pupil services providers should maintain the results of such assessment measures in their clinical notes.

We believe that suicide assessment is best done by a crisis team. Cornell and Sheras (2006) recommend that these teams always include a school administrator, school resource officer, and pupil services provider(s). School administrators are involved because of their responsibility for maintaining a safe school environment. School resource officers are responsible for investigating the location of weapons in the school or obtaining a search warrant for the home, if necessary. Pupil services providers should handle the clinical aspects of the assessment, de-escalation of the student's agitation, family assistance, and coordination of cooperating community agencies. We recognize that many pupil services providers must cover multiple schools (U.S. Department of Education, 2007b). Ideally, they will coordinate their schedules so that there is always at least one clinician on hand. Minimally, a pupil services professional should be available to go to a school immediately as part of a crisis response. Teachers should only be included if they have a special relationship with the student at risk. In addition to these team members recommended by Cornell and Sheras, we also recommend that parents be involved whenever possible. While their willingness and capacity to participate may be diminished by a sudden notification of their child in crisis, we must remember it is their child and in most cases, the child will be released into their custody.

Roberts (2006) offers a seven-step plan for crisis intervention. First, practitioners should assess lethality by immediately talking to parents and patiently to the student. Parents should be asked to make collateral contacts with ex- and current romantic partners as well as ex- and current friends to inquire about any recent changes (e.g., breakups, illegal drugs, unusual behavior). If these individuals are present in the school, these contacts can be made by a pupil services member of the crisis team. Cooper and Lesser (2002) recommend that a lethality assessment include determining the student's suicidal ideation (frequency and duration of thoughts); concreteness of the plan (lethality, locality, imminence, and plausibility); extent of preparation; impulsivity; and use of substances as disinhibitants. Students should also be asked about positive aspects of their life such as future plans, upcoming celebrations, social supports, and happy events that are recurrent. Second, school-based mental health providers should establish rapport with the student. Initially this means creating a common bond with the student around favorite interests, such as movies, music, TV shows, or video games. Genuine engagement, however, requires demonstration of respect, active listening, warmth, and empathy (Brock et al., 2006; Raines & Ahlman, 2004). Third, practitioners should identify the major problem, including immediate precipitants and triggering incidents. During this time, clinicians should inquire directly about suicidal or homicidal ideation and/or nonverbal gestures. Brock, Sandoval, and Hart (2006) recommend exploration of five areas. *Current suicide plan* questions focus on the presence of active intent and extent of preparation. *Pain* questions center on desperation and observation of physical agitation (i.e., the compulsion to do something to end suffering). *Resources* questions concentrate on interpersonal relationships and reasons for living. *Prior suicidal behavior* questions converge on the history and frequency of past attempts. *History of mental illness* questions focus on mental disorders, personality problems, substance abuse, and trauma. Fourth, practitioners should address the student's feelings. This includes helping the student identify what she is feeling, differentiating between surface affects and underlying moods, and validation of emotions. This step also involves helping the student identify emotional coping methods that have worked in the past that may help in the present. Fifth, practitioners should explore possible alternatives. This should include the use of a strengths-based assessment such as Graybeal's (2001) ROPES model or solution-focused assessment (Murphy, 2008; Sklare, 2005; Teall, 2000). This should also include an assessment of the success or failure of past therapeutic interventions. Sixth, practitioners should formulate an immediate action plan (see Fig. 5.1). This plan should include a discussion of short-term goals, mutual commitment to tasks, and guidelines for termination. Finally, practitioners should end the crisis intervention with their door ajar. The student should be encouraged to call, drop-in, e-mail, or text-message if another crisis arises. The practitioner should schedule a checkup for the near future to ensure changes and referrals are still on track. A two-way release of information and follow-up by phone with community providers can confirm the student's self-report.

High-risk threats are both serious and imminent (Cornell & Sheras, 2006). The student should be escorted to a prearranged safe room with a phone. Parents should be called immediately (in the presence of the student) and invited to participate in team decisions. The student should never be left alone even for a few minutes. Determined adolescents intent on suicide have been effective even when placed on round-the-clock suicide watches (Busch, Fawcett, & Jacobs, 2003). A study by Swahn and Potter (2001) of 153 near-lethal suicide attempters (adolescents and young adults) found 25% acted within 5 minutes of the impulse to take their lives, while 71% acted within 1 hour. If the student attempts to leave, block the door and warn that physical restraint may occur before imposing it. Do not deceive the student

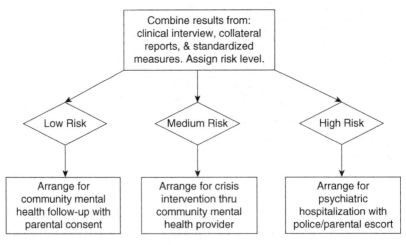

FIGURE 5.1 Suicide Action Plan Flowchart.

about confidentiality; it is better for the student to be angry than to lose trust in the integrity of the mental health providers. If the student refuses to relinquish a weapon or other lethal means at his or her disposal, police should be contacted and medical personnel notified (Brock et al., 2006). Inform the youth in a matter-of-fact tone about all actions taken or about to take place. Transportation should be arranged in accordance with student cooperation. Students who object to hospitalization should be taken in a squad car for safety reasons. Cooperative students can be transported in their parent's vehicle.

Triage for students who are deemed an immediate danger to themselves should include short-term psychiatric hospitalization combined with psychosocial therapy and pharmacological therapy (Roberts, 2006). It is vitally important that psychotropic medication does not occur in isolation from psychosocial treatment. Adolescents who only receive antidepressant medication sometimes feel just good enough to do something to end their suffering and this can increase the likelihood of suicide. Birmaher and colleagues (2007) recommend that psychosocial intervention should include four aspects. *Psychoeducation* should present depression as a disease that is no one's fault, neither a manipulation nor a sign of moral weakness. *Supportive management* includes active listening, restoration of hope, problem solving, and training in coping skills. *Family involvement* includes strengthening the student's relationship with parents as well as referrals for conflictual issues (e.g., marriage therapy). *School involvement* includes temporary accommodations to the student's workload (a 504 plan) and referral for school-based services (such as counseling).

Threats Against Others

We think that it is significant that both the Federal Bureau of Investigation (O'Toole, 1999) and the joint U.S. Secret Service and Department of Education (Fein et al., 2002) reports take an ecological approach to school violence. In other words, threat assessment requires both an evaluation of the student(s) involved and the milieu in which the threat occurs. This further implies that approaches such as zero-tolerance policies, prospective behavioral profiling, and actuarial decision making should be rejected in favor of a more contextualized perspective (Reddy et al., 2001). The FBI report states this well:

> Educators, mental health professionals, legislators, law enforcement officers, parents, students, and the rest of the public all

share a sense of frustration and helplessness and a compulsion to take some quick action that can prevent similar incidents in the future. Though understandable, this impulse can lead communities to forget the wisdom of H. L. Mencken's aphorism: "For every problem, there is a solution which is simple, neat, and wrong." (O'Toole, 1999, p. 2)

Generally, schools are safe places for children, since less than 1% of the violence against children occurs on campus, even during the year of the Columbine massacre (U.S. Department of Education & U.S. Department of Justice, 2000).

The FBI report (O'Toole, 1999) recommended a four-point assessment approach to identifying violent students. The first factor is the *personality of the student*. Consideration should be given to how the student copes with conflict, disappointment, or insults; how he expresses anger and frustration; how he responds to criticism; how he responds to authority figures; and his ability to demonstrate empathy or respect for others. For example, Newhill (2003) discusses the concept of emotional dysregulation. This includes a student's emotional reactivity, emotional intensity, and inability to regain emotional balance. The second factor is the *family dynamics of the student*. Issues such as family patterns of behavior and thinking, beliefs and values, and customs and traditions are important. For example, exposure to child abuse and domestic violence at home increases the likelihood of student-initiated school violence (Baldry, 2003; Szyndrowski, 1999). The third factor is *school dynamics*. While school administrators may have their own view of the school climate, students may have a completely different experience. For example, students often perceive a pecking order among cliques and experience bullying in less supervised locations (Barnes, 2005; Meyer-Adams & Conner, 2008; Roou, 2004). A large discrepancy between the student and staff viewpoints is important because it implies that much of the problem is occurring outside the awareness of school officials. The fourth factor is the *social dynamics of the community*. What are the attitudes toward alcohol, drugs, entertainment, racism, social status, and weapons? For example, in many communities a lack of athletic proclivity and physical prowess may leave an artistic adolescent feeling marginalized (Brooks & Magnussen, 2006; Meador, 2005). Within the larger community, a teen's choice of an immediate peer group plays an important role in shaping attitudes and behavior (O'Toole, 1999).

Targeted threat assessment has five guiding principles (Borum & Verhaagen, 2006). First, violence is the final result of a discernible process of thinking and acting. Students seldom just "snap" and engage in random acts of violence. Practitioners should focus on understanding the motives and behavior of the hostile student (see Box 5.2). Second, violence results from the interplay between the perpetrator, recent past events, current precipitants, and the intended target. There is a complex and contextualized interaction that cannot be blamed on just one "deranged" student. Third, practitioners

---

Box 5.2 Threat Assessment Interview of the Hostile Student

1. If you had to name people at school who have made it hard for you, who would they be? (Purpose: to identify potential targets)
2. Have you ever daydreamed about how you could get even with people at school who have done you wrong? (Purpose: to identify potential acts of violence)
3. Have you shared with anyone how you would like to deal with such people? What advice did they give? (Purpose: to determine social support for plans)
4. Are you the kind of person who will let someone know you are angry with them? (Purpose: to determine pent-up aggression)
5. Would you describe yourself as average, or do you think you stand out as different? (Purpose: to determine how well the student "blends in" with the crowd)
6. What have you been doing to stay busy over the past several days? (Purpose: to determine preparatory signals for violence)
7. Have you been feeling discouraged and let down lately? (Purpose: to determine level of depression and hopelessness)
8. Tell me about people that you have lost in your life that you really miss? (Purpose: to determine how recent and painful losses have been)

---

9. What failure did you have in school that really hit you hard? (Purpose: to determine how the student copes with disappointment)
10. Which students have really bugged you with snide remarks? (Purpose: to determine the student's level of resentment about bullies)
11. If this country were under attack and you had to get a gun to defend yourself, how would you go about it? (Purpose: to determine the student's access to weapons)
12. If you were in a tight spot, what friend would you like to have with you? Why? (Purpose: to determine possible collaborators)

Source: Patrasso (2005).

should investigate the facts using critical thinking to guide them. Clinicians should be skeptical about hearsay and focus on the evidence at hand. Don't be afraid to challenge how people "know" something to be true. Fourth, an integrated systems perspective should guide the investigation. Parents, friends, probation officers, teachers, employers, and other informants will all have information for the assessment and a part of the solution. Fifth, the essential question is not whether the student has made a threat, but whether he truly intends to carry it out. Students often make idle threats that they have no real intention of carrying out.

Borum and Verhaagen (2006) suggest that in a *Tarasoff*-type situation that clinicians should consider six factors known by the mnemonic acronym ACTION.

Attitudes that justify violence (e.g., victims are considered subhuman)
Capacity to carry out violence (e.g., possession of weapons and ammunition)
Thresholds or rules broken to further the plan (e.g., stealing a gun or bullets)

Ethical Decision Making in School Mental Health

Intent or commitment to the plan (e.g., resolute about violent objectives)

Others' reactions or responses to the plan (e.g., fear that student can be lethal)

Noncompliance with risk reduction interventions (e.g., refusal to de-escalate)

Similarly, the joint report of the U.S. Secret Service and U.S. Department of Education (Fein et al., 2002) recommends that the team discern the answers to 11 questions in a targeted risk assessment (see Box 5.3). The threat assessment report can be organized into seven parts: (1) precipitating events; (2) identifying information about the subject; (3) background information; (4) current situation; (5) attack-related preparation; (6) motives; and (7) target selection (Borum & Verhaagen, 2006).

Clinicians may also want to employ risk assessment questionnaires to structure their investigation and ensure that nothing is missed. There are six validated risk assessment measures for violence specifically for youth. The *Structured Assessment of Violence Risk in Youth* (SAVRY; Bartel, Borum, & Forth, 2000) has been tested in juvenile detention facilities, residential psychiatric placements, correctional schools, and forensic units (Gammelgard, Koivisto, Eronen, & Kaltiala-Heino, 2008). It is best at predicting physical violence, good at predicting violence against objects, verbal threats, and rule violations, but not for verbal abuse (Lodewijks, Doreleijers, de Ruiter, & Borum, 2008). The *Life Challenges Questionnaire-Teen* form is a 120-item self-report inventory for youth with 53 scattered items that are categorized into the Risk Assessment Index. It successfully differentiated Christian high school youth from those in a juvenile detention facility (Grinberg, Dawkins, Dawkins, & Fullilove, 2005). The *Early Assessment Risk List for Boys* (EARL-20B; Augimeri, Webster, Koegl, & Levene, 2001) is a Canadian tool used to identify violent boys, ages 6–12 years old (Enebrink, Langstrom, Hulten, & Gumpert, 2006). The *Youth Level of Service/Case Management Inventory* (Hoge & Andrews, 1995) has been useful in predicting both juvenile recidivism (Bechtel, Lowenkamp, & Latessa, 2007; Onifade et al., 2008; Thompson & Pope, 2005) and institutional misconduct in youth ages 10–16 years (Holsinger, Lowenkamp, & Latessa, 2006). The *Violence Risk Scale* (Wong & Gordon, 2006) has a youth version in the draft stage that has been used with 133 youth in Canada (Stockdale, 2008). Finally, the *Child and Adolescent Risk for Violence* (CARV; Seifert, Phillips, & Parker, 2001) has only been tested in

Box 5.3 Eleven Team Questions for Threat Assessment Against Others

1. What are the student's motive(s) and goals? What function does he or she hope to accomplish?
2. Have there been any communications suggesting ideas or intent to attack?
3. Has the subject shown inappropriate interest in any of the following: school attacks, weapons, mass violence?
4. Has the student engaged in attack-related behaviors such as developing a plan, acquiring weapons, practicing, casing the site, or rehearsing?
5. Does the student have the capacity to carry out an act of targeted violence (organization and means)?
6. Is the student experiencing hopelessness, desperation, and/or despair?
7. Does the student have a trusting relationship with at least one responsible adult?
8. Does the student see violence as an acceptable or desirable or only way to solve problems?
9. Is the student's conversation and story consistent with his or her actions?
10. Are other people concerned about the student's potential for violence due to recent changes or escalations in mood or behavior?
11. What circumstances or environmental factors might affect the likelihood of an attack?

Source: Fein et al. (2002).

a pilot study on 37 youths, ages 2–20 years. As with the suicidal measures, the results of these violence instruments should be recorded in clinical records.

Growth Through Crisis

For both suicide and threat assessments, it is understandable that students would be upset at being told that their confidentiality might be violated.

First, it is crucial to tell students that their confidentiality is going to be broken *before* doing so. They should never find out "after the fact" if at all possible. The NASW (2008) *Code of Ethics* makes this explicit, "Social workers should inform clients, to the extent possible, about the disclosure of confidential information and the potential consequences, when feasible before the disclosure is made" (§1.07(d)). Second, it is important to anticipate that they are likely to feel angry, hurt, and betrayed by the clinician. It helps to honestly acknowledge these feelings and remind the student of the ethical orientation discussed in Chapter 2. For example, a practitioner might tell a student, "I understand how desperately you want to end your pain, but right now your life is more important to me than keeping confidentiality." Third, students commonly feel like the situation has been taken out of their hands at these times. It is important to give the student as much control as is reasonable given these dire circumstances. Such control might include who should be told first, how much detail should be shared, and how such disclosures should occur (by phone, in-person, etc.). While it may be tempting to disclose all the details during a crisis, this is antithetical to our ethical obligations. As the NASW (2008) *Code of Ethics* states:

> The general expectation that social workers will keep information confidential does not apply when disclosure is necessary to prevent serious, foreseeable, and imminent harm to a client or other identifiable person. In all instances, *social workers should disclose the least amount of confidential information necessary to achieve the desired purpose*; only information that is directly relevant to the purpose for which the disclosure is made should be revealed. (§1.07(c), emphasis added)

Fourth, we have found that the student's presence during these disclosures actually serves to strengthen the therapeutic bond. For example, the professional may turn to the student and ask, "Should I go into more detail about...?" All of these considerations are consistent with ASCA (2004) *Ethical Standards* when they state that when the student is a danger to self or others, the professional counselor:

> Will attempt to minimize threat to a student and may choose to 1) inform the student of actions to be taken, 2) involve the student in a three-way communication with parents/guardians when breaching confidentiality, or 3) allow the student to have input as to how and to whom the breach will be made. (§A.7.b)

Finally, at some later point, a discussion about the student's reasons for divulging a threat can be thoroughly explored. For example, did the student secretly desire to be stopped or to externalize an internal conflict? Asking students to reflect on why they disclosed a plan to hurt themselves or others instead of just carrying the plan out deepens their self-awareness. The ultimate goal of all intervention should be client growth, and crisis intervention is no different (Raines, 2004).

Developmental Decision Making

All of the major ethical codes have an ethical requirement for developmentally appropriate services. If students are to participate in ethical decision making as we have recommended in Chapter 4, then this process becomes one of the services offered. The developmental research on student readiness to participate in ethical decision making is mixed (Halpern-Felsher, 2009). On the one hand, many teenagers appear cognitively mature enough to contribute to ethical deliberations. Developmental research suggests that adolescents, 14 years and older, are as capable as adults at understanding medical information and weighing the risks and benefits of therapy (Bastiaens, 1995; Kaser-Boyed, Adelman, & Taylor, 1985; Weithorn & Campbell, 1982). This research serves as a warning against paternalism. *Paternalism* occurs whenever adults assume they know what is in the "best interests" of the child without ever consulting that child. While this may be completely justified for preverbal infants and children with severe mental retardation, developmental delay, or psychosis, it is not justifiable for normal children who can reason and communicate without difficulty (Schacter, Kleinman, & Harvey, 2005). As the Center for Mental Health in Schools (2004) states:

> It is a paternalistic act whenever a child is made to undergo unwanted assessment, even though the activity is viewed as in the child's "best interests." Whether stated or not, when such actions are taken, the child's autonomy is made less important than the possible harm to the child or others if the child is not assessed or the possible benefits to be gained if the child is assessed. (p. 6)

In short, decisions made by adults to abrogate a child's autonomy sometimes send the message: Your rights are less important than what I believe to be in your best interests. On the other hand, however, there is substantial research that demonstrates adolescents' proclivity toward excessive risk-taking behavior, such as criminality, reckless driving, substance abuse, and unprotected sex (Reyna & Rivers, 2008). For example, the Josephson Institute (2008) found that while 98% of youth agreed that it was important to be a "person of good character," 60% thought that sometimes people had to lie and cheat in order to succeed, and 90% thought that this was necessary in sports! This research serves as a warning to maintain a consistent concern for students' readiness to participate in ethical decision making. It may help to inquire what factors serve to increase the likelihood of risk taking in youth and what can be done to assist them in making the best possible ethical decisions.

Risk Factors

There are eight factors that predispose youth to make risky decisions. First, personality characteristics play an important role. Emotional intensity, especially anger as a personality trait, distinguishes youth who engage in behaviors that jeopardize their own well-being (Figner, Mackinlay, Wilkening, & Weber, 2009). Dispositional anger leads children to minimize information use and to engage in high-arousal activities, evaluating risky situations as simultaneously fun and fearful (Gambetti & Giusberti, 2009). Similarly, children with externalizing tendencies demonstrate higher risk taking (Hooper, Luciana, Wahlstrom, Conklin, & Yarger, 2008). Second, substance abuse serves as a disinhibitant to normal caution. It is especially associated with poor sexual decisions—both to initiate a sexual relationship and to engage in sex with multiple sexual partners (Cooper, 2002; Crockett, Raffaelli, & Shen, 2006). Third, some disabilities increase the tendency of youth to choose risky behavior. Rasmussen and Wyper (2007) found that children who were prenatally exposed to alcohol have greater incidence of abnormalities in the prefrontal cortex, which resulted in executive functioning deficits. A lack of activity in the prefrontal cortex has been associated in greater risk taking through functional magnetic resonance imaging (MRI) tests (Eshel, Nelson, Blair, Pine, & Ernst, 2007). Fourth, researchers have found that males are consistently more prone to risk than females, although this improves for both genders with age (d'Acremont & Van der Linden, 2006; Huizenga, Crone, & Jansen, 2007; Van Leijenhorst, Westenberg, & Crone, 2008). Fifth, youth who have never had a serious or life-threatening illness are at greater risk than survivors of severe or chronic disease, perhaps because the latter recognize their greater vulnerability to health-related dangers (Burns, Sadoff, & Kamat, 2006; Hollen, Hobbie, Donnangelo, Shannon, & Erickson, 2007;

Tercyak et al., 2005). Sixth, a lack of social skills (especially negotiation and peer-refusal skills) is associated with greater risk taking. These skills seem especially important for girls when making decisions about sexual activity and condom use (Pearson, 2006). Seventh, youth with mental health problems, especially thought disorders, make riskier decisions than comparable adolescents without these problems (Kester et al., 2006). Finally, there are environmental risk factors. A lack of appropriate leisure activities in the community lends itself to greater juvenile delinquency (Caldwell & Smith, 2006) as does negative peer pressure (Crockett, Raffaelli, & Shen, 2006; Gardner & Steinberg, 2005). Despite all of these risk factors, we strongly believe that all students should be involved in some aspects of the ethical quandary, consistent with their capacity and willingness to participate.

Working in the Zone

Vygotsky (1934/1987) was the first observer of children to note that children's decision making was improved when others helped them. He postulated that there was a *zone of proximal development* wherein children were unable to do a task alone but could do it with the support of others. This kind of helping is often called *scaffolding* because it adjusts the amount of support to the current needs of the student (Berk, 2004). Using a combination of direct instruction and partialization, mentors both teach and break the task into its component parts to enable the student to solve the problem (Berk, 2004). For example, Martenson and Fagerskiold (2008) systematically reviewed the research on children's decision making in health care. They concluded that children's competence was dependent on the caregiving adults around them, such as parents or professionals. Children are social beings and rely on relationships to make their best decisions (Laible, Eye, & Carlo, 2008). Accordingly, some researchers have called for an approach called "supported decision making" for youth who may not be completely competent to make their own decisions (Bielby, 2008; Finken, 2009). As we have discussed in Chapter 4, collaborative decision making neither forfeits responsibility to the student nor bullies the student into acquiescing to the professional's point of view.

Working in the zone of proximal development has five implications for ethical decision making. First, it means supporting the student's capacity and information by providing developmentally appropriate explanations so that they can meaningfully participate in the process (Wolfe, Jaffe, & Crooks, 2006). Second, it means that we titrate the complexity of the predicament so that students are not overwhelmed by the details but get the "gist" of the problem. Rivers, Reyna, and Mills (2008) define gist as "the meaning an individual extracts from information which reflects the individual's knowledge, understanding, culture, and developmental level" (p. 109). In brief, we think of it as the cognitive-emotional gestalt of the quandary. Third, they need to role play key social skills such as assertiveness, conflict resolution, and peer refusal techniques. Each role play needs to be initially scripted, rehearsed, replayed, and debriefed (Wolfe, Jaffe, & Crooks, 2006). Fourth, practitioners need to motivate youth to make healthy choices. Programs that attempt to scare youth seldom work and often backfire (Beutler, 2000; Petrosino, Turpin-Petrosino, & Buehler, 2003; Verhulst, 2002). A motivational interviewing approach works better. Students can be asked to list the pros and cons of each option both emotionally and cognitively as well as short term and long term (Miller & Rollnick, 2002). Finally, youth need peer groups that provide protection from exposure to antisocial activities and reinforcement for prosocial choices (Wolfe, Jaffe, & Crooks, 2006). Participation in a group of mature ethical decision makers tends to improve the quality of subsequent decisions even when the other group members are absent.

Cultural Sensitivity

All of the major theories discussed in Chapter 1 are, in fact, Western approaches to ethics. Assuming that all students and especially all families will accept these perspectives without question is unwarranted. While all of the codes of ethics espouse support for cultural sensitivity, they seldom go so far as to recognize that the tacit assumptions, such as individualism, objectivity, and rationality, which undergird ethical decision making, are ethnocentric values (Herlihy & Watson, 2003; Pettifor, 2004; Zhong, 2007). In general, there are three possible approaches to cultural issues in practice. *Absolutism* assumes that the same ethical principles can apply across all cultures. This perspective minimizes the significance of the cultural context for ethical behavior and emphasizes objectivity. *Relativism* assumes that all ethical norms originate in a specific cultural context. This approach avoids between-group comparisons based on standard criteria and emphasizes subjectivity. *Universalism* posits an ontology of moral realism while admitting to epistemic fallibility (Bhaskar, 1989). Thus, it holds to certain moral truths but acknowledges cultural differences (Hathaway, 2001; Ridley, Liddle, Hill, & Li, 2001). For example, universalism may hold that child abuse is always wrong (e.g., the U.N.'s *Convention on the Rights of the Child*, 1989) but allow that child abuse may be defined differently across cultures (see Exercise 3 at the end of the chapter).

Cultural Ethics

Houser, Wilczenski, and Ham (2006) present nine alternative cultural theories of ethics. Here we will divide these into two broad categories—cultural and religious—and briefly outline the major concepts of each one.

Houser and colleagues suggest that alternative ethics exist for three broad ethnic groups. For *Native Americans*, the major principles are (1) respect of people and nature; (2) truthfulness; (3) service to others; (4) moderation and balance; and (5) responsibility for their actions. The concept of balance is symbolized by the medicine wheel's four components of the mental, spiritual, emotional, and physical parts of life. For *Hispanic or Latino* cultures, the major concepts are (1) harmony with self and the universe; (2) focus on the present with a consequential tendency to fatalism regarding the future; (3) familism over individualism; (4) machismo, not in the hypermasculine sense, but emphasizing honor, integrity, effectiveness, and responsibility; (5) marianismo, the feminine ideal of chastity, nurturance, self-sacrifice, and submission; and (6) solidarity, a sense of collective camaraderie for love and justice. *Pan-African* values include (1) community—"it takes a village..."; (2) nonmaleficence or doing no harm to others; (3) truthfulness; (4) integrity or keeping one's word; (5) patience or submission to God's timing; (6) generosity and gentleness; and (7) fulfilling one's social duties.

Houser and colleagues also posit that alternative ethical values exist for six major religious faiths. *Confucian* values include (1) socially prescribed behavior according to one's role as a parent, child, spouse, sibling, friend, ruler, or subject; (2) reciprocity and sincerity toward others; (3) empathy for humanity; (4) ability to feel shame; and (5) deference to authority figures (leaders, parents, and husband). *Taoist* tenets incorporate (1) the Tao or the true and desirable path; (2) yin and yang, or the harmony of opposites; (3) simplicity; (4) reversal and cyclicity; (5) natural nonaction (going with the flow); and (6) emotional control. *Hindu* virtues consist of (1) purity; (2) self-control; (3) detachment; (4) truthfulness; and (5) nonviolence. Emotional control is expected because feelings can lead to lust, anger, egotism, and jealousy. Eventually, all our thoughts and action lead to karma in which the universe gives back as we have given. *Buddhism* holds four noble truths: (1) truth of humanity that misery and suffering are a part of life; (2) truth from knowing that suffering comes from the craving for pleasure; (3) truth that this craving can be eradicated; and (4) truth that this eradication is the result of the noble path. This noble path has eight aspects: right understanding or perception, right thought or mental purity, right speech or truthfulness, right action, right livelihood or occupation, right effort or mental discipline, right mindfulness or attention, and right concentration or meditation. *Judaism* may be most famous for the Ten Commandments, but there are actually 613 commandments in the Torah. Jews emphasize the following values: (1) family and community; (2) social action; (3) humility; (4) honesty and truthfulness; and (5) beneficence or nonmaleficence. *Islam* has five pillars or duties: (1) Shahada or faith in the creed; (2) Salah or prayers; (3) Zakat or charity; (4) Sawm or fasting (during Ramadan); and (5) the Hajj or pilgrimage (to Mecca). Islam also has five categories of behavior: (1) forbidden acts that cause harm to self or others; (2) undesirable acts or unintentional misdeeds; (3) neutral acts that disturb no one; (4) desirable acts that create positive outcomes; and (5) required acts that benefit others, such as charity to those in need.

Cultural Differences

This brief review allows us to reflect on some important differences with dominant Western perspectives. Here we will address six common disparities.

First, family/community is often more important than the individual. Thus, ethical concepts such as client "self-"determination or therapeutic ideals of "self-"actualization are likely to create confusion for people who value communitarianism (Palmer & Kaufman, 2003). Ideas of privacy or confidentiality may be culturally understood to include the family group or entire clan (Meer & VandeCreek, 2002; Monshi & Zieglmayer, 2004; Pettifor & Sawchuk, 2006; Sori & Hecker, 2006). Dishion and Stormshak (2007) argue for a family-centered approach, pointing out that polarized solutions rarely resolve the ethical issues: "Practitioners who are rigid on either end of the spectrum— that is, disclosing all information to adults or refusing to disclose any information to adults—will probably make poor ethical decisions" (p. 258). They further note that "when therapists work within an ecological framework, strict confidentiality may not always be possible or advisable" (p. 259). Taylor and Adelman (1989/2003) identify two problems with rigid confidentiality. First, parents who are dissatisfied with the level of cooperation they experience with the practitioner may decide to withdraw from the helping process or even remove the child from counseling. This obviously thwarts the purpose of counseling altogether. Next, some youth may deliberately misuse confidentiality as a weapon against their parents. Naïve therapists may unwittingly collude with the adolescent and inadvertently cut off an important natural helping source for the child and aggravate an already difficult relationship (Dishion & Stormshak, 2007). The optimal solution is to balance the needs of the child with those of the parents (see Box 5.4).

If modified confidentiality is the best solution, then how should it work? Raines (2004) recommends making this part of the ethical orientation given to minor clients. He suggests three "routine" disclosures to caregivers: (1) the

---

Box 5.4 Korean American Student

Lyn Park is a 16-year-old second-generation Korean American student who was born and raised near Chicago. Both of her parents are professionals; her father is a dentist and her mother is an accountant. At home, the family speaks Korean, but they enjoy American TV programs. One day, she drops into her high school counselor's office and asks if she can talk. After a few minutes of chit-chat, Lyn says she has a friend who wants to know where she can get birth control pills without her parents' knowledge. The counselor initially suggests that she should ask her friend to come by, but then Lyn begins to cry, admitting that she is really talking about herself. She reveals that she has been dating a boy 3 years older and, while they have not had sex yet, they have begun to do some heavy petting and she is worried that it could go "too far." In Illinois, the "age of consent" for intercourse is 17 (Avert, 2009), but minors are allowed to get prescription birth control with a physician referral (Guttmacher Instititut, 2009). The school counselor knows that Koreans are very family-centered and her parents would probably not approve of their daughter having access to contraceptives without their knowledge and permission. Lyn further divulges that, to keep her parents in the dark, she would prefer to obtain the pills during school hours. School policy, however, forbids students from leaving school grounds for a medical appointment unless signed out and accompanied by a parent. Other pupil services providers have pointed out that this local policy serves as a barrier to some students getting confidential reproductive medical care as allowed by state law.

Ethical Decision Making in School Mental Health

Questions

1. What further information does the counselor need to make a good decision?
2. What effects does the student's culture have on this issue?
3. What weight should be given to the age difference between Lyn and her boyfriend?
4. To avoid polarization of the issue, identify at least three possible courses of action.
5. What clinical issues are implied in her anxiety about going "too far"?
6. What are the legal issues when one partner is above the age of consent and one partner is below the age of consent?
7. What would you recommend around the school policy regarding medical appointments?

child's actual attendance record at sessions (number, frequency, and duration); (2) the issues or topics being discussed (but not details); and (3) progress reports on how the child is moving toward therapeutic goals. Ideally, written child assent is sought for these customary disclosures (Dishion & Stormshak, 2007). Parents who are dissatisfied with such an arrangement may be offered either a parent guidance session or a family session with the child present. Parent guidance sessions are most appropriate when the parents desire greater intimacy at a time when the student is seeking greater independence. Parents can be educated that adolescence is a natural time for seeking more autonomy even when students still have dependency needs. One helpful approach is to ask the parents which adults (other than their parents) they sought out for support during this phase of their life and point out that their child is continuing the same tradition. Another approach is to normalize the acculturation process for second-generation minority youth who often opt for more American values and seek some compromise with the culture of origin. Stewart and Tan (2007) explain that "families often make decisions in groups and it is important that the integrity of the family unit should be respected where possible and appropriate, which also helps to support the young person while promoting his or her development of autonomy" (p. 342).

Second, in many cultures, emotional self-control is often more important than affective catharsis. Talking about one's feelings may seem self-indulgent or egoistic to some families. Combined with a sense of deference to authority figures, families may expect the school-based clinician to give information, advice, or concrete assistance rather than try to elicit discussion about feelings (Jue & Lewis, 2001). Professionals should consider three adaptations for families where emotional restraint is the norm. Counselors can ask about parents' thoughts about an issue rather than their "feelings" about it. Practitioners can also inquire about family stories or legacies related to the topic of discussion, including best-case and worst-case scenarios. Finally, pupil services providers can provide some psychoeducational information about the issues that students commonly face and how these impact family and school relationships. The American Academy of Child and Adolescent Psychiatry, for example, provides nearly a hundred Facts for Families brochures designed for parents in multiple languages (see Internet Resources at the end of this chapter).

Third, the idea of reciprocity for services rendered without a fee may create ethical problems for therapists who usually decline proffered gifts (Brown & Trangsrud, 2008; Herlihy & Watson, 2003). For example, in New York City, a middle-class Puerto Rican family wanted to know how they could "repay" a counselor for helping their children. Rather than insult them by refusing a gift, it was suggested that they could give a gift to the school. The next day, a huge fruit basket was delivered to the front office and then placed in the teachers' lounge for everyone to enjoy. The staff was only informed that it came from a "grateful family." Likewise, in an upper-class Jewish community where teachers regularly received hundred-dollar gift certificates to upscale stores, the male school social worker was asked what he might like. Rather than refuse their generosity, he replied that he would most appreciate a thank-you note to the district superintendent for social work services. Since the superintendent usually only received complaints from parents, this note was not only appreciated but widely distributed throughout the district office. Brown and Trangsrud's (2008) research found that it was more common for professionals to accept gifts when they were inexpensive, culturally appropriate, and given in gratitude at the end of the relationship. Gifts that were costly, given during treatment, or had coercive potential were generally declined.

Fourth, professional boundaries and clinical distance may seem odd to families who have accepted the therapist as a member of the family replete with invitations to dinner or graduation celebrations. This brings up "dual relationship" issues for many American practitioners (Durodoye, 2006; Gabriel & Davies, 2000; Kertesz, 2002; Parham, 1997; Zur, 2002). For example, one Middle Eastern family invited the school psychologist to attend the high school graduation party of their first child to ever complete this level of education in the United States. After consultation with a supervisor, it was decided that the practitioner should honor their hospitality and offer to take pictures of the event, emphasizing family solidarity. The clinician hoped in this way to "hide" behind the camera and be an unobtrusive participant-observer. The family, however, had other ideas and insisted that the practitioner be included in some of the pictures due to her contribution to the student's achievement. Ridley, Liddle, Hill, and Li (2001) use a similar example of a Taiwanese client inviting his therapist to an opera as a means of expressing gratitude. In this case, however, the female therapist declined and the client felt that he had been insulted (Sue, 1997). Both cases illustrate the delicate nature of finding a balance between appropriate professional behavior and cultural sensitivity.

Fifth, similar to both issues above, the family may expect a certain amount of reciprocity from the practitioner in terms of self-disclosure, such as the practitioner's own experiences as a parent or experiences with oppression (Burkard, Knox, Groen, Perez, & Hess, 2006; Cashwell, Shcherbakova, & Cashwell, 2003; Kim et al., 2003). The primary danger of such disclosures is that they can divert attention away from the clients' needs and focus on the clinician. Some research, however, suggests that therapist self-disclosure with minority clients is likely to increase clinicians' credibility as culturally sensitive and enable them to model appropriate self-disclosure on the part of the client (Constantine & Kwan, 2003). This strategy seems to be particularly effective with African American clients (Burkard et al., 2006), but not as effective with Asian American clients (Kim et al., 2003). The astute practitioner will recognize that this cultural expectation may well have a parallel process with their U.S.-raised children. This leaves the bicultural student in the awkward predicament of either having to share more than he or she would prefer or developing subversive strategies for concealment, such as lying to his or her parents (Tasapoulos-Chan, Smetana, & Yau, 2009). Neither of these tactics is conducive to healthy parent–child relationships, so school-based practitioners will need to help such students find middle ground.

Finally, certain ethnic child-rearing practices engender clinical concerns about possible child abuse (Congress, 2001; Fontes & O'Neill-Arana, 2008; Merali, 2002). The following example illustrates this.

> One Haitian parent, whose child had an untreated attention-deficit disorder, came to school brandishing a switch after learning of her son's difficulties during his first day at school. Hearing her thick French accent, the school nurse invited her into the office and inquired about when the family had immigrated to the United States. She gently removed the green branch from the mother's hand and explained that in the United States parents were not allowed to use punishments that might leave a mark on their child. She then explored other disciplinary measures that the mother had tried and whether she had discussed her son's problems with their pediatrician. Upon learning that her son had never seen a doctor since his birth, she explained the medical requirements for school enrollment and asked if the mother would like a referral to a local physician.

Merali (2002) mentions the Vietnamese practice of Cao Gio, which entails heating a coin and pressing it against the skin, resulting in marks that resemble bruising. Fontes (2005) mentions African coming-of-age rituals involving scarification. Some parents bite their children to demonstrate affection, leaving dental imprints. Some families practice co-sleeping until their children are 6–7 years old.

Professionals must engage in critical thinking about cultural explanations (Fontes, 2005). There are four possible criteria for assessing such culturally sanctioned practices. First, is the intent of the parent to harm or help? A closely related issue is the mood of the parent—does the parent deliver the punishment out of anger, sadness, or shame? Second, what are the effects on the child—both physically and psychologically? Punishments that result in serious bodily injury such as blood, brain damage, broken bones, or bruising cannot be tolerated. Likewise, punishments that destroy the child's sense of self as a person of dignity and worth cannot be overlooked (U.N., 1989, Preamble). Third, how normative or common is the practice in the minority culture? For example, there are many American adults who recall having their mouths washed out with soap when they were young, but that custom is not widespread in the contemporary culture. Fourth, do the parent's actions conform to acceptable cultural practice? Again, many American households believe in corporal punishment, but even proponents would probably not condone the use of a baseball bat. Likewise, seclusion is often considered an acceptable punishment, but it is never appropriate to lock a child in an attic, basement, cage, or hot car. For cases like the Haitian mother whose intent to help the child fails the test of effects on the child, parenting education should be the primary intervention. If parent education fails to provide sufficient safety for the child, however, then stronger measures must be taken, including contact with child welfare authorities. Reports to child protective services should include any relevant cultural context of the family and may help to shape a culturally sensitive response. For practitioners wishing to explore this issue in depth, we strongly recommend Fontes' (2005) book on the subject of culture and child abuse.

The most important aspect of making culturally sensitive ethical decisions is making the implicit explicit (Ridley, Liddle, Hill, & Li, 2001). We like to compare one's native culture to the air that we breathe—it is invisible to us, it surrounds us, we inhale (internalize) it and exhale (externalize) it without thinking about it. When working with clients of other cultures, however, we must make our tacit assumptions obvious to ourselves and enable them to describe their understandings to us. Evans (2008) phrases it well: "Ethical professional practice with children requires the clinician to understand his or her own culture and not assume that it represents some basic standard or core values against which other groups can be evaluated or judged" (p. 185).

Ethical Guidelines

- Remember that clinical competence requires lifelong learning. Keep current with new research and regularly attend professional development seminars.
- Know the warning signs for suicide, but do not assume that an additive approach will identify the students most at risk. Triangulate the sources of information, including the use of a standardized scale to systematize suicide risk assessment. Determine the composition of a crisis team ahead of time with specific roles prescribed for each member. Ensure all members are properly trained and prepared. The team should follow a specific crisis assessment plan to determine the level of danger. High-risk students should never be left alone and should be informed of all actions prior to their occurrence, if at all possible. Triage should include trustworthy

transportation to a hospital and a combination of psychosocial therapy and psychotropic medication. Psychosocial intervention should include psychoeducation about depression, supportive therapy, family involvement, and school advocacy.

- Threats against others should include a four-pronged threat assessment, including personality factors, family dynamics, school climate, and community environment. Like suicide assessment, the crisis team should take an orderly approach to threat assessment to ensure completeness of both the assessment and the intervention plan.

- Both suicide assessments and violence assessments should be carefully documented in case there is a review of the decision.

- Crisis teams may also want to consider including a standardized instrument to systematize their data collection. Throughout both types of threat assessment, the final goal should be to help the student grow and heal through the experience.

- Professionals should carefully consider students' developmental level when determining the extent of their involvement in ethical decision making. Be aware of the factors that place students at risk for poor decision making. Nonetheless, all students should be involved in some aspects of the ethical predicament. The adults involved should offer developmentally appropriate explanations of the issues involved both at the cognitive and emotional levels.

- Practitioners should be aware that even their ethical principles are culturally determined. When working with diverse families, it helps to approach universal values with an attitude of epistemic fallibility and honor cultural differences. Clinicians should be aware that minority families may operate with completely different ethical priorities than the dominant culture. Practitioners should be aware that there are common differences about ethical values and be prepared to compromise while maintaining their professionalism. Clinicians should not simply accept cultural explanations at face value, but think critically about their implications for students.

Exercises

1. Breaking Confidentiality

In which of the dozen situations below would you be likely to break a student's confidentiality?

- Student is drinking alcohol at parties on the weekend.
- Student is having unprotected sex with a steady boyfriend.
- Student is painfully thin and was found purging in the school bathroom.
- Student is having sporadic suicidal ideations after a romantic breakup.
- Student is making threats to "get even" after losing a ballgame.
- Student is gay and HIV positive.
- Student admits he vandalized the principal's car last week.
- Student is experimenting with methamphetamine.
- Student has a sexually transmitted disease and several sexual partners.
- Student is getting drunk every day after school.
- Student has a plausible plan to commit suicide.
- Student talks about bringing his dad's gun to school to get revenge.

What decision rules did you intuitively use as you thought about each situation? What laws or local policies apply to each situation? This exercise can be done with fellow colleagues or with a class. Did most others agree or disagree with your judgments? What might this suggest about your opinions?

2. Disclosure to Parents

How would you involve the children below in an ethical quandary that involved disclosing a secret to their parent?
- A gifted third grader
- A sixth grader with Asperger's syndrome

- A ninth grader adjudicated as a delinquent
- An 18-year-old twelfth grader with a substance abuse disorder

3. Child Maltreatment Reports

Which of the following 20 cultural practices would you be likely to report as child abuse?

- Allowing a child to watch 40 hours of TV per week
- Biting a child (without breaking the skin)
- Bracing teeth with sharp metal wires
- Bruising a child with a heated coin
- Child labor (under the age of 14)
- Child marriage (under the age of 14)
- Circumcisions for boys
- Clitorectomies for girls
- Corporal punishment
- Co-sleeping (above the age of 5 years)
- Cures involving lead, mercury, or other toxic substances
- Dieting or purging food to lose weight for wrestling or gymnastics
- Jaw expansion (in preparation for bracing teeth)
- Overfeeding a child to the point of morbid obesity
- Piercing of ears, nose, or tongue
- Psychotropic medication with potentially lifelong side effects
- Scarification of the face
- Swaddling of infants to prevent movement
- Tattoos (under the age of 14 years)
- Washing out a child's mouth with salt or soap

Would you be more likely to report common customs in our culture or other cultures? Why? Are you surprised that the United States (unlike 183 other nations) has never ratified the U.N. Convention on the Rights of the Child (Congressional Research Reports, 2009)? What would you propose doing about this?

Internet Sources

Adolescent Coping with Depression Course
http://www.kpchr.org/public/acwd/acwd.html
American Academy of Child & Adolescent Psychiatry Facts for
Families
http://www.aacap.or/cs/root/facts_for_families/facts_for_families
American Academy of Child & Adolescent Psychiatry Practice
Parameters
http://www.aacap.org/cs/root/member_information/practice_
information/practice_parameters/practice_parameters
American Association of Suicidology
http://www.suicidology.org
Balancing Student Privacy and School Safety
http://www.ed.gov/policy/gen/guid/fpco/brochures/elsec.pdf
DOE and U.S. Secret Service Threat Assessment Guide
http://www.pent.ca.gov/thr/11questions.pdf
FBI School Shooter: Threat Assessment
http://www.fbi.gov/publications/school/school2.pdf
Josephson Institute—Ethics of American Youth
http://www.charactercounts.org/programs/reportcard/
Motivational Interviewing
http://www.motivationalinterview.org/
National Child Traumatic Stress Network
http://www.nctsn.org
National Organization for People of Color Against Suicide
(NOPCAS)
http://www.nopcas.com
National Suicide Prevention Lifeline
http://www.suicidepreventionlifeline.org/
Secret Service Threat Assessment in Schools Guide
http://www.secretservice.gov/ntac/ssi_guide.pdf
Signs of Suicide Program
http://www.mentalhealthscreening.org/sos_highschool/kits/
index.htm
Suicide Awareness/Voices of Education (SAVE)
http://www.save.org

United Nations Convention on the Rights of the Child
http://www.unicef.org/crc/
Virginia's Guidelines for Responding to Student Threats of
Violence
http://youthviolence.edschool.virginia.edu/threat-assessment/
guidelines-manual.html
Youth Suicide Prevention School-Based Guide
http://theguide.fmhi.usf.edu/

6

Implementing the Decision

In Chapter 4, we made the case for collaborative decision making to manage an ethical predicament. While other ethical decision-making models in the literature assume a single ethical agent, we believe there are both ethical and clinical reasons to engage the student, and sometimes other stakeholders, in the decision-making process. We noted the two National Association of Social Workers' (NASW, 2008) ethical principles related to self-determination and partnering with clients and the Introduction to the American School Counselor Association's (ASCA, 2004) *Ethical Standards*, which cites the student's right to move toward self-direction and self-development. We discussed how engaging a student in the decision-making process can help her become more autonomous and can strengthen the relationship between the pupil services professional and the student at the very time that relationship may be stressed or even threatened. We believe the relationship between the pupil services professional and the student is both therapeutic and educational; the pupil services professional is both a school-based mental health professional and an educator. Both roles can and should be embraced when we work with students.

In Chapter 5, we included a section we called Growth Through Crisis, in which we talked about how students can and should be involved in implementing the decision. This partnership can help preserve the relationship between the pupil services professional and the student and can help the student begin to regain some control over his life at a very difficult time.

Throughout this book we have talked about "managing" the ethical predicament, rather than "resolving" the quandary. There are two very important reasons for this. First, using the verb "manage" implies a truly active engagement with the ethical quandary. We do the best we can to produce the best outcomes we can for the student and the stakeholders. However, that does not mean that we can necessarily prevent all negative outcomes. Second, to use the verb "resolve" implies that ethical predicaments can be reconciled to everyone's complete satisfaction. The implication is that all of the competing values and other responsibilities can be honored. The reality is when a decision is implemented to manage an ethical quandary, one or more ethical values and competing responsibilities will be given more weight than others (Mattison, 2006). The tension or competition between these considerations is what makes the decision difficult.

In Chapter 2, we discussed common competing ethical values and other competing responsibilities: the student's right to privacy and confidentiality, self-determination and autonomy; our concern with the student's health and well-being; the rights of parents to be informed of and to determine services for their children; and our responsibility to follow the law and our employer's policies and procedures. At the root of an ethical predicament is our inability, at least in our initial review and consideration, to honor all of these important values and responsibilities. Scrutiny of the quandary may occasionally reveal an elegant solution that mediates all of the variables. For instance, in Chapter 4, we included a scenario in which a father confronts a school social worker to learn what his daughter has revealed in small group sessions. Alternatives 3 and 4 successfully mediated all of the competing values and responsibilities. While we can certainly strive for these elegant solutions, as was stated earlier, in many of the ethical predicaments pupil services professionals encounter, whatever course of action is eventually chosen, some values and responsibilities will be given more weight than others (Mattison, 2006).

Review and Consideration of the Decision

The next step in our process to manage ethical predicaments is to implement the decision (Cottone & Claus, 2000; Koocher & Keith-Spiegel, 2008; Mattison, 2006; McNamara, 2008; Nasser-McMillan & Post, 1998; Pope & Vasquez, 2007; Reamer, 2006; Stone, 2005; Van Divner & Champ Morera, 2007). Pope and Vasquez (2007) recommend that the selected course of action be reviewed and reconsidered. This allows you to essentially "double-check" what you plan to do before you do it. There are a variety of ways that you can "screen" the selected course of action prior to implementation. Stadler (1986) recommends actually testing the course of action. Van Divner and

Champ Morera (2007) suggest envisioning the outcome once a course of action has been selected. Is this outcome acceptable? How will this outcome affect the student, other stakeholders, and me? Can and should the course of action be modified to improve the outcome? They also recommend negotiating obstacles through anticipation of these obstacles. This is another strategy to minimize the conflict between the different competing values and other responsibilities. For instance, anticipate how the stakeholders may respond. Will some people be upset? What can you do to address their concerns, either before or after the course of action is implemented?

Testing the Courses of Action

One of the best ways to review and reconsider the selected course of action is to reframe it and examine it from a completely different perspective. In the Introduction, we discussed both a moral and legal foundation for professional practice.

The moral foundation is what is commonly referred to as the "Golden Rule." If you were the student, would you want someone to handle this situation with the proposed course of action? If you were the student's parent, would you want someone to follow this course of action on behalf of your child? If we are engaging the student as a partner in the decision-making process, the first question may not be that hard to answer. However, the second question can be much harder to resolve, especially if the pupil services professional has children of her own. In our role as parent, we want to protect and care for our children. In our role as a pupil services professional, we must also consider the student's right to confidentiality and autonomy. While the pupil services professional with children may have special insight into a parent's view of a particular situation, that insight should not inappropriately affect what decision is selected and enacted. The downside to this test is that the decision can change dramatically depending on whom the professional identifies as the other person in the Golden Rule.

The legal foundation is the fiduciary relationship. Here pupil services providers must ask themselves if they have discharged their fiduciary responsibility to their primary client. No other person has this "hold" on the professional. Remember that the fiduciary relationship is between two people with unequal power in the situation. Clients depend on the integrity of the professional to act in their best interests. *Burdett v. Miller* (1992) described this as acting with the "utmost candor, rectitude, care, loyalty, and good faith" for one's client (p. 1381).

There are other "tests" you can perform to help review the proposed course of action. One test addresses justice and generalizability (Raines, 2009; Stone, 2005). The practitioner should assess his own sense of fairness by determining if he would treat other students in this same situation in this same manner. If your answer is no, what is the reason? Is there a legitimate practice reason to treat this student differently? For instance, a student with less maturity and competence may be involved in the decision making differently than another student who is more able to make independent decisions. Or is there some personal bias that may be interfering in the decision-making process? You should always check to ensure that personal bias is not adversely affecting the selected course of action (e.g., your insight as a parent). Several years ago, one of the authors was providing training on ethics and professional boundaries to school social workers. Part of the training involved participants working in small groups to discuss real-life ethical predicaments experienced by school social workers and other pupil services professionals. During a break, one of the participants approached the author and expressed his concern about the inclusion of an ethical quandary in which a student seeking an abortion approaches a school social worker with questions. The participant believed it was wrong to have included that ethical quandary in the training. It was apparent to the author that this participant had very strong personal opinions about abortion, which was his personal right. It was also apparent that, if the participant were in this situation, he would have great difficulty responding objectively to the student's questions about abortion. This does not mean this school social worker cannot provide high-quality school social work services to students. However, he does need to be aware of his strong personal feelings about abortion and refer any students who need assistance in this area to another competent professional. Or he may wish to practice in a setting where he is less likely to encounter this predicament (e.g., an elementary or parochial school).

Another test is publicity (McNamara, 2008; Stone, 2005). Are you comfortable with others knowing your decision? Apart from the obvious concern for the confidentiality of the student, would you want your professional conduct in this situation reported publicly? In one of our communities, a community-based counselor was accused of having sex with an underage student he was counseling at the high school. The case details were reported in the local paper. While he strenuously denied the allegations against him, he admitted to "poor judgment" for allowing the girl in his home (see Maroda, 2007). His case was doomed, however, when she could accurately describe the furniture in his bedroom.

Would you anticipate your professional colleagues would congratulate you on your management of the ethical quandary when you encounter them at work? Or would you cringe at the thought your co-workers had learned about this situation and your actions? Gabbard (1997) found that therapists who withheld information from supervisors or consultants were at higher risk for ethical boundary violations. Welfel (1998) recommends informing your supervisor when you take action to manage an ethical quandary. Not being willing to fully disclose case details and considered courses of action compromises the benefit of consultation and supervision and implies the practitioner has significant concerns about what to do. Ideally, other pupil services professionals, while identifying with the challenges of the ethical predicament, would respect (and learn from) your decisions about how you manage the situation.

The last test is universality (McNamara, 2008; Stone, 2005). Assess whether you would recommend the same course of action to another pupil services professional in the same situation. If a professional colleague facing the same ethical quandary sought you out for professional consultation, would your conclusions be the same? Would you help your colleague to work toward the same course of action? Would your professional association support how you handled this predicament? Remember that the "standard of care" is what an ordinary, reasonable, and prudent professional with similar training would do in similar circumstances (Reamer, 2005). If you believe that you would hesitate to suggest this course of action to a professional colleague facing the same ethical quandary, that is a signal that you have real reservations and should reconsider that course of action.

If your responses to all of these tests are positive, then you are ready to proceed with the selected course of action. However, if any of these tests have raised concerns, you should revisit one or more of the earlier steps in this decision-making process (e.g., analyzing the predicament, seeking consultation). Not to do so risks adverse outcomes for your student, stakeholders, and/or you.

Case Example

The school social worker in Box 6.1 is initially identifying only two courses of action that are polar opposites, something we cautioned against in Chapter 4. These two courses of action are to (1) view the new student as her

A high school has a treatment foster home within its attendance area that specializes in juvenile sex offenders. Most residents of this foster home have attended the high school without any significant problems. However, two juveniles committed serious sexual offenses after being enrolled in the high school. One incident occurred in a high school lavatory, while another happened on a school bus. A county social worker contacts the school social worker about enrolling a new resident of the treatment facility. He is a 16 year-old male who is exiting a secure treatment facility after being adjudicated as a sexual offender for multiple offenses in which the minor victims' participation was not voluntary. When the building principal hears about the new student, he contacts the county social worker and tells her that the school will provide an alternative educational program for this individual. He will be assigned to the local police department for computerized instruction, facilitated by a teacher who will come in 1–2 hours each day. The county social worker protests, but the building principal states the school district is putting the safety of students first. The student victimized in the lavatory by a previous resident of the treatment foster home was a client of the school social worker who still suffers from the trauma of that incident. The school social worker is torn between advocating for a full-day, in-school educational program for the new student and just keeping silent, because she fears that severe budget constraints will not allow the school to be able to monitor the new student adequately.

client and advocate for a full-day educational program with access to the range of classes that other students enjoy, or (2) accept a restricted educational placement for the student due to the real danger of sexual assault to students in the high school if this new student is allowed to attend without adequate monitoring and supervision.

Clearly, the potential danger in this situation if the new student is placed in the high school is real. Regardless of the progress this new student may have made in previous treatment, there can be no guarantees that he will not reoffend, if given the opportunity. It has happened before with youth from this treatment foster home with similar backgrounds and it could happen again. Students enrolled at the high school have a fundamental right to learn in a physically and emotionally safe environment. School officials have a fundamental responsibility to establish and maintain a safe learning environment for students. In light of this, the building principal's reaction and proposal are understandable, regardless of whether we agree with it.

On the other hand, all but two youth from this treatment foster home have been successfully placed in the high school without further incidents of sexual offenses. The treatment foster home is an interim placement between the secure facility they have exited and an eventual return to their respective home communities and families. Participation in an educational environment that is less structured and secure than the secure facility they exited is part of a successful transition. The two sexual offenses by previous residents of the treatment foster home are being projected onto this youth by the building principal. If the building principal has his way, this youth will suffer consequences for the misconduct of two other people he does not even know.

Let's apply the tests from earlier to these two possible courses of action. In the Golden Rule test, the school social worker would ask, If I were this youth, would I want the school social worker to keep silent and allow me to be assigned to the police station for computerized instruction? If I were this youth's parent, would I want the school social worker to keep silent? On the other hand, the school social worker could ask the same questions with respect to the other high school students and their parents. The responses will probably be very different. The youth and his parents may want the school social worker to fulfill her responsibility as an advocate, while other students and their families may want the safety of the student body given the highest priority. This review of the possible courses of action finds great competition among the values and other responsibilities, making choosing either course of action very difficult.

The fiduciary test, however, is less ambiguous. If the new student is the primary client, then the school social worker's primary obligation belongs to him. Here the focus is on the school social worker's need for honesty, integrity, care, and faithfulness to this student. The school social worker concerned about candor might ask a question such as, "Have I been forthright with the student about the severity of the consequence that might ensue if he reoffended in the school?" Arranging a three-way face-to-face meeting with the principal, for example, would make this extremely clear. Another question could be related to personal integrity: "Have I satisfied my own concerns that this student will safely interact with my other students, or am I inadvertently setting up this student to fail?" The school social worker may want to obtain clinical consultation with an expert in the field (e.g., Rich, 2009), as discussed in Chapter 3, or conduct her own risk assessment using some of the tools discussed in Chapter 5, such as the SAVRY (Fannif & Becker, 2006; Viljoen et al., 2008).

The next test is justice and generalizability. In this test, the school social worker would ask, "What would I do if this were another student transferring into the high school? Would I keep silent or advocate for an inclusive educational placement?" As shown in Box 2.3 in Chapter 2, school social workers and other pupil services professionals believe advocacy is a fundamental part of their role as educators in schools. The school social worker in this scenario is considering not just the youth, but the other high school students as well. Her concern for the lingering trauma of the student who was previously sexually assaulted weighs on her decision making. Unless the school social worker can honestly justify legitimate professional practice reasons to place the youth at the police station for computerized instruction and limited teacher contact, the conclusion must be that the test of justice and generalizability is not met by keeping silent.

The next test is publicity. Here the school social worker would ask, "What if the high school principal's insistence on an alternative placement for this youth was reported to the local newspaper? Would I want the paper to report I advocated for this youth's right to an education or that I accepted and supported the building principal's recommendation?" Or alternatively, "If I was attending a conference with colleagues from my profession and we were asked to share an ethical quandary and how we managed it, would I be willing to share that I advocated for this youth's education, even though it may endanger other students? Or that I chose to place the safety of the student body as more important than the individual rights of the youth?" The fact that the school social worker is struggling so much with these two alternatives leads us to believe she may not want others to know about her actions in either course of action.

The last test is universality. The school social worker would ask herself, If a professional colleague approached me for consultation with this same ethical predicament, would I recommend he keep silent in support of the building principal's decision? Or would I recommend he advocate for the inclusive education of the youth? If the pupil services provider was sued for

Ethical Decision Making in School Mental Health

malpractice, could she honestly state that she met the standard of care? The fact that the school social worker is so conflicted about either course of action leads us to believe she would hesitate to offer either alternative to a colleague facing the same situation.

Applying these tests can help to determine whether you are ready to proceed with a selected course of action. In this case, these tests raised some serious concerns about either alternative. That is, advocating for a fully inclusive education for this youth without adequate supervision puts the other students in the high school at risk, especially in light of the youth's history of forced sexual encounters. In addition, by placing the youth in a setting in which he may be more likely to reoffend, this course of action increases the possibility he will be reincarcerated, which is not what he would want. At the same time, keeping silent in this situation may result not just in this youth being placed at the police station for computerized instruction, but other youth placed in the treatment foster home in the future could have limited educational services imposed on them as well. Their respective successful re-entry into their home communities may be endangered if the transition from more to less supervision is not managed properly. If they return home before they are ready for a less supervised setting, they may reoffend. This puts the members of their home communities at risk and increases potential costs to society for reincarceration.

Neither of these courses of action should be considered to be acceptable. There simply are too many adverse consequences if either is implemented. The school social worker should resist any temptation to succumb to the "either-or" polarity of these two alternatives. Rather, the school social worker should take the time to follow a decision-making process designed to manage ethical predicaments. The ethical quandary has not yet been fully analyzed. For instance, the building principal's proposal may well be illegal, depending upon the education laws in that state. Federal education laws (i.e., IDEA, Section 504) probably also apply. It is not clear yet what the response will be from the county department of social services, once the county social worker notifies her supervisor of the building principal's ultimatum. The county may acquiesce in order to maintain good relations with the school district, or the county's legal counsel may be brought in to bring legal pressure on the school district.

Other courses of action that respect the rights of the youth, the students in the high school, and other stakeholders need to be explored. According to IDEA, if the student has been identified as having a disability, the only persons who can determine the sexual offender's educational placement is the IEP team, not the principal. The possibility of legal action against the school may make the building principal more amenable to considering alternatives other than placement at the local police station. For instance, Horton (1996) identifies some intermediate placement options such as an alternative school setting, a self-contained special education class, or supported placement in a regular education setting with an aide (to monitor bathroom or locker room behavior). If the student is allowed to attend the high school, regular ongoing two-way communication with the treatment foster home and clinical therapist should occur on a weekly basis. Furthermore, teachers should receive special training to support the student's recovery. This training might cover removal of sexual stimuli from the educational environment, strict rules about sexual jokes or innuendoes, and more attention to modest dress for both teachers and classroom peers. These precautions are in the best interests of the youth and other students.

Be Prepared to Justify the Decision

Despite all of your efforts to mediate the tensions between the ethical values, consider your competing responsibilities to stakeholders, and manage obstacles through anticipation, there may be some who are unhappy with how this ethical quandary was managed. Even though you engage the student as a partner in the decision making and reach agreement on how to proceed together, if there are unanticipated, negative outcomes, the student may blame you. Family members may feel that you should have involved them more. The building principal may feel the course of action did not provide for adequate safety or failed to honor the school's disciplinary code. Mattison (2006) recommends being prepared to justify your decision. Strom-Gottfried (2008) recommends documenting the entire decision-making process. Van Divner and Champ Morera (2007) and Pope and Vasquez (2007) believe the pupil services professional should take responsibility for the decision. This preparation can help you to deal with criticism after the course of action is implemented.

Managing Criticism

Raines (2009) suggests focusing on protection, the present, and the positive aspects of the decision as one way to deal with criticism. First, protection of the student and others from harm is paramount. The federal Family Educational Rights and Privacy Act (FERPA) specifically allows schools to

The U.S. Department of Education (2007a) has issued guidance to schools in the form of a brochure entitled *Balancing Student Privacy and School Safety: A Guide to the Family Educational Rights and Privacy Act for Elementary and Secondary Schools*. This brochure states: "In an emergency, FERPA permits school officials to disclose without consent education records, including personally identifiable information from those records, to protect the health and safety of students or other individuals. At such times, records and information may be released to appropriate parties such as law enforcement officials, public health officials, and trained medical personnel. *See* CFR §99.31(a)(10) and §99.36. This exception is limited to the period of the emergency and generally does not allow for a blanket release of personally identifiable information from a student's records."

share education records without consent in order to address a health and safety emergency (see Box 6.2). To the extent your actions have kept people safe, this can be used to justify your decision.

Second, management of the ethical predicament in the immediate present should take priority over past considerations or possible future considerations that may never occur (i.e., second-guessing). While you need to be mindful of what might happen in the future, dealing with immediate concerns comes first. If necessary, you can re-engage the ethical quandary in the future to manage it once again. We will discuss this more in Chapter 7.

Finally, while the critics will focus on what they perceive to be the negative outcomes of the decision, you need to be prepared with the aspects of the decision that were positive. It is likely that other courses of action that you did not select may have had negative outcomes that were avoided by the course of action you did select. The critics may not perceive and appreciate the challenges of the ethical predicament. To the extent you can help them to understand that there was no ideal alternative in this situation, this may help you to justify your decision. Recently, one of the authors attended a school board meeting where parents were invited to comment on several versions of a redistricting plan. Some parents wanted to make sure that their younger children attended the same school as their older children. Some parents wanted their children to attend the school closest to home. Still others wanted their children to be able to attend the schools with the highest test scores. Toward the close of the meeting, it appeared that the school board was exasperated—there was simply no way they were going to satisfy even a majority of the parents. At this point, the author stood up and pointed out how great it was to have so many concerned parents in the district and that the school was a year away from having to enact the decision, leaving plenty of time to consider all of the possibilities. The school board was pleasantly surprised when all of the parents applauded this summary of the meeting.

Documenting the Process

You can help to prepare to justify your decision if you have documented the decision-making steps you have taken (Barnett & Johnson, 2008b; Doverspike, 2008; Mitchell, 2007; Reamer, 2005b; Zur, 2007). You can use our (or some other) ethical decision-making model as a template to document how you came to the decision you did.

1. *Knowing yourself and your professional responsibilities.* Are you aware of your ethical orientation and preferences? Have you taken time to consider how your personal values may be influencing your decision making in this situation? Have you considered how your personal feelings about this particular client might have affected your decision? Are you familiar with your profession's ethical standards? Do you understand the requirements and expectations of the federal and state laws that govern your pupil services practice?

2. *Analyzing the predicament.* What did you do to analyze the quandary? Who did you determine to be your primary client and why? What other stakeholders did you identify? What responsibilities to the student and the stakeholders did you consider? What were the ethical values and other competing responsibilities that you identified as being relevant in this situation?

3. *Seeking consultation.* Did you seek out consultation? From whom? Was it just colleagues from your own profession? Did you seek out anyone else who may have more clinical or

legal expertise in this situation? What feedback and advice did you get from these individuals?

4. *Identifying different courses of action.* What different courses of action did you identify? Did you take care to avoid the trap of "either-or" thinking? Who did you work with to generate the different courses of action? The student? Stakeholders? How did you assess these different courses of action? Did you consider the likely outcomes of each course of action and how they will impact the student, stakeholders, and you?

5. *Managing the clinical concerns.* If applicable, did you do any risk assessments for possible self-harm to the student or student harm to others? If so, did you use any evidence-based tools, as well as your clinical judgment? Did you include others in the risk assessment to ensure your conclusions are sound? Did you assess the student's ability to make sound decisions? Did you work within the student's zone of proximal development so that he was able to participate in some aspects of the ethical decision making? Did you consider the family's culture when making the decision?

6. *Implementing the decision.* Did you submit the selected course of action to the five tests (i.e., Golden Rule, fiduciary responsibility, justice and generalizability, publicity, and universality)? Did the selected course of action pass all five tests? If not, what parts of the ethical decision-making process did you revisit? How did you modify the selected course of action to pass all five tests? Or did you select a new course of action?

Established Parameters to Help Justify Decisions

To the extent that you can demonstrate that you are acting within established parameters, you can also help to justify your decision and satisfy your critics. We have identified the following hierarchy of parameters: federal and state law, state education rules, school board policy, administrative procedures, group practice decisions, and individual practice decisions. These are separate from any ethical considerations that are outlined in a profession's established ethical standards, which apply and must be considered across all of these parameters.

Laws can prohibit, require, or allow specific behavior in given situations. More than half of states prohibit the use of corporal punishment in schools (McCarthy, 2005). All states mandate the reporting of suspected child maltreatment by the members of some professions (e.g., physicians, teachers), consistent with the intent of the federal Child Abuse Prevention and Treatment Act (Smith, 2009). The Family Educational Rights and Privacy Act (FERPA) allows education records to be shared without consent to address a health and safety emergency (see Box 6.3). Some states have unique laws that grant students additional rights. For instance, Wisconsin prohibits a pupil services professional from sharing student-disclosed information regarding use of alcohol or other drugs by the student or some other student, unless the student gives written permission, there is serious and imminent danger, or a report is required for suspected child maltreatment (§118.126, Wis. Stat.). To the extent that actions to manage an ethical predicament are consistent with the law, these are strong justifications that can be shared with the student and stakeholders. This underscores the importance of pupil services professionals being knowledgeable about school law related to their professional practice.

As with all government organizations, school boards are expected to operate within the parameters established in federal and state law (Amundson, Ficklen, Maatsch, Brody Saks, & Banks Zakariya, 1996). Sometimes these laws may be extremely specific and require no clarification in order for the school employees to understand how to comply with these laws. Other laws may be stated in broad terms that are open to interpretation or require additional specificity in order for school boards to communicate to school employees what their associated responsibilities are. School boards may pass policies to provide direction to their employees that are consistent with federal and state law (Amundson et al., 1996). School administrators are charged with the responsibility to operate the school district within the parameters of local school board policy (Amundson et al., 1996). To the extent that actions to manage an ethical predicament are compliant and/or consistent with school board policy, the pupil services professional can use these parameters to help justify the decision with the student and stakeholders. The focus of the objections can then be redirected to the school board policy and away from the pupil services professional. That is, the discussion can then be shifted to whether the school board policy should be changed or maintained in its present form, rather than whether the pupil services professional made the correct professional judgment in this situation.

Box 6.3 Student Confidentiality Versus Parental Rights

An elementary school counselor is providing individual counseling to a student whose parents are in the midst of a contentious divorce. The girl is keeping a journal of her experiences and feelings, which she and the school counselor discuss. The journal is kept in the school counselor's office. The family court has appointed a guardian ad litem to make recommendations to the court regarding the custody of the girl. He interviews the school counselor and learns of the journal. The school counselor allows the guardian ad litem to read the journal, after obtaining the permission of the student. The girl's mother learns of the journal from the guardian ad litem and contacts the school to have the journal copied and sent to her attorney.

1. Not everything that a school possesses regarding a student is considered an education record under FERPA (e.g., a drawing or some other work or art produced by a student). Do you think this student's journal is an education record?
2. Since the school counselor stores the journal in her office, could the she consider it a personal record under FERPA?
3. Does the mother have the legal right to compel the school to have the journal copied and given to her attorney?
4. Is there some way the school counselor can manage this situation to protect the student's right to confidentiality and respect the mother's rights as a parent?

While school boards may enact policies that are highly specific and require no additional direction to implement, the recommended practice is to create general policies with positive directions for the superintendent and staff (Amundson et al., 1996). School administrators may establish administrative procedures to ensure that broadly stated school board policies are implemented consistently in all school buildings across the school district. An Internet search by one of the authors using the key terms "school board policy" and "administrative procedures" yielded more than 2.7 million hits, with many being from local school districts. To the extent that actions to manage an ethical quandary are consistent with administrative procedures, the pupil services professional can also use these parameters to help justify the decision with the student and stakeholders. The focus of any objections can be redirected to the administrative procedures and away from the pupil services professional. That is, the discussion can then be shifted to whether the administrative procedures should be changed or maintained in their present form.

Much of the professional practice of pupil services professionals is outside what is typically included in school board policies and administrative procedures, so practitioners may not find much support for justification for their decisions in these parameters. However, that does not mean that pupil services professionals should be content to rely solely on legal and ethical parameters. Reamer (2005b) notes that judgments regarding how a social worker handles an ethical predicament are based upon the social worker's adherence to prevailing professional practice and what ethicists and lawyers refer to as "standards of care." Specifically, how would "an ordinary, reasonable, and prudent professional" with similar training act under similar circumstances (p. 117)? Within the school setting, school counselors, school nurses, school psychologists, and school social workers would be considered to have similar training in how they treat confidential student information and manage ethical predicaments. Some professions publish standards for school-based practitioners (see Internet Sources at the end of the chapter). Pupil services professionals may also choose to collaborate with each other to establish group practice protocols that form local "standards of care" to apply in a given situation. That way, if actions are called into question afterwards, the pupil services professional has already established that he has acted in accordance with the standard against which he will be judged. For instance, the pupil services professionals within a school district could choose to establish a specific protocol to follow when presented with a student who has made comments about possible self-harm. If all pupil services professionals follow the same protocol in this situation and concerns are expressed afterwards, the focus of the criticism can be shifted to the protocol and away from the individual pupil services professional.

Despite these parameters and how they can be used to help justify decisions, pupil services professionals will always be faced with ethical predicaments where there is no guidance from the law, school board policy, administrative procedures, or group practice decisions. The decision will ultimately fall to the individual pupil services professional. Following the steps outlined in this book and utilizing a collaborative, decision-making approach that involves the student and stakeholders can make individual practice decisions more manageable.

Ethical Guidelines

1. Remain empathic about the client's feelings regarding the problem.
2. Maintain positive regard for the client even if you disagree on the ethical issue.
3. Focus on managing, not solving, the ethical predicament in the best possible manner. While an elegant solution may present itself, usually the best available course of action will have some less desirable outcomes for the student and/or other stakeholders.
4. Screen the selected course of action before you implement it by examining it from five different perspectives. Consider the "Golden Rule," fiduciary responsibility, justice and generalizability, publicity, and universality tests. If your selected course of action does not pass all five of these tests, revisit one or more of the earlier steps in the decision-making process.
5. Try to anticipate possible criticism from the student and/or stakeholders and be prepared to respond. Focus on the three Ps of protection, present, and positives.
6. Use the seven steps of the decision-making process to structure your documentation in your personal notes for selecting the course of action.
7. Use available parameters to help justify your decision: laws, school board policies, administrative procedures, and group practice decisions and protocols.
8. Override client self-determination only in extraordinary circumstances.

Exercises

1. Alternative Courses of Action

Review the case example in Box 6.1 again. Other than an alternative school setting, what other potential courses of action can you think of? Apply the tests of the Golden Rule, fiduciary responsibility, justice and generalizability, publicity, and universality to your new ideas.

2. Criticism Management

Think of a time when you were criticized for a decision you made or action you took. How could focusing on the three Ps of protection, present, and positives have made a difference?

3. Standard of Care Protocol

Organize a group of pupil services professionals in your school district or fellow students who are also participating in a practicum in schools. Create a protocol you will all agree to follow to address a particular kind of situation that you all may face.

Internet Resources

ASCA National Model: A framework for school counseling programs
http://www.schoolcounselor.org/files/
Natl%20Model%20Exec%20Summary_final.pdf
Balancing Student Privacy and School Safety
http://www.ed.gov/policy/gen/guid/fpco/brochures/elsec.pdf
NASP School Psychology: A blueprint for training and practice II
http://www.nasponline.org/resources/blueprint/blue2.pdf
NASW Standards for School Social Work
http://www.socialworkers.org/practice/standards/NASW_SSWS.pdf
National School Boards Association
School Law: http://www.nsba.org/MainMenu/SchoolLaw.aspx
School Board Policies: http://www.nsba.org/MainMenu/
SchoolBoardPolicies.aspx

7

Reflecting on the Process

Many ethical decision-making models conclude with the practitioner moving forward with the selected course of action. We believe that to end the ethical part of the process at that point is actually unethical. The fact that the practitioner is managing a complex ethical quandary increases the possibility of unforeseen consequences and missed clinical concerns compared to other "routine" decisions. In previous chapters we have talked about how stakeholders may not be happy with the outcomes of the decision and there may indeed be some less desirable outcomes, including to the student, which could not be avoided. Assuming the pupil services professional continues to practice in schools, the same situation could arise again with another student. These are powerful reasons why the ethical decision-making process should continue through implementation of the course of action.

The ethical standards for all of the pupil services professions call upon the members of these professions to continue their professional growth throughout their professional careers (see Box 2.3 in Chapter 2). Continuing education is commonly associated with attendance at specific events (e.g., conference, training, university course). Indeed, one of the conditions of license renewal typically requires the documentation of formal credits and/or clock hours. However, professional growth occurs in informal settings as well as formal ones. For instance, consultation with professional colleagues is a way of increasing our ethical and clinical skills. Several states have moved away from requiring credits and clock hours for license renewal in favor of practice-based professional development designed by and for the individual educator called a *professional development plan* (Constable & Alvarez, 2006). Professional development plans focus on improving the educator's professional knowledge, skills, and dispositions by embedding the learning experience in the educator's daily work. Extending the ethical decision-making process through the implementation of the course of action is a form of practice-based, professional development in that the pupil services professional can learn how to better manage similar ethical predicaments in the future. Goldstein (1998) refers to this as "ontological learning." This form of education occurs in two ways. First, we can learn vicariously by pondering the experiences of others. Second, we can learn experientially by "reflective and critical thought about what we did" (p. 250).

Postdecision Activities

There are notable references in the literature, including the authors' work, that include important postdecision activities that we believe can serve to improve the practitioner's ethical and clinical skills:

- The implementation of the selected course of action should be monitored (Dibble, 2006; Reamer, 2006; Tymchuk, 1986). This can be done primarily through checking in with the student and the other identified stakeholders.
- The implementation of the selected course of action should also be evaluated (Dibble, 2006; McNamara, 2008; Pope & Vasquez, 2007; Reamer, 2006; Stadler, 1986; Strom-Gottfried, 2008; Tarvydas, 1998). The pupil services professional can ask these questions to evaluate the selected course of action: What were the outcomes? What feedback have I received from the student and other stakeholders on the course of action? Is the student satisfied with the outcomes? Are the other stakeholders satisfied with the outcomes?
- Van Divner and Champ Morera (2007) call on school psychologists to re-engage in the ethical decision-making process if the ethical quandary is not resolved. There may be additional actions that can and should be taken to improve outcomes for the student and/or stakeholders after the course of action has been implemented. Later in this chapter we share more about re-engaging the decision-making process when the outcomes of the decision are not acceptable.
- The implementation of the selected course of action should be reflected upon (Dibble, 2006; Mattison, 2000;

Raines, 2009; Welfel, 1998). Reflection can briefly be described as assessment in hindsight. It is an opportunity to look into the "rearview mirror" of the process we followed to come to the decision we did. How did we do? With the benefit of hindsight, would we do things differently? Mattison (2000) shares a cycle of reflection that the practitioner utilizes throughout the decision-making process. The cycle concludes with reflection that goes beyond the implementation of the course of action: (1) compare the current decision to past decisions, and (2) use the ethical predicament and the decision to better understand your value patterning. This action cycles back to the first step in our ethical decision-making model discussed in Chapter 1.

Reflections on an implemented course of action can be guided through a series of questions based upon the authors' previous work. *To what degree did personal values influence this decision?* We all have personal values. Some of these we may believe in passionately. We devoted Chapter 1 in this book to helping the pupil services professional recognize his personal values and ethical preferences. Ethical standards for school counselors, school nurses, school psychologists, and school social workers are all in agreement that the practitioner should not impose her value system on the student (see Box 2.3 in Chapter 2). The more passionate we are about a particular value, the greater the potential struggle to manage the ethical quandary. Personal experiences can also affect our ability to work with students objectively (see Box 7.1). We will use this case example to help expound on the reflection questions presented next.

To what extent and how did other participants influence this decision? How was the decision-making process collaborative involving the student and perhaps other stakeholders? Were there any ways the student was "herded" toward a decision that she was not satisfied with? In Box 7.1, the school nurse knows the decision to leave the relationship belongs to the student. Any attempts to force the student to end the relationship are more likely to backfire and strengthen the student's resolve to maintain the relationship. However, the school nurse is concerned that her recent personal experience may not allow her to objectively support the student, as Evelyn did her, to make her own decision. Lasser and McGarry Klose (2007) review social psychological phenomena and analyze how they can inappropriately affect ethical decision making in

Box 7.1 Personal Experience: Bias or Asset?

A 16-year-old student approaches the school nurse for information about contraception. The student is not yet sexually active, but her boyfriend is pressuring her to have sex and she wants to be sure she avoids pregnancy. Through discussion with the student, the school nurse learns that the student is in an emotionally abusive relationship. Her empathy for the student rises rapidly, as she has just exited a 10-year marriage that gradually became more emotionally abusive over time. The school nurse understands that her personal experience gives her a special "window" into the student's relationship that other pupil services professionals in the school will not have. She recalls how much Evelyn, a woman who works in the local domestic abuse center, was able to help her, because of her own past abusive relationship. The school nurse's friends had been telling her to leave her husband for years, but the decision wasn't that easy. Evelyn had supported her journey into recovery and allowed her to make her own decision when she was ready. On the other hand, the school nurse understands that the emotional wounds from her past abusive relationship are still fresh. She is still healing and, she asks herself, "Can I be objective in this situation?" The school nurse knows the student will likely cling to the relationship with her boyfriend, even though it is not a healthy relationship. She also knows a decision by the student to end the relationship may never come. The school nurse struggles with the decision to work with the student or refer her to another pupil services professional in the school or the local domestic abuse center.

the school setting. One of these phenomena is authority and obedience. In this case study, the student may perceive the school nurse as an authority figure and may be predisposed to perceive an alternative shared by the school nurse as a strong recommendation or even a directive. Another phenomenon is fear appeals. The school nurse needs to take care not to allow her personal experience to exaggerate the potential dangers to the student, as this could also "herd" the student to a particular decision.

Ethical Decision Making in School Mental Health

How was the student's self-determination balanced with concerns for her safety and well-being? If the student had shared information that described a physically abusive relationship, the school nurse must then call upon her knowledge of state laws regarding child abuse reporting to determine whether a report is necessary. If not, she still needs to assess the potential for physical harm to the student. Adults in physically abusive relationships clearly have the legal autonomy to determine how they will manage the relationship, including if and when to leave the relationship. The risk for serious injury or death to a woman actually increases in the aftermath of her leaving an abusive spouse or partner (Campbell et al., 2003; Kyriacou et al., 1999; Wilson & Daly, 1993). Minors, however, do not have that same legal autonomy nor do they necessarily have the maturity of an adult to determine how to manage the relationship safely and whether to end it. It is likely the student's parents would want to know about any kind of abuse in their daughter's social relationships. A sudden and intrusive intervention on the parents' part, however, could drive the student deeper into the relationship with her abusive boyfriend. She may even perceive him as a victim in this situation. Balancing the student's right to self-determination and the school nurse's concern for the safety of the student is a difficult ethical challenge.

What administrative pressures were exerted in the situation (e.g., contacting the police-school liaison officer)? If the school nurse chose to consult with the building principal, there may have been a strong suggestion (or even a directive) to contact law enforcement authorities to protect the student and perhaps charge the boyfriend with a crime. Any decision to involve law enforcement should be rooted in a concern for the safety of the student and any legal requirement to report the situation. While many school districts treat police-school liaison officers as members of the crisis team, pupil services professionals need to remember that these individuals are first and foremost law enforcement officers who have been assigned to "patrol" the school buildings and campus. They are not professional educators (i.e., teacher, pupil services professional, administrator). Police officers take an oath to uphold the law, an oath which they do not check at the school door. Furthermore, many police officers are trained to deceive suspected perpetrators in order to secure voluntary admissions of guilt (Skolnick & Leo, 1992). For a list of deceptive practices used by police, see Box 7.2. While the focus of the school nurse in this case study is on what is in the best interests of the student, a police-school liaison officer may perceive this

Box 7.2 Deceptive Interrogation Practices

Skolnick and Leo (1992) identified eight commonly employed deceptive interrogation tactics used by police investigators. Practitioners concerned about the conduct of police-school liaison officers need to be familiar with them.

1. *Reframing the interrogation as an interview.* Interviews are considered noncustodial and suspects are told they can "leave at any time." Police are not required give Miranda warnings in an interview. A more recent version of this tactic is reframing a suspect as merely a "person of interest" in the case.
2. *Delivering the Miranda warning as a bureaucratic requirement.* When suspects perceive their rights to remain silent as a mere ritual, they are more likely to waive their Miranda rights.*
3. *Misrepresenting the seriousness of the crime.* Police may underestimate or exaggerate the crime to get the suspect to talk. Telling a perpetrator that the victim is not as badly hurt, for example, may persuade them to admit to what they think is a "lesser" crime.
4. *Feigning empathy.* Police may pretend to be the suspect's friend and help them "clear their conscience" through a confession.
5. *Offering justification for the crime.* Police may offer excuses for the suspect such as telling a rapist that "the girl wanted it" or a violent bully that "the kid was a punk."
6. *False promises.* Suspects may be told that remorse will be a "mitigating" factor in sentencing or that the court will probably just impose treatment rather than incarceration.
7. *Misrepresentations.* Police officers sometimes plant an undercover operative in the same holding cell as the suspect to elicit self-incriminating statements.

Ethical Decision Making in School Mental Health

8. *Fabricating evidence.* Police may tell suspects that they have DNA evidence or fingerprints that confirm their guilt. Alternatively, they may claim that a partner has already confessed or that a polygraph machine has indicated they're not telling the whole truth.

---

* Miranda rights are usually stated as follows: "You have the right to remain silent. Anything you say can and will be used against you in a court of law. You have the right to an attorney. If you cannot afford an attorney, one will be appointed to you. Do you understand these rights as they have been read to you?" An affirmative response gives police the right to interrogate the suspect. This warning stems from the U.S. Supreme Court case, Miranda v. Arizona, 1966.

situation as one that requires an investigation to determine whether a crime was committed, with a possible arrest to follow.

How was the advice received from the consultants considered? The school nurse may decide to check with respected colleagues before making a decision about whether to refer the student or work with her. Evelyn may have particular insight into whether the school nurse's recent personal experience may be an asset or a bias in the school nurse's work with the student. The police-school liaison officer can share what the legal requirements are in this situation without the school nurse having to reveal the student's identity. The school nurse should approach consultation with an open mind, which may lead her to courses of action that may not have been identified before.

What clinical concerns were missed or underestimated? What areas of professional competence needed improvement to address the ethical predicament in the best interests of the student? If the school nurse had not had the previous personal experience of seeking support for an abusive relationship, she would need to assess her level of expertise in working with students in abusive relationships. Does she understand the cycle of violence in abusive relationships? Does she understand the differences between abusive teen relationships and abusive adult relationships (Foshee & Reyes, 2009; Theriot, 2008)? The answers to these questions help to determine whether to seek out consultation to enhance competence or to refer this student to another professional with more expertise.

What knowledge of the law, school board policies, and administrative rules could have been increased to address the ethical predicament in the best interests of the student? If the relationship described in Box 7.1 is emotionally, but not physically abusive, there may be not a legal requirement to report this situation. However, the school district may have a policy that prohibits harassment against students. That policy may require school employees to report any incidents of harassment to the school administration. The school nurse needs to understand the policy and associated administrative procedures, in order to take those parameters into consideration in the ethical decision-making process.

In hindsight, was the selected decision the best one available? If you took a challenging ethical quandary and managed it to produce the best possible outcomes for the student and other stakeholders, celebrate that accomplishment. You may wish to share your success with fellow colleagues to help them learn from your excellent work, but check to make sure the decision was right for the right reasons. That is, were the outcomes successful due to how the ethical predicament was managed, or were you simply lucky in how everything worked out? If the outcomes were positive for some chance reasons, you may not be as fortunate the next time. You can take advantage of the opportunity to reflect upon the decision and how you might handle this situation differently in the future.

If the answer is no, ask yourself, was my decision-making process flawed in any way? Did I skip any steps or fail to adequately carry out any of these steps? For instance, should I have consulted other people? Did I miss any stakeholders? Did I fail to seek out the necessary information to manage the clinical concerns well? If the process is flawed in any way, the selected course of action may not be successful. In addition, a flawed process will not help to justify your course of action (see Box 7.3).

You can improve your chances of success by taking care to follow and implement the steps of an ethical decision-making process that fits your professional practice well. Revisiting these steps can help to identify where your process may have fallen short.

Had the decision making been handled differently, what different course of action would have been selected? Were there courses of action that were not considered that would have resulted in more acceptable outcomes? Which consequences were not anticipated? The process guides and leads you to the eventual decision. Once again, avoid the obvious "either-or" choices. Look for alternatives that minimize the competition between the relevant ethical values and other responsibilities.

Box 7.3 Managing Mistakes

O'Donohue and Henderson (1999) argue that scientific decision making in clinical practice requires epistemic fallibilism:

> Science begins when one realizes that one's current beliefs—no matter how "commonsensical," no matter how well they seem to cohere with other beliefs, no matter how much they are generally accepted by others, and no matter how many times they have appeared to be confirmed by one's experience—may still be false. Science begins with the epistemologically humble attitude of "I may be wrong." (p. 17)

In Pope and Vasquez' (2007) first chapter, they universalize ethical errors as follows: "None of us is infallible. Whatever our experience, accomplishments, or wisdom, all of us can—and do—make mistakes, overlook something important, and reach conclusions that are wrong" (p. 14).

Reamer (2008) identifies three kinds of errors. First, there are inadvertent mistakes. For example, a school counselor openly alludes to an adolescent's pregnancy without realizing that no one else knew her secret. Second, there are well-intentioned mistakes. For example, the school psychologist recommends a self-contained program for antisocial youth for an adjudicated adolescent without realizing that such interventions have been found to be not only ineffective, but harmful to youth (Dishion, McCord, & Poulin, 1999). Third, there are intentional deviances from accepted standards of conduct. For example, a school social worker deliberately misdiagnoses a child to help the family obtain Medicaid to pay for his therapy. Any of these mistakes can create an adverse event that requires further intervention. If we are bound to have ethical lapses, what should we do about it after the fact? Hopefully, there are two main goals in managing mistakes. First, we want to improve the situation either by mitigating any harm or by coming to a more satisfactory resolution of the problem. Second, we want to learn from our mistakes so that we are less likely to commit the same *faux pas* in the future. Let's examine each of these in more detail.

Gutheil (2006) argues that clients experiencing adverse events need acknowledgment, remorse, and remedy. Accordingly, there are three steps in meeting the first goal of improving the situation: they must acknowledge, apologize, and act. First, practitioners must take responsibility for and honestly acknowledge their mistakes (Boyle, O'Connell, Platt, & Albert, 2006; Kelley, 2002). The importance of assuming responsibility is mentioned in multiple ethical codes. The ASCA (2004) *Ethical Standards* state that a professional counselor "accepts responsibility for the consequences of his/her actions" (§E.1.a). The NASP (2000) *Principles* state that "School psychologists accept responsibility for the appropriateness of their professional practices (§III.A.1). Finally, the NASW (1999) *Code of Ethics* expects social workers to "act honestly and responsibly" (p. 8). Faunce and Bolsin (2005) argue that such admissions are part of one's fiduciary responsibility to the client. Some clinicians may object that this kind of disclosure exposes them to negative consequences. Those in doubt would be well advised to consult an attorney, insurance provider, or supervisor. There is some research, however, that full disclosure actually reduces one's risk of being sued or brought before a licensing board (Mazor et al., 2004; Pelt & Faldmo, 2008). Luce (2006) lists another benefit as well: disclosure reduces further injury to the client. Second, it is common decency to apologize for the mistake (Cravens & Earp, 2009; Finkelstein et al., 1997; Zimmerman, 2004). Luce (2008) suggests that a sincere apology can reduce practitioner guilt, facilitate absolution from clients, and restore confidence that the mistake has been handled honorably. Third, if the mistake resulted in adverse consequences for the client or others, the practitioner must take action to make the situation right (Berlinger, 2004; Finkelstein et al., 1997; Kraman & Hamm, 1999). Clients should be re-engaged as partners in the new decision-making process (Reamer, 2008; Van Divner & Champ Morera, 2007). One of the byproducts of our sharing mistakes with student-clients is that it helps them to become resilient and responsible citizens (Curwin, 2003; Goldstein, & Brooks, 2002).

One essential prerequisite to learning from our mistakes is having a supportive environment in which to discuss and work through the error without being subjected to blame or punishment (Hendin, Maltsberger, & Haas, 2004; Tjosvold, Yu, & Hui, 2004). Edmondson (2004) identifies four sources of error in clinical decision making. First, the individuals involved may be prone to cognitive distortions. According to schema theory, we all see what we expect to see even in our relationships with other people (Baldwin, 1999). This results in overlooking evidence to the contrary or doing things without thinking about it. For example, one of our children was recently putting away groceries and accidentally placed a box of fish sticks in the cereal cupboard. He was simply used to putting boxes in this location and hadn't bothered to notice the label! Second, the individuals may be so emotionally intense that they do not think clearly (Figner, Mackinlay, Wilkening, & Weber, 2009). This is the reason we suggested that practitioners think about their level of involvement and attitudes toward clients in Chapter 2. In fact, all of the factors that impair adolescent decision making mentioned in Chapter 5 can do the same to adults. Third, in complex systems, it is nearly impossible to both know and predict all of the mediating variables. Most school-based clinicians know how the student functions at school, but little about how the same student behaves at home or in the community. This is an excellent reason to involve parents as partners in the process, as we have suggested at several points. Likewise, we may be able to provide adequate structure and support at school during instructional periods but have little control over nonacademic times (e.g., bus rides, cafeteria, hallways, or playground). This is a strong reason to think broadly about which stakeholders are affected by the ethical decision. Finally, authoritarian systems are likely to suppress divergences of opinion leading to impoverished decision making because of a failure to adequately consider multiple alternative actions (Son Hing, Bobocel, Zanna, & McBride, 2007). Furthermore, they create a climate of fear in which mistakes are less apt to be disclosed and corrected. This is why it is important to conduct a power analysis of the stakeholders in the system. Clinicians can be coerced into making decisions that are not in the best interests of their clients if they feel threatened with firings or lawsuits.

What precautions might prevent problems in the future? If you study why the outcomes of the decision were not what you had anticipated or hoped for, this can lead you to what can be done differently in the future if you encounter a similar situation. Did the parents vehemently object to the course of action and their lack of involvement? Is the building principal seeking to implement new administrative procedures that will limit the clinical judgment of pupil services professionals in similar situations? Was the student harmed in some way, due to your failure to disclose information that could have protected him? Answering and reflecting on these questions may help you to learn better ways to manage this or a similar ethical quandary in the future.

Through your reflection, you may find that you actually did follow the ethical decision-making process faithfully. You may find that, given the circumstances, the decision was the best that could be made, but the outcomes were still not acceptable to the student and/or to important stakeholders. In this case, it is critical that you take steps to avoid being placed in this situation in the future, because the outcomes are likely to be unacceptable again. You may wish to partner with other pupil services colleagues to attempt to change school board policy or administrative procedures. You may wish to work with your colleagues to create a group practice protocol (see Chapter 6) to establish a standard of care that would guide professional practice in this situation. Another strategy is to seek out better understanding of the professional competencies and legal parameters that guide other pupil services professionals and community-based mental health professionals. For instance, one of the authors used a technique he called "protective interrupting" whenever a student below the age of consent for sexual activity would begin to talk about sexual behavior. Because the student's disclosure of sexual activity to a school social worker might trigger a legal requirement to make a report to child protective services in that state, the author would interrupt the student and walk the student down the hall to the school nurse. The law in that state grants the student additional legal rights to confidentiality working with a school nurse that the student did not have with the school social worker. The student's health and safety is still protected since the school nurse is a mandated reporter under the law. In addition, the student's right to confidentially seek out information to protect her health is preserved. The school nurse welcomed the referrals and the opportunity to deliver important health care services to students in need.

Case Study

Clearly, there were some adverse outcomes that resulted from the decisions made by the educators in the case example described later in Box 7.4. The student was expelled from school. Even though the school district is providing alternative educational services, this choice was forced on the student and

---

Box 7.4 Cutting at School

A principal receives a call from a parent saying that her child heard that a seventh grade girl was thinking about cutting herself. The principal contacts the school social worker and the school psychologist. They jointly interview the seventh grade girl about this report. The girl shares that she was not cutting herself and had never cut herself. She is nervous about her mother being notified about this suspicion. The principal, school social worker, and school psychologist discuss the situation and decide to call the seventh grade girl's community-based therapist, instead of the mother. (Note: the mother had previously given written consent for the school and the therapist to communicate.) The school social worker calls the mother to share that she is worried about her daughter's having negative coping strategies and suggests the mother talk with her daughter about positive ways to handle stress. About a week later, the girl brings several razor blades to school and distributes them to other students, not with the intent to physically harm others, but to "cut" with them. Consistent with school board policy, the school administration brings the student forward for expulsion. At the expulsion hearing, the hearing officer asks the principal whether she had any prior knowledge of this girl cutting and the principal shares that she had received a phone call from a concerned parent. The girl is expelled from school and is receiving education at an alternative school in the school district. The mother of the seventh grade girl is furious that school personnel knew of a suspicion of her daughter cutting and did not relay that information to her. She believes that had the school contacted her, she could have prevented her daughter from taking the razor blades to school and her daughter would not have been expelled. She plans to contact an attorney.

---

the mother through the expulsion. We can surmise that the working relationship between the mother and the school had been at least adequate, since the mother had agreed to ongoing communication between the school and her daughter's therapist. Now that relationship has been devastated, perhaps beyond repair. In addition to seeking out legal advice to perhaps sue the involved educators and the school district, the mother may revoke her permission to share information between the school and the therapist, reducing their ability to coordinate services in the best interests of the student.

Let's use the case study to apply the reflection questions from earlier in this chapter.

To what degree did personal values influence this decision? We do not know whether any of the personal values of any of these three educators in this case study inappropriately influenced this decision. However, it appears that the decision was made collaboratively among the three of them consistent with a team approach to pupil services delivery. This approach can help minimize the possibility of any individual decision maker's personal values encroaching on the decision, since there are other decision makers who can keep this in check.

To what extent and how did other participants influence this decision? Was the decision-making process collaborative, involving the student and perhaps other stakeholders? How was the student's self-determination balanced with concern for her safety and well-being? How was the consultative advice considered? It does appear that the decision making was done in a collaborative manner among the three educators. In addition, the student's wishes were respected when the educators decided not to fully inform the mother of their concerns. However, in hindsight, it is clear that these educators gave too much weight to the student's right to self-determination and not enough weight to the ethical standard of concern for the student's safety and well-being. A decision was made not to fully involve the mother, even though she is a critical stakeholder. There may indeed have been legitimate clinical reasons for not fully informing the mother of the raised concerns. For instance, the educators may have been concerned about the student engaging in other high-risk behaviors (e.g., running away, suicide attempt). However, the mother has taken steps to ensure the emotional well-being of her daughter by involving her daughter in therapy and allowing the therapist and school to communicate on an ongoing basis. While the therapist was notified of the situation with the student, it is not clear whether the therapist's clinical expertise and professional knowledge about the student was actively sought out. Finally, the student's friends may have been able to share additional information

Ethical Decision Making in School Mental Health

about the student's potential for self-harm that was not available from any other source.

What clinical concerns were missed or underestimated? What areas of professional competence needed improvement to address the ethical predicament in the best interests of the student? What knowledge of the law, school board policies, and administrative rules could have been increased to address the ethical predicament in the best interests of the student? In this case, we do not know what, if any, special training the school psychologist and/or school social worker have to assess risk for self-harm. We do not know whether they used any standardized tool(s) or protocols to enhance their clinical judgment. We do know that these steps would help to ensure that the clinical concerns in this case study would be managed as well as possible, especially when applied collaboratively by the two pupil services professionals.

In hindsight, did these three educators make the right decision? Was the decision-making process flawed in any way? Did they skip any steps or fail to adequately carry out any of these steps? Looking back, it is clear that the decision made by these educators resulted in negative outcomes for the student, the mother, and the educators. Consultation with the therapist is critical to help make the best possible decision in the student's best interests. Use of appropriate standardized tools and protocols may have resulted in additional information that may have prompted a different choice of action by the three educators. Since the building principal had been originally contacted by the parent of one of the student's friends, the school psychologist and school social worker had at least one peer they could have interviewed about the student's potential for harm. Finally, it is not clear whether the school psychologist or school social worker continued to monitor the student in the week following the decision before she brought the razor blades to school. When the three educators decided not to fully inform the mother, they in essence assumed the parental responsibility to keep the student safe.

Had the decision making been handled differently, what different course of action would have been selected? Were there courses of action that were not considered that would have resulted in more acceptable outcomes? Which consequences were not anticipated? The outcomes in this case study were so negative that we must assume the three professionals did not anticipate them. The decision not to fully inform the mother of her daughter's potential for self-harm was critical in this situation. The student spends significant but not all of her time in school. Her time with the therapist is minimal. These professionals, while sincerely concerned with the student's health and well-being, cannot ensure her safety outside of the time they spend together. One can argue that the mother cannot ensure her daughter's safety all of the time either, but as the daughter's legal guardian, the mother has options open to her that the educators and school do not. In addition, the educators, therapist, and mother working together extend the time frame when the student can be monitored to ensure safety.

What precautions should these educators take to prevent problems in the future? The mother's anger with the school district and the three professionals, in particular, is understandable. Her lawsuit may ultimately be successful. It is not clear whether they took responsibility for their decision and the unintended consequence of the student's expulsion, as is recommended by some (Pope & Vasquez, 2007; Van Divner & Champ Morera, 2007), but a lawsuit would bring their actions to light. Regardless, steps can be taken to minimize the possibility of such adverse outcomes in similar situations in the future:

1. Pupil services professionals in the school that have the necessary expertise to assess students for the risk of self-harm should be identified. Only those individuals with that particular competence should be allowed to perform this function.
2. These designated individuals should work together to identify what evidence-based standardized instruments will be used to assess students that may be at risk for self-harm.
3. Likewise, these pupil services professionals should collaborate to adopt or develop a standardized protocol to interview the student. Guidelines for parental notification should be included.
4. The clinical expertise of any student's therapist should be actively sought out and considered, consistent with state and federal laws governing sharing of confidential information.
5. The interview protocol and instruments should be incorporated into the school's crisis response plan and procedures to ensure consistent application.

The collaborative decision making utilized by these three educators is generally considered to be a preferred strategy that will arrive at better decisions, despite the fact the outcomes were not acceptable in this case. Lasser and McGarry Klose (2007) identify three possible social psychological phenomena that can inappropriately affect group ethical decision making in the school setting:

1. Decisions made by groups may involve greater risk than decisions made by individuals (i.e., the risky shift).
2. Pressure to conform may cause a group member to go along with a decision that conflicts with his better judgment.
3. If one member of the group presents herself as "the expert" in a given situation, other members of the group may accept her recommendation and ignore other valid information (i.e., information influence).

Pupil services professionals need to be aware of these social psychological phenomena to ensure "groupthink" dynamics do not result in decisions with less acceptable outcomes being selected (Gambrill, 2005). Lasser and McGarry Klose (2007) offer the following recommendations:

1. Take the initiative to promote independent thought among team members, especially if someone may be nonverbally signaling a lack of comfort with a proposed course of action.
2. Informally in-service teachers and administrators about social psychological phenomena and how they can adversely impact group decision making.
3. Work to reduce power differentials on teams by rotating duties (e.g., leading meetings, taking notes).
4. If you notice that some social psychological phenomenon may be interfering with how the group conducts its decision making, bring your observation to the group's attention.

Re-Engaging the Ethical Decision-Making Process

As we stated earlier in this chapter, Van Divner and Champ Morera (2007) call on school psychologists to re-engage the ethical decision-making process if the ethical predicament is not resolved. Let's consider how the three practitioners in Box 7.4 could continue to work for the best possible outcomes for the student.

The working relationships between the three educators and the student and the identified stakeholders have clearly been damaged. The mother is understandably upset about these three educators choosing not to notify her about her daughter's potential risk for cutting, believing that she could have prevented her daughter from bringing razor blades to school and the resulting expulsion. The student may also blame them, even though they respected her wish not to have her mother notified, because she may see them as the cause for her expulsion and subsequent removal from her school-based, social network of friends. Finally, the therapist may find the school district's decision to expel the student to be unnecessary and counterproductive to the therapeutic process. In short, the student and the other stakeholders may feel that the trust in the relationship has been seriously violated.

These three educators may seek to express a sincere apology to the mother, the student, and the therapist, including remorse for how the whole situation unfolded, resulting in the student's expulsion. However, the school district may have a concern over the potential for the mother perceiving the school district as having liability, if an apology is issued (i.e., an apology could be perceived as some kind of admission of fault). The reality is the working relationships described earlier may be damaged beyond repair, at least in the present.

There are two primary concerns that ethically must be addressed by these three educators. First, the student's academic progress in school must be supported. Fortunately, the student in this case study was placed into an interim alternative educational setting following the expulsion. This allows her to continue to make academic progress during the expulsion, leading to a greater likelihood of a more successful re-entry into the regular school setting. Second, whatever emotional problems that have prompted the student to use cutting as a coping mechanism are still present. Although the community-based therapist may have the primary responsibility for the student's treatment in this regard, continued communication between the therapist and the school to support the therapeutic effort is still in the student's best interests.

The student's placement in the alternative school for the remainder of the school year offers the opportunity for these three practitioners to refer the student to their professional counterparts who work in the alternative school. A meeting should be scheduled to allow the newly designated practitioners in the alternative school to learn more about the student's situation and ensure an appropriate transition. While the student and the mother may be reluctant to continue to allow the school and the therapist to communicate directly, the possibility of the early reinstatement at the beginning of the next school year is clearly an incentive. The therapist has done nothing to betray the trust of the mother or the student, so enlisting her help in this endeavor would be important. However, her willingness to work collaboratively with the school may be diminished following the school district's expulsion of her client. The principal, school psychologist, and school social worker can agree to designate one of them to stay in contact with the staff at the alternative school, in order to help facilitate a successful transition back into the regular school setting following the completion of the early reinstatement conditions or the conclusion of the expulsion period.

Ethical Guidelines

1. Monitor and evaluate the implementation of the selected course of action to determine whether the outcomes for the student and other stakeholders are acceptable.
2. Re-engage in the ethical decision-making process if outcomes are not acceptable for the student and/or other stakeholders.
3. Reflect on how the ethical predicament was managed to determine whether a same or similar situation should be managed differently in the future.
4. Take proactive steps to ensure that social psychological phenomena are not inappropriately affecting decisions made with students or other stakeholders, resulting in less acceptable outcomes.

Exercises

1. Asset or Bias?

What other ways could the school nurse in Box 7.1 determine whether her personal experience with domestic violence will be an asset or a bias if she works with the student?

2. Management of Mistakes

Take a look at the suggestions in Box 7.3 for managing mistakes. Which of the three steps do you follow most often? Which of the three steps are you most likely to neglect?

3. Re-engagement

What are other ways the three educators in Box 7.4 could re-engage the ethical decision-making process, in order to help improve the outcomes for the student and stakeholders?

4. Social Psychological Phenomena

Share the possibilities of social psychological phenomena adversely affecting group decision making with the other members of a team on which you serve (e.g., building consultation team). Discuss any team members' observations and how to avoid the pitfalls of these phenomena.

Internet Resources

Self Injury
http://helpguide.org/mental/self_injury.htm
http://www.selfinjury.com/
http://www.healthyplace.com/abuse/self-injury/self-injury-homepage/menu-id-65/
Dating Violence
http://www.thedatesafeproject.org/sharing.htm
http://www.safeyouth.org/scripts/faq/datingwarning.asp
Collaborative Pupil Services
http://www.dpi.wi.gov/sspw/pdf/pscandc.pdf
http://www.napso.org/
Groupthink & Social Psychology
http://www.spring.org.uk/2009/07/fighting-groupthink-with-dissent.php
Police-School Liaison Officers
http://www.nassleo.org/
http://www.ifpo.org/articlebank/school_officers.html

Conclusion

Our goal in writing this book was to make it fundamentally different from most other books on ethics. First, we focused on sharing a process of making ethically sound and justifiable decisions, rather than addressing specific issues that require ethical judgments. The process involves taking proactive steps to be as well-prepared as possible to manage ethical predicaments. The pupil services professional should analyze the situation fully, followed by seeking out consultation from authoritative and objective sources, before identifying a full range of possible courses of action. Those courses of action and their anticipated outcomes for both the student and stakeholders are carefully considered. The selected course of action is "tested" before implementation to help ensure the best possible outcomes for the student and other stakeholders and avoid unanticipated, adverse outcomes. The pupil services professional documents the steps taken to make the decision and is prepared to justify the decision, should any criticism arise. Finally, the implemented course of action is monitored and reflected upon to protect the student and improve future professional practice.

Second, we did not write this book for a specific profession but for the four, school-based pupil services professions of school counseling, school nursing, school psychology, and school social work. While each of these professions has its own ethical standards, we have demonstrated that they have much in common, while at the same time having unique features that the other professions can learn from (see Box 2.3 in Chapter 2). Because these four professions all practice in the school setting, the ethical challenges they face have more in common with each other than they do with their mental health colleagues practicing in community-based settings.

Finally, unlike other books on ethics that assume the mental health professional must make the eventual decision of how to manage the ethical dilemma individually, we have made the case for working in collaboration with others, most importantly the student. This collaboration honors the school-based, pupil services professional's role as both a mental health professional and an educator. The student is empowered to participate in and own the selected course of action. In addition, by including the family and other educators in the decision-making process, there is a greater likelihood the selected course of action will be supported by all of the important adults in the student's life.

While some may claim that a school's academic mission does not include delivery of mental health services, this position ignores the dramatic impact personal issues such as violence, mental illness, and substance abuse have on a student's academic performance and progress. If mental health services were abundantly available in the community and students were able to seamlessly flow back and forth from the school to community-based treatment settings, the need for pupil services would be reduced, but that is not the case in any community we know of. School counselors, school nurses, school psychologists, and school social workers are in a unique position to support the academic development of students because of their mental health expertise and their understanding of the school environment.

We have used real-life scenarios that have challenged practicing pupil services professionals as a means to illustrate the application of our ethical decision-making process. We have summarized each chapter with ethical guidelines, included exercises that can be done with groups of fellow colleagues or students, and shared relevant Web sites for the reader to explore.

It is our sincere hope that you have enjoyed reading this book and have benefited from it both professionally and personally. Regardless of whether you choose to adopt our ethical decision-making model, we hope that you embrace a consistent process that will enable you to improve the delivery of your services to your students and the other important adults in their lives.

Glossary

Absolutism	The belief in unconditional and objective moral truths that are unaffected by cultural, religious, or personal differences.
Altruism	Acting only in selfless concern for others rather than egoism. *See* Egoism.
Aspirations	Norms that aim at the highest expression of behavior, going "above and beyond" one's obligations. *See* Obligations.
Assent	A minor's affirmative agreement to participate in assessment, research, or treatment. This is usually accompanied by the express permission of the parents. *See* Informed consent.
Beneficence	A moral value that professionals should always act in the best interests of others. This may conflict, however, with self-determination. See *Self-determination.*
Beneficiaries	People who benefit from a decision or course of action. All beneficiaries are stakeholders, but not all stakeholders are necessarily beneficiaries. See *Stakeholders.*
Candor	The characteristic of being honest and open. It is one of the duties of a fiduciary agent. See *Fiduciary agent.*
Capacity	The ability to comprehend the information and appreciate the consequences of a decision.
Care	A relationship-based approach to ethical issues emphasizing concern for self and others.
Categorical imperative	Kant's phrase for an unconditional moral rule. His first principle was, "I ought never to act in such a way that I could not also will that my maxim should be a universal law."

Chance locus of control	The belief that luck or fate is in control of the outcome regardless of one's actions.
Civil disobedience	The deliberate and open defiance of social law because of its violation of an ethical principle.
Client	The person who knowingly enters into a fiduciary relationship with a professional. Clients may be voluntary or involuntary, but they should normally be aware that they are the recipients of professional services unless they have some type of cognitive disability resulting in a loss of awareness. *See* Fiduciary relationship.
Communitarianism	The belief in the central importance of the group or community rather than the individual citizen. *See* Individualism.
Complementary identifications	The process of identifying primarily with others in the client's life or placing oneself in others' positions when viewing a particular situation.
Concordant identifications	The process of identifying primarily with the client or placing oneself in the client's position when viewing a particular situation.
Confidentiality	Information that is communicated to another with the understanding that the disclosure is not meant to be shared with others.
Consequentialism	An ends-based approach to ethical issues aimed at good outcomes. Sometimes called teleological ethics. *See* Utilitarianism.
Consultation	The act of conferring with other persons in order to deepen or broaden our understanding of the issues—ethical, clinical, and/or legal.
Countertransference	The therapist's total emotional response (both positive and negative) to a client that originates in the therapist's unique experience or the client's usual presentation or both.
Deontology	A duty-based approach to ethical issues founded on moral principles.

Dilemma	Greek: "two assumptions." A problem assumed to have only two unsatisfactory options.
Due process	A rules-based procedure used to ensure justice and fairness.
Egoism	Acting only out of self-interest, never altruism. *See* Altruism.
Epistemicfallibilism	The belief that all knowledge is transient and that rational criteria do not exist outside of historical time. *See* Moral realism.
Ethics	A set of norms, both obligatory and aspirational, that guide behavior in accordance with shared values.
Eudaimonia	Greek: "flourishing." Aristotle's term for living well or harmoniously.
Fiduciary relationship	A trust-based relationship between a principal with less expertise or power and a fiduciary agent with greater expertise or power.
Golden Rule	Stated in the positive as "Do unto others as you would have them do unto you."
Groupthink	A faulty group process resulting from an emphasis on group cohesion leading to a failure to think critically about the ideas of other group members. It leads to premature consensus and erroneous decision making.
Individualism	The belief in the central importance of the individual person rather than the collective group or society. *See* Communitarianism.
Information	The adequacy of one's knowledge about the nature of proposed services; potential benefits, risks, and side effects; likelihood of achieving goals; reasonable alternatives; relevant benefits, risks, and side effects of the alternatives; and limitations on confidentiality.
Informed consent	An adult's affirmative agreement to participate in assessment, research, or treatment when possessing capacity, information, and voluntariness. *See* Assent. *See* Informed dissent.

Informed dissent	An adult's negative refusal to participate in assessment, research, or treatment when possessing capacity, information, and voluntariness. *See* Informed dissent. *See* Assent.
In loco parentis	Latin: "In place of parents" the doctrine that schools act as surrogate parents to students entrusted into their care.
Integrity	Moral wholeness that integrates a moral agent's attitudes, beliefs, and behavior into a consistent character.
Malpractice	Mistreatment of a client due to abuse or neglect of one's fiduciary duty to act in accordance with a professional standard of care. *See* Fiduciary relationship.
Minor	Someone who has not yet reached legal maturity. This state may depend on the situation, such as when a minor is charged as an adult for a crime.
Moral realism	The belief in intransitive moral absolutes that exist independently of human belief. *See* Epistemic fallibilism.
Negligence	A failure to exhibit sufficient care about a situation in which one has an ethical obligation to act.
Norms	Stated or tacit standards that are expected of members belonging to a group that serve to guide or regulate acceptable behavior.
Nonmaleficence	A moral value that professionals should at least "do no harm" to others.
Obligations	The minimal duties associated with a person's knowledge, position, or relationships that may lead to sanctions if not met (e.g., professionals have obligations to their clients, colleagues, employers, profession, and society). *See* Aspirations. *See* Fiduciary relationship.

Parens Patriae	Latin: "parent of the nation." The doctrine that state-sponsored institutions, such as schools, should act in the best interest of minors entrusted into their care. This doctrine is sometimes used to both protect and punish students.
Passive consent	The practice of assuming that those who do not actively object are tacitly giving affirmative agreement. *See* Assent. *See* Informed consent.
Paternalism	Acting as if one is a parent to another person, resulting in both concerned nurture and regulated restriction of the other's right to self-determination.
Permission	Also known as surrogate consent; authorization of assessment and/or services for another. In schools, parents are asked to give express (oral or written) permission for their minor children. *See* Informed consent. *See* Informed dissent.
Power	The ability to influence the behavior of others through legitimate position, rewards, coercion, expertise, referent relations, information, affiliation, and group association.
Prima facie	Latin: "At first glance." Prima facie duties are ones that seem superficially true but may not endure deeper examination.
Privacy	The right or value to maintain personal control of one's belongings, body, decisions, information, and thoughts against unauthorized intrusions by others. *See* Confidentiality.
Privilege	The legal right to refuse to disclose or prevent others (e.g., licensed therapists) from disclosing confidential communications.
Profession	A vocation that requires specialized knowledge and skills involving a combination of higher education and practical experience.

Relativism	The belief that each culture, faith, or person has its own ethical values that cannot be judged by others external to that experience.
Risk	The likelihood of potential harm or injury resulting from a decision or act.
Risk factors	Group characteristics that are statistically associated with greater risk (e.g., age or gender). Risk factors may not be helpful in identifying specific individuals at risk. *See* Warning signs.
Self-determination	The autonomy to make decisions and choose a course of action so long as there is no infringement on the rights of others to do the same.
Stakeholders	Parties with a vested interest in a decision because they are affected by the outcome. The client is the primary stakeholder, but there are many others that have a stake in the conclusion. *See* Client.
Standard of care	The concerned conduct exercised by an ordinary, reasonable, and prudent professional with similar training in a similar situation.
Supplicant	The person requesting help from a professional. This could be the same as a self-referred client or someone asking the professional to help someone else such as when parents or teachers refer a student for services. *See* Client. *See* Stakeholders.
Targets	People, organizations, or communities that are the focus of a professional change effort.
Trait cynicism	The tendency toward disillusionment or distrust of other people.
Trust	Confident reliance reposed on others because of their presumed beneficence. *See* Beneficence.
Universalism	The belief in consensual moral truths that may be expressed differently in diverse cultures (e.g., the Golden Rule or the United Nations Declaration of Human Rights).

Utilitarianism	A moderate form of consequentialism that espouses acting for the greatest good for the greatest number of people. *See* Consequentialism.
Values	Principles or qualities held in high esteem that inform our attitudes and behavior.
Virtue	A habitual disposition to conduct oneself in a meritorious manner or a character trait such as courage, justice, self-control, or wisdom.
Voluntariness	The freedom from coercion, constraint, or compulsion, including the right to participate or not to participate without any negative repercussions.
Warning signs	Signals that an individual is escalating his or her level of dangerousness, such as rehearsing for a violent act. *See* Risk factors.

Appendix

U.S. Supreme Court Case	Legal Question	Decision
1st Amendment Cases (freedom of religion, speech and press, assembly and petition)		
Abington School District v. Schempp, 374 U.S. 203 (1963)	Did a state law that requires public school students to participate in Bible reading violate their religious freedom?	Yes (8-1)
Agostini v. Felton, 521 U.S. 203 (1977)	Is an arrangement to have public school teachers instruct in parochial schools a violation of the establishment of religion clause?	No (5-4)
Aguilar v. Felton, 473 U.S. 402 (1985)	Does a city's decision to use Title I funds to pay salaries of parochial school teachers violate the establishment of religion clause?	Yes (5-4)
Bethel School District No. 403 v. Fraser, 478 U.S. 675 (1986)	Does a school district that disciplines high school students for giving a lewd speech at a high school assembly violate their right to free speech?	No (7-2)
Board of Education v. Allen, 392 U.S. 236 (1968)	Does a state law requiring that public school boards loan textbooks to parochial school students without cost violate the establishment of religion clause?	No (6-3)
Board of Education Kiryas Joel Village School v. Grumet, 512 U.S. 687 (1994)	Does a state law that intentionally draws boundaries in accordance with a religious sect's boundaries violate the establishment of religion clause?	Yes (6-3)

Board of Education v. Pico, 457 U.S. 853 (1982)	Does a school district's decision to ban certain books from its school libraries, based on their content, violate the freedom of speech?	Yes (5-4)
Board of Education of Westside Community Schools v. Mergens, 496 U.S. 226 (1990)	Is a school district's prohibition against the formation of a Christian club consistent with the establishment of religion clause?	No (8-1)
Committee for Public Education v. Nyquist, 413 U.S. 756 (1973)	Does a state law providing state aid to parochial schools violate the establishment of religion clause?	Yes (6-3)
Edwards v. Aguillard, 482 U.S. 578 (1987)	Does a state law that prohibits the teaching of evolution in public schools unless accompanied by instruction in "creation science" violate the establishment of religion clause?	Yes (7-2)
Elk Grove Unified School District v. Newdow, 542 U.S. 1 (2004)	Does a public school district policy that requires students to recite the Pledge of Allegiance that includes the words "under God," violate the establishment of religion clause?	No (8-0)
Engle v. Vitale, 370 U.S. 421 (1962)	Does starting the school day with a voluntary nonsectarian prayer violate the establishment of religion clause?	Yes (6-1)
Epperson v. Arkansas, 393 U.S. 97 (1968)	Does a state law prohibiting the teaching of evolution violate the establishment of religion clause?	Yes (7-2)
Everson v. Board of Education of the Township of Ewing, 330 U.S. 1 (1947)	Does a state law that reimburses parents for the transportation by public carrier of children attending public and Catholic schools violate the establishment of religion clause?	No (5-4)

Garcetti v. Ceballos, 547 U.S. 410 (2006)	Is a public employee's job-related speech on a matter of public concern protected by the freedom of speech?	No (5-4)
Good News Club v. Milford Central School, 533 U.S. 98 (2001)	Does a school violate the free speech rights of a religious group when it excludes the group from meeting after school?	Yes (6-3)
Grand Rapids School District v. Ball, 473 U.S. 373 (1985)	Does a school district's provision of classes to nonpublic school students at public expense in classrooms in religious schools violate the establishment of religion clause?	Yes (5-4)
Grayned v. City of Rockford, 408 U.S. 104 (1972)	Is a city law prohibiting picketing near a school a violation of free speech rights?	Yes (9-0)
Hazelwood School District v. Kuhlmeier, 484 U.S. 260 (1988)	Does a principal's deletion of the inappropriate articles in a student newspaper violate the students' rights to freedom of speech?	No (5-3)
Illinois ex rel. McCollum v. Board of Education of School District, 333 U.S. 203 (1948)	Does the use of the public school facilities for voluntary religious classes during school hours violate the establishment of religion clause?	Yes (5-4)
Lamb's Chapel v. Center Moriches School District, 508 U.S. 384 (1993)	Does a school district that denies a religious organization the use of school premises after school violate the freedom of religion clause?	Yes (9-0)
Lee v. Weisman, 505 U.S. 577 (1992)	Does the inclusion of clergy who offer prayers at official public school ceremonies violate the establishment of religion clause?	Yes (5-4)
Lemon v. Kurtzman, 403 U.S. 602 (1971)	Do state laws that provide financial aid to church related educational institutions violate the establishment of religion clause?	Yes (8-0)

McCreary County v. ACLU, 545 U.S. 844 (2005)	1. Do displays of the Ten Commandments in public schools violate the establishment of religion clause?2. Was a determination that the display's purpose was to advance religion sufficient for its invalidation?	Yes and Yes (5-4)
Minersville School District v. Gobitis, 310 U.S. 586 (1940)	Does the mandatory flag salute violate the right to free speech?	No (8-1)
Mitchell v. Helms, 530 U.S. 793 (2000)	Does a state law that provided secular aid to private schools violate the establishment of religion clause?	No (6-3)
Morse v. Frederick, 551 U.S. 393 (2007)	Can public schools prohibit students from displaying messages promoting the use of illegal drugs at school events without violating their freedom of speech?	Yes (5-4)
Mueller v. Allen, 463 U.S. 388 (1983)	Does a state law allowing parents to deduct expenses for "tuition, textbooks, and transportation" for their children attending public or parochial schools violate the establishment of religion clause?	No (5-4)
Pickering v. Board of Education of Township High School District 205, 391 U.S. 563 (1968)	Is a school board's dismissal of an employee for writing a letter to the newspaper critical of the board's decisions a violation of the right to free speech?	Yes (8-1)
Pierce v. Society of Sisters, 268 U.S. 510 (1925)	Does a state law requiring parents or guardians to send children between the ages of 8 and 16 years old to public school violate the religious freedom of parents to direct the education of their children?	Yes (9-0)

Santa Fe Independent School Dist. v. Doe, 530 U.S. 290 (2000)	Does a school district's policy permitting student-led, student-initiated prayer at football games violate the establishment of religion clause?	Yes (6-3)
Stone v. Graham, 449 U.S. 39 (1980)	Does a state law mandating the posting of a copy of the Ten Commandments in each public school classroom violate the establishment of religion clause?	Yes (5-4)
Tinker v. Des Moines Ind. Comm. School District, 393 U.S. 503 (1969)	Does a school district's prohibition on the wearing of armbands in public school as a form of symbolic protest violate the freedom of speech?	Yes (7-2)
Wallace v. Jaffree, 472 U.S. 38 (1985)	Does a state law authorizing a 1-minute period of silence in all public schools "for meditation or voluntary prayer" violate the establishment of religion clause?	Yes (6-3)
West Virginia State Board of Education v. Barnette, 319 U.S. 624 (1943)	Does a state law that compels public school students to salute the flag violate the freedom of speech?	Yes (6-3)
Wisconsin v. Yoder, 406 U.S. 205 (1972)	Does a state law mandating school attendance until the age of 16 years against parents' religious objections violate the freedom of religion clause?	Yes (7-0)
Zelman v. Simmons-Harris, 536 U.S. 639 (2002)	Does a state's school voucher program that provides tuition aid for certain students to attend participating public or private schools of their parent's choosing violate the establishment of religion clause?	No (5-4)

| Zobrest v. Catalina Foothills School District, 509 U.S. 1 (1993) | May a school district deny an interpreter to a deaf child (placed by parents in a parochial school) based on the establishment of religion clause? | No (5-4) |
| Zorach v. Clauson, 343 U.S. 306 (1952) | Does a state law that permits students to leave school grounds during school hours to go to religious centers for religious instruction violate the establishment of religion clause? | No (6-3) |

4th Amendment
(unreasonable search and seizure)

Board of Education of Independent School Dist. No. 92 of Pottawatomie Cty. v. Earls, 536 U.S. 822 (2002)	Is a student activities drug testing policy that requires all students who participate in competitive extracurricular activities to submit to drug testing, consistent with unreasonable search protections?	Yes (5-4)
Doe v. Renfrow, 451 U.S. 1022 (1981) 631 F.2d 91 (1980)	Does a school acting in loco parentis that conducts a strip search of students targeted by police dogs violate their rights against unreasonable search?	Yes, Certiori denied (8-1)
New Jersey v. T.L.O., 469 U.S. 325 (1985)	Does the school's search of a student's purse for drugs violate her rights against unreasonable search?	No (6-3)
Safford Unified School District v. Redding, 557 U.S. __ (2009) 129 S. Ct. 2633	Does the prohibition against unreasonable search bar school officials from strip searching students suspected of possessing drugs in violation of school policy?	Sometimes (7-2)
Vernonia School District v. Acton, 515 U.S. 646 (1995)	Does random drug testing of high school athletes violate the reasonable search and seizure clause of the 4th Amendment?	No (6-3)

5th Amendment
(right to due process in federal law)

Bolling v. Sharpe, 347 U.S. 497 (1954)	Does the segregation of the public schools of Washington D.C. violate the due process clause?	Yes (9-0)

8th Amendment
(prohibition against cruel and unusual punishment)

Atkins v. Virginia, 536 U.S. 304 (2002)	Is the execution of people with mental retardation a violation of their rights against cruel and unusual punishment?	Yes (6-3)
Baker v. Owen, 423 U.S. 907 (1975) Aff'd 395 Fed Supp. 294	Can school administrators administer corporal punishment against parental wishes?	Yes
Ingraham v. Wright, 430 U.S. 651 (1977)	Does a state law permitting the corporal punishment of students for disciplinary purposes violate their rights against cruel and unusual punishment?	No (5-4)

11th Amendment
(sovereign immunity for states)

Milliken v. Bradley–II, 433 U.S. 267 (1977)	1. Can a federal district court order remedial education programs for students who had been subjected to segregation? 2. Can a federal district court order a state to bear partial costs of these remedial programs without violating the state's immunity from lawsuits?	Yes and Yes (9-0)

14th Amendment
(right to due process and equal protection under state laws)

Brown v. Board of Education of Topeka–I, 347 U.S. 483 (1954)	Does the segregation of public school children on the basis of race deprive minority children of the equal protection clause?	Yes (9-0)

Brown v. Board of Education of Topeka–II, 349 U.S. 294 (1955)	Should children previously segregated on the basis of race be admitted to public schools on a racially nondiscriminatory basis with all deliberate speed?	Yes (9-0)
Carey v. Population Services International, 431 U. S. 678 (1977)	Does a state law that forbids minors from obtaining nonprescription contraceptives violate the due process clause?	Yes (7-2)
Freeman v. Pitts, 503 U.S. 467 (1992)	Is a federal district court permitted to withdraw supervision of a school system gradually before full compliance with racial desegregation is achieved?	Yes (9-0)
Goss v. Lopez, 419 U.S. 565 (1975)	Do schools that suspend students without a preliminary hearing violate their due process rights?	Yes (5-4)
Green v. County School Bd. of New Kent County, 391 U.S. 430 (1968)	Does a school district that allows students the freedom to choose whether they attend a predominantly White or Negro school violate the court's decision in Brown v. Board of Ed.?	Yes (9-0)
H. L. v. Matheson, 450 U.S. 398 (1981)	Is a state law requiring parental notification for minors who wish to have an abortion a violation of the due process clause?	No (6-3)
In re Gault, 387 U.S. 1 (1967)	Does a juvenile court that commits a minor to a state industrial school without parental notification violate the due process clause?	Yes (8-1)
Keyes v. School District No. 1, 413 U.S. 189 (1973)	Does partial segregation in a city involve all of the city's schools and violate the equal protection clause?	Yes (7-1)

Martinez v. Bynum, 461 U.S. 321 (1983)	Did a state law violate the equal protection clause when it denies tuition-free admission to minors living apart from their parents if their primary purpose of living in the district was to attend school free of charge?	No (8-1)
Meyer v. Nebraska, 262 U.S. 390 (1923)	Does a state law prohibiting the teaching of modern foreign languages to elementary school children violate the due process clause?	Yes (7-2)
Milliken v. Bradley–I, 418 U. S. 717 (1974)	May a federal court impose a multidistrict, area-wide remedy for single-district de jure school segregation violations?	No (5-4)
North Carolina State Bd. of Educ. v. Swann, 402 U.S. 43 (1971)	Does a state law prohibiting the busing of students to achieve racial balance in schools violate the due process clause?	Yes (9-0)
Lau v. Nichols, 414 U.S. 563 (1974)	Does a school district that teaches only in English violate the rights of non-English-speaking students under the Civil Rights Act of 1964?	Yes (9-0)
Parents Involved in Community Schools v. Seattle School District No. 1, 551 U.S. 701 (2007)	Does a school district that allows students to attend the high school of their choice violate the equal protection clause when it denies students admission in order to achieve a desired racial balance?	Yes (5-4)
Planned Parenthood of Missouri v. Danforth, 428 U.S. 52 (1976)	Is a state law requiring parental consent for minors who wish to have an abortion a violation of the due process clause?	Yes (5-4)
Plessy v. Ferguson, 163 U.S. 567 (1896)	Is a state law requiring separate but equal segregation on public transportation a violation of the equal protection clause?	No (7-1)

Plyler v. Doe, 457 U.S. 202 (1982)	Does a state law allowing the state to withhold funds from local school districts for educating children of illegal aliens violate the equal protection clause?	Yes (5-4)
San Antonio Independent School District v. Rodriguez, 411 U.S. 1 (1973)	Does a state public education finance system violate the equal protection clause by failing to distribute funding equally among its school districts?	No (5-4)
Swann v. Charlotte-Mecklenburg Board of Education, 402 U.S. 1 (1971)	Are federal courts authorized to oversee and create remedies for state-supported segregation under the equal protection clause of the 14th Amendment?	Yes (9-0)

Article 1 of the U.S. Constitution
(Congress's power to regulate commerce)

United States v. Lopez, 514 U.S. 549 (1995)	Is the 1990 Gun-Free School Zones Act, which prohibits anyone from carrying a handgun in a school zone, unconstitutional because it exceeds Congress's Commerce Clause authority?	Yes (5-4)

Family Educational Rights and Privacy Act (FERPA)
(maintenance and dissemination of student records)

Gonzaga University v. Doe, 536 U.S. 273	Can students whose privacy was violated sue a university for damages under the Family Educational Rights and Privacy Act of 1974?	No (7-2)
Owasso Independent School Dist. No. I-011 v. Falvo, 534 U.S. 426 (2002)	Does the practice of peer grading violate the Family Educational Rights and Privacy Act (FERPA) of 1974?	No (9-0)

Federal Rules of Evidence
(admissibility of evidence in federal trials)

Jaffee v. Redmond, 518 U.S. 1 (1996)	Can psychotherapists be forced to disclose evidence about their patients in federal court cases under the Federal Rules of Evidence (i.e., Rule 501)?	No (7-2)

Individuals with Disabilities Education Act
(rights of students with disabilities)

Arlington Central School District Board of Education v. Murphy, 548 U.S. 291 (2006)	Does IDEA permit parents to recover fees they pay to experts during legal actions against school districts?	No (6-3)
Board of Education of the Hendrick Hudson Central School District v. Rowley, 458 U.S. 176 (1982)	Does the "free appropriate public education" promised under IDEA require a school district to educate children with disabilities to reach their full academic potential?	No (6-3)
Burlington School Comm. v. Massachusetts Dept. Of Education, 471 U.S. 359 (1985)	Can parents be reimbursed for unilaterally placing a child with disabilities in a private school if that school is the appropriate placement under IDEA?	Yes (9-0)
Cedar Rapids Comm. School District v. Garrett F. and Charlene F., 526 U.S. 66 (1999)	Do schools that receive federal funding under IDEA have to pay for one-on-one nursing assistance for certain of their disabled students?	Yes (7-2)
Florence County School District Four v. Carter, 510 U.S. 7 (1993)	May a court order reimbursement for parents who withdrew their child from a public school providing an inappropriate education under IDEA and put the child in a private school?	Yes (9-0)

Forest Grove School District v. T.A. 557 U.S. __ (2009), 129 S. Ct. 2484	Must a school district reimburse a former student for his tuition at a private school when the student never received special education services at the public school and withdrew for reasons unrelated to his disability?	Yes (6-3)
Honig v. Doe, 484 U.S. 305 (1988)	Do schools that suspend students for behavior related to their disability violate their rights under IDEA?	Yes (6-2)
Irving Independent School Dist. v. Tatro, 468 U.S. 883 (1984)	Is clean intermittent catheterization (CIC) a related service under IDEA?	Yes (9-0)
Winkelman v. Parma City School District, 550 U.S. 516 (2007)	May a non-lawyer parent of a child with a disability under IDEA argue in federal court either on his own behalf or on behalf of his child?	Yes (7-2)

Reconstruction Civil Rights Act
(qualified immunity for public officials)

Safford Unified School District v. Redding, 557 U.S. __ (2009) 129 S. Ct. 2633	Are school officials individually liable for damages in a lawsuit filed under 42 U.S.C §1983?	No (7-2)
Morse v. Frederick, 551 U.S. 393 (2007)	Does a school official have qualified immunity from a damages lawsuit under 42 U.S.C. 1983 when she disciplines a student for displaying a banner supporting drug use at a school event?	Undecided (5-4)
Wood v. Strickland, 420 U.S. 308 (1975)	Are school officials entitled to a qualified good faith immunity from liability for damages under 42 U.S.C. §1983?	Yes (5-4)

Rehabilitation Act of 1973
(Section 504)

School Board of Nassau County v. Arline, 480 U.S. 273 (1987)	Does Section 504 extend relief to individuals afflicted with contagious diseases (e.g., tuberculosis)?	Yes (7-2)

Title IX of the Educational Amendments of 1972
(sexual discrimination)

Davis v. Monroe County Board of Education, 526 U.S. 629 (1999)	Can a school board be liable for "student-on-student" sexual harassment?	Yes (5-4)
Fitzgerald v. Barnstable School Committee 555 U.S. __ (2009) 129 S. Ct. 788	Does Title IX's private remedy preclude the use of 42 U.S.C. §1983 to advance sex discrimination claims against federally funded educational institutions?	No (9-0)
Franklin v. Gwinnett County Public Schools, 503 U.S. 60 (1992)	Is a school district liable for the sexual harassment of a student by a teacher?	Yes (9-0)
Gebser v. Lago Vista Ind. School District, 524 U.S. 274 (1998)	Can a federally funded educational program be required to pay sexual harassment damages to a student who was involved in a secret relationship with a member of its staff?	No (5-4)

Sources: http://www.oyez.org, http://www.law.cornell.edu/supct/, http://www.supremecourtus.gov

References

Abdel, A., & Lester, D. (2007). The psychometric properties of the Reynold's Suicide Ideation Questionnaire with Kuwaiti and American students. *Archives of Suicide Research, 11*(3), 309–319.

Abramson, M. (1996). Reflections on knowing oneself ethically. *Families in Society, 77*(4), 195–202.

Achenbach, T. M., & Rescorla, L. A. (2001). *Manual for the school-age forms and profiles: Child behavior checklist, teacher's report form, youth self-report. An integrated system of multi-informant assessment.* Burlington: University of Vermont.

Advocates for Youth. (1998). Legal issues and school-based and school-linked health centers. Retrieved June 13, 2007, from http://www.advocatesforyouth.org/PUBLICATIONS/iag/sbhcslhc.htm

Aebi, M., Metzke, C. W., & Steinhausen, H-C. (2009). Prediction of major affective disorders in adolescents by self-report measures. *Journal of Affective Disorders, 115*(1–2), 140–149.

Agosta, A. (2003). Spirituality in GLBT clients. *Social Work Today, 3*(17), 28–29.

Alkhatib, A., Regan, J., & Jackson, J. (2008). Informed assent and informed consent in the child and adolescent. *Psychiatric Annals, 38*(5), 337–339.

American Association of School Administrators. (2007). *Code of Ethics.* Arlington, VA: Author.

American Bar Association. (1998). State of the First Amendment: Freedom of religion. *Update on Law-Related Education, 22*(1), 10–16.

American Counseling Association. (2005). *Code of Ethics.* Alexandria, VA: Author.

American Nurses Association. (2001). *ANA Code of Ethics for Nurses.* Silver Spring, MD: Author.

American Psychological Association. (2002). *Ethical principles of psychologists and code of conduct.* Washington, DC: Author.

American Psychological Association. (2008). *Health and mental health association codes of ethics: Provisions regarding conflicts between ethics and law.* Retrieved April 7, 2010, from http://www.apa.org/ethics/code/associations.pdf

American Psychological Association Committee on Professional Practice and Standards. (2003). Legal issues in the professional practice of psychology. *Professional Psychology: Research and Practice, 34*(6), 595–600.

American School Counselor Association. (2004). *Ethical standards for school counselors.* Alexandria, VA: Author.

Amundson, J. K., Daya, R., & Gill, E. (2000). A minimalist approach to child custody evaluation. *American Journal of Forensic Psychology, 18*(3), 63–87.

Amundson, K.J., Ficklen, E., Maatsch, J.T., Brody Saks, J., & Banks Zakariya, S. (1996). *Becoming a better board member*. Alexandria, VA: National School Boards Association.

Anderson, J. (2000). The revolution against evolution, or "Well, Darwin, we're not in Kansas anymore." *Journal of Law and Education, 29*(3), 398–404.

Angeles, J., Tierney, M., & Osher, D. (2006). How to obtain Medicaid funding for school-based health and mental health services. In C. Franklin, M. B. Harris, & P. Allen-Meares (Eds.), *The school services sourcebook: A guide for school-based professionals* (pp. 1093–1110). New York: Oxford University Press.

Annas, J. (2006). Virtue ethics. In D. Copp (Ed.), *The Oxford handbook of ethical theory* (pp. 515–536). New York: Oxford University Press.

Appelbaum, P. S. (2008). Privilege in the federal courts: Should there be a "dangerous patient exception"? *Psychiatric Services, 59*(7), 714–716.

Arnold v. Board of Education of Escambia, 754 F. Supp. 853 (S.D. Ala. 1990).

Atkins v. Virginia, 536 U.S. 304 (2002).

Augimeri, L. K., Webster, C. D., Koegl, C. J., & Levene, K. S. (2001). *Early Assessment Risk List for Boys (EARL-20B). Version 2*. Toronto, Ontario: Earlscourt Child & Family Centre.

Avert. (2009, August 12). *Worldwide ages of consent*. Retrieved August 29, 2009, from http://www.avert.org/age-of-consent.htm

Avildsen, J. (Producer & Director), & Schiffer, M. (Writer). (1989). *Lean on me* [Motion picture]. United States: Warner Bros.

Baker v. Owen, 437 U.S. 907 (1975).

Baker, S. B., & Gerler, E. R. (2004). *School counseling for the twenty-first century* (4th ed.). Upper Saddle River, NJ: Merrill.

Baldry, A. C. (2003). Bullying in schools and exposure to domestic violence. *Child Abuse and Neglect, 27*(7), 713–732.

Baldwin, M. W. (1999). Relational schemas: Research into social-cognitive aspect of interpersonal experience. In D. Cervone & S. Yuichi (Eds.), *The coherence of personality: Social-cognitive bases of consistency, variability, and organization* (pp. 127–154). New York: Guilford.

Banks, S. (2008). Critical commentary: Social work ethics. *British Journal of Social Work, 38*(6), 1238–1249.

Barbee, P. W., Combs, D. C., Ekleberry, F., & Villalobos, S. (2007). Duty to warn and protect: Not in Texas. *Journal of Professional Counseling: Practice, Theory, and Research, 35*(1), 18–25.

Barnes, P. (2005). The cool vs. the uncool. *Teaching Pre-K - 8, 36*(1), 42.

Barnett, J. E., & Johnson, W. B. (2008a). Making an ethical decision: A process model. In J. E. Barnett & W. B. Johnson (Eds.), *Ethics desk reference for psychologists* (pp. 177–180). Washington, DC: American Psychological Association.

Barnett, J. E., & Johnson, W. B. (2008b). Responding to an ethics complaint, licensure board complaint, or malpractice suit. In J. E. Barnett & W. B. Johnson (Eds.), *Ethics desk reference for psychologists* (pp. 201–203). Washington, DC: American Psychological Association.

Bartel, P., Borum, R., & Forth, A. (2000). *Structured Assessment for Violence Risk in Youth (SAVRY), Consultation ed.* Tampa, FL: University of South Florida.

Bartell, R. (1996). The argument for a paradigm shift or "What's in a name?". *Canadian Journal of School Psychology*, *12*(2), 86–90.

Bastiaens, L. (1995). Compliance with pharmacotherapy in adolescents: Effects of patients' and parents' knowledge and attitudes toward treatment. *Journal of Child and Adolescent Psychopharmacology*, *5*(1), 39–48.

Bechtel, K., Lowenkamp, C. T., & Latessa, E. (2007). Assessing the risk of re-offending juvenile offenders using the Youth Level of Service/Case Management Inventory. *Journal of Offender Rehabilitation*, *45*(3–4), 85–108.

Beck, A. T., Steer, R. A., & Brown, G. K. (1996). *Manual for the Beck Depression Inventory-II*. San Antonio, TX: Psychological Corporation.

Beck, J. S., Beck, A. T., & Jolly, J. B. (2001). *Beck Youth Inventories*. San Antonio, TX: Psychological Corp.

Bellah v. Greenson, 141 Cal. App. 92 (1977).

Benfari, R. C., Wilkinson, H. E., & Orth, C. D. (1986). The effective use of power. *Business Horizons*, *29*, 12–16.

Berchman, R. M. (2009). The Golden Rule in Graeco-Roman religion and philosophy. In J. Neusner & B. Chilton (Eds.), *The Golden Rule: Analytical perspectives* (pp. 9–44). Lanham, MD: University Press of America.

Berk, L. E. (2004). Development through the lifespan (3rd ed.). Boston: Pearson/Allyn & Bacon.

Berkowitz, M. W., & Schwartz, M. (2006). Character education. In G. G. Bear, & K. M. Minke (Eds.), *Children's needs III: Development, prevention, and intervention* (pp. 15–27). Bethesda, MD: National Association of School Psychologists.

Berlinger, N. (2004). Fair compensation without litigation: Addressing patients' financial need in disclosure. *Journal of Healthcare Risk Management*, *24*(1), 7–11.

Bersoff, D. N. (2008). Some contrarian concerns about law, psychology, and public policy. In D. N. Bersoff (Ed.), *Ethical conflicts in psychology* (4th ed., pp. 175–179). Washington, DC: American Psychological Association.

Bethel School District 403 v. Fraser, 478 U.S. 675 (1986).

Beutler, L. E. (2000). Empirically-based decision making in clinical practice. *Prevention and Treatment*, *3*, Article 27. Retrieved April 7, 2010, from http://psycnet.apa.org/index.cfm?fa=buy.optionToBuy&id=2000-02994-001&CFID=7734381&CFTOKEN=42145769

Bhaskar, R. (1989). *Reclaiming reality: A critical introduction to contemporary philosophy*. London: Verso.

Bielby, P. (2008). *Competence and vulnerability in biomedical research*. New York: Springer.

Birmaher, B., Brent, D., Bernet, W., Bukstein, O., Walter, H., Benson, R. S., Chrisman, A., Farchione, T., Greenhill, L., Hamilton, J., Keable, H., Kinlan, J., Schoettle, U., Stock, S., Ptakowski, K. K., & Medicus, J. (2007). Practice parameter for the assessment and treatment of children and adolescents with depressive disorders. *Journal of the American Academy of Child and Adolescent Psychiatry*, *46*(11), 1503–1526.

Black, D. M. (2004). Sympathy reconsidered: Some reflections on sympathy, empathy and the discovery of values. *International Journal of Psychoanalysis*, *85*(3), 579–596.

Blase, J. J. (1990). Some negative effects of principal's control oriented and protective political behavior. *American Educational Research Journal*, *27*(4), 727–753.

Board of Education of the Hendrick Hudson Central School District v. Rowley, 102 S. Ct. 3034 (1982).

Boland-Prom, K., & Anderson, S. C. (2005). Teaching ethical decision making using dual relationship principles as a case example. *Journal of Social Work Education, 41*(3), 495–510.

Borum, R., & Verhaagen, D. (2006). *Assessing and managing violence risk in juveniles.* New York: Guilford.

Bouchoux, D. E. (2008). *Legal research explained.* Austin, TX: Wolters Kluwer: Law & Business.

Bowers, M., & Pipes, R. B. (2000). Influence of consultation on ethical decision making: An analogue study. *Ethics and Behavior, 10*(1), 65–79.

Boyle, D., O'Connell, D., Platt, F. W., & Albert, R. K. (2006). Disclosing errors and adverse events in the intensive care unit. *Critical Care Medicine, 34*(5), 1532–1537.

Boynton v. Burglass, 590 So.2d 446 (Fla. 1991).

Brandell, J. R. (1992). *Countertransference in psychotherapy with children and adolescents: A powerful therapeutic resource.* Northvale, NJ: Jason Aronson.

Bridges, N. A. (2001). Therapist's self-disclosure: Expanding the comfort zone. *Psychotherapy: Theory, Research, and Practice, 38*(1), 21–30.

Brock, S. E., Sandoval, J., & Hart, S. (2006). Suicidal ideation and behaviors. In G. G. Bear & K. M. Minke (Eds.), *Children's needs III: Development, prevention, and intervention* (pp. 225–238). Bethesda, MD: National Association of School Psychologists.

Broidy, S., & Jones, S. (1998). Sources of professional ethics. *Educational Studies, 29*(1), 3–13.

Brooks, F., & Magnussen, J. (2006). Taking part counts: Adolescents' experiences of the transition from inactivity to active participation in school-based physical education. *Health Education Research, 21*(6), 872–883.

Brown v. Board of Education, 347 U.S. 483 (1954).

Brown v. Wells Fargo Bank, NA, 168 Cal.App.4th 938, 85 Cal.Rptr.3d 817 Cal.App.2d Div. 3. (2008).

Brown, C., & Trangsrud, H. B. (2008). Factors associated with acceptance and decline of client gift giving. *Professional Psychology: Research and Practice, 39*(5), 505–511.

Brown, M. M., & Grumet, J. G. (2009). School-based suicide prevention with African American youth in an urban setting. *Professional Psychology: Research and Practice, 40*(2), 111–117.

Buchanan-Barrow, E., & Barrett, M. (1996). Primary school children's understanding of the school. *British Journal of Educational Psychology, 66*(1), 33–46.

Buchanan, D., & Badham, R. (1999). *Power, politics, and organizational change: Winning the turf game.* Thousand Oaks: Sage.

Buckley, M., Storino, M., & Saarni, C. (2003). Promoting emotional competence in children and adolescents: Implications for school psychologists. *School Psychology Quarterly, 18*, 177–191.

Burdett v. Miller, 957 F.2d 1375 (7th Cir. 1992).

Burkard, A. W., Knox, S., Groen, M., Perez, M., & Hess, S. A. (2006). European American therapist self-disclosure in cross-cultural counseling. *Journal of Counseling Psychology, 53*(1), 15–25.

Burns, B. J., Costello, E. J., Angold, A., Tweed, D., Stangl, D., Farmer, E., & Erkanli, A. (1995). Children's mental health service use across service sectors. *Health Affairs, 14*(3), 147–159.

Burns, J. J., Sadof, M., & Kamat, D. (2006). Managing the adolescent with a chronic illness. *Psychiatric Annals, 36*(10), 715–719.

Busch, K. A., Fawcett, J., & Jacobs, D. G. (2003). Clinical correlates of inpatient suicide. *Journal of Clinical Psychiatry, 64*(1), 14–19.

Buser, L. (November 11, 2009). Memphis city schools students truant; 19 parents charged. *Commercial Appeal.* [Electronic version] Accession # 2W62204984886.

Bush, S. S., Grote, C. L., Johnson-Greene, D. E., & Macartney-Filgate, M. (2008). A panel interview on the ethical practice of neuropsychology. *Clinical Neuropsychologist, 22*(2), 321–344.

Caldwell, L. L., & Smith, E. A. (2006). Leisure as a context for youth development and delinquency prevention. *Australian and New Zealand Journal of Criminology, 39*(3), 398–418.

Campbell, J., Webster, D., Koziol-McLain, J., Block, C., Campbell, D., Curry, M., et al. (2003). Risk factors for femicide in abusive relationships: Results from a multi-site case control study. *American Journal of Public Health, 93*(7), 1089–1097.

Campbell, L. (2003). Ethical and legal issues in working with children and adolescents. In L. Van de Creek & T. Jackson (Eds.), *Innovations in clinical practice: Focus on children and adolescents* (pp. 153–166). Sarasota, FL: Professional Resource.

Carey v. Population Services International, 431 U.S. 678 (1977).

Carns, A. W., & Carns, M. R. (1997). A systems approach to school counseling. *School Counselor, 44*(3), 218–223.

Cashwell, C. S., Shcherbakova, J., & Cashwell, T. H. (2003). Effect of client and counselor ethnicity on preference for counselor disclosure. *Journal of Counseling and Development, 81*(2), 196–201.

Cedar Rapids Community School District v. Garrett F., 526 U.S. 66 (1999).

Center for Mental Health in Schools at UCLA. (2004). *An introductory packet on confidentiality and informed consent.* Los Angeles, CA: Author. Retrieved August 7, 2005, from http://smhp.psych.ucla.edu/pdfdocs/confid/confid.pdf

Chafouleas, S., Riley-Tillman, T. C., & Sugai, G. (2007). *School-based behavioral assessment: Informing intervention and instruction.* New York: Guilford.

Chamiec-Case, R. (2010). Ethical integration of Christian faith and social work practice: The excellence and Christian virtues models. *NACSW Catalyst, 53*(1), 3.

Cheating young cheaters. (2002, February 11). *Chicago Tribune* (electronic version). Accession # 2W72537898774

Clark, J. J., & Croney, E. L. (2006). Ethics and accountability in supervision of child psychotherapy. In T. K. Neill (Ed.), *Helping others help children: Clinical supervision of child psychotherapy* (pp. 51–71). Washington, DC: American Psychological Association.

Coeckelbergh, M. (2007). Who needs empathy? A response to Goldie's arguments against empathy and suggestions for an account of mutual perspective-shifting in contexts of help and care. *Ethics and Education, 2*(1), 61–72.

Cohen, D. K., Moffitt, S. L., & Goldin, S. (2007). Policy and practice: The dilemma. *American Journal of Education, 113*(4), 515–548.

Concepcion, M., Murphy, S., & Canham, D. (2007). School nurses' perceptions of family-centered services: Commitment and challenges. *Journal of School Nursing, 23*(6), 315–321.

Congress, E. P. (2000). What social workers should know about ethics: Understanding and resolving practice dilemmas. *Advances in Social Work, 1*(1), 1–25.

Congress, E. P. (2001). Ethical issues in work with culturally diverse children and their families. In N. B. Webb (Ed.), *Culturally diverse parent-child and family relationships: A guide for social workers and other practitioners* (pp. 29–53). New York: Columbia University Press.

Congressional Research Reports for the People. (April 1, 2009). *The United Nations Convention on the Rights of the Child: Background and policy issues.* Retrieved August 5, 2009, from http://opencrs.com/document/R40484

Conroy, H., & Harcourt, D. (2009). Informed agreement to participate: Beginning the partnership with children in research. *Early Child Development and Care, 179*(2), 157–165.

Constable, R. T. (1989). Relations and membership: Foundations for ethical thinking in social work. *Social Thought, 15*(3/4), 53–66.

Constable, R. T., & Alvarez, M. (2006). Moving into specialization in school social work: Issues in practice, policy, and education. *School Social Work Journal* (Special issue), 116–131.

Constantine, M. G., & Kwan, K-L. K. (2003). Cross-cultural considerations of therapist self-disclosure. *Journal of Clinical Psychology, 59*(5), 581–588.

Cooper, M. G., & Lesser, J. G. (2002). *Clinical social work practice: An integrated approach.* Boston: Allyn & Bacon.

Cooper, M. L. (2002). Alcohol use and risky sexual behavior among college students and youth: Evaluating the evidence. *Journal of Studies on Alcohol and Drugs, Suppl. 14*, 101–117.

Cornell, D. G., & Sheras, P. L. (2006). *Guidelines for responding to student threats of violence: A manual for school-based teams to assess and respond effectively to students who threaten violence.* Longmont, CO: Sopris West/Cambium Learning.

Corrao, J., & Melton, G. B. (1988). Legal issues in school-based behavior therapy. In J. C. Witt, S. N. Elliott, & F. M. Gresham (Eds.), *Handbook of behavior therapy in education* (pp. 377–399). New York: Plenum.

Cottone, R. R., & Claus, R. E. (2000). Ethical decision-making models: A review of the literature. *Journal of Counseling and Development, 78*(3), 275–283.

Covey, S. R. (1989). *The 7 habits of highly effective people: Restoring the character ethic.* New York: Simon & Schuster.

Cravens, C., & Earp, J. A. (2009). Disclosure and apology: Patient-centered approaches to the public health problem of medical error. *North Carolina Medical Journal, 70*(2), 140–146.

Crockett, L. J., Raffaelli, M., & Shen, Y-L. (2006). Linking self-regulation and risk proneness to risky sexual behavior: Pathways through peer pressure and early substance use. *Journal of Research on Adolescence, 16*(4), 503–525.

Crone, D. A., & Horner, R. H. (2003). *Building positive behavior support systems in schools: Functional behavioral assessment.* New York: Guilford.

Crosby, J., Lonetree, A., Brown, C., & Ross, J. (2009, May 26). Daniel Hauser faces custody hearing today: Colleen and Daniel Hauser, who ended a dramatic weeklong manhunt

Monday, were back at home this morning and facing a court hearing this afternoon to clarify Daniel's custody and the next steps in his medical care for Hodgkin's lymphoma. *Star Tribune* [Electronic version, Accession #: 2W62515934729]

Cull, J. G., & Gill, W. S. (1988). *Suicide Probability Scale (SPS) manual.* Los Angeles: Western Psychological Services.

Curwin, R. L. (2003). *Making good choices: Developing responsibility, respect, and self-discipline in grades 4-9.* Thousand Oaks, CA: Corwin.

d'Acremont, M., & Van der Linden, M. (2006). Gender differences in two decision-making tasks in a community sample of adolescents. *International Journal of Behavioral Development, 30*(4), 352–358.

Dalen, K. (2006). To tell or not to tell, that is the question: Ethical dilemmas presented by Norwegian psychologists in telephone counseling. *European Psychologist, 11*(3), 236–243.

Darden, E. C. (2009). The paddle problem. *American School Board Journal, 196*(1), 39–40.

Darlington, Y., Feeney, J. A., & Rixon, K. (2005). Interagency collaboration between child protection and mental health services: Practices, attitudes, and barriers. *Child Abuse and Neglect, 29*(10), 1085–1098.

Davis v. Monroe County Board of Education, 526 U.S. 629 (1999).

Davis, C. (1988, February 1). Getting tough. *Time,* pp. 52–58.

Day, P. (2005). "Coping with our kids:" A pilot evaluation of a parenting programme delivered by school nurses. *Groupwork, 15*(1), 42–60.

Day-Vines, N. L., & Terriquez, V. (2008). A strengths-based approach to promoting prosocial behavior among African American and Latino students. *Professional School Counseling, 12*(2), 170–175.

deChiara, J. (2007). *The right of way: Ethical decision making of selected elementary school principals.* Unpublished doctoral dissertation, Lesley University, Cambridge, Massachusetts. Retrieved August 29, 2009, from Dissertations & Theses: Full text (Publication No. AAT 3275001).

Deigh, J. (1999). Ethics. In R. Audi (Ed.), *The Cambridge Dictionary of Philosophy* (2nd ed., pp. 284–289). Cambridge, England: Cambridge University Press.

deKemp, R. A. T., Overbeek, G., deWied, M., Engels, R. C. M. E., & Scholte, R. H. J. (2007). Early adolescent empathy, parental support, and antisocial behavior. *Journal of Genetic Psychology, 168*(1), 5–18.

Demac, D. (1997). *Freedom of religion: State of the First Amendment.* Arlington, VA: Freedom Forum.

Denig, S. J., & Quinn, T. (2001). Ethical dilemmas for school administrators. *The High School Journal, 84*(4), 43–49.

Dennison, S. (2008). Measuring the treatment outcome of short-term school-based social skills groups. *Social Work with Groups, 31*(3–4), 307–328.

Detert, J. R., Treviño, L. K., & Sweitzer, V. L. (2008). Moral disengagement in ethical decision making: A study of antecedents and outcomes. *Journal of Applied Psychology, 93*(2), 374–391.

Devine, J. (2004). The discourse on violence prevention: What are the implications for smaller schools? In J. Devine, J. Gilligan, K. A. Miczek, R. Shaikh, & D. Pfaff (Eds.),

Youth violence: Scientific approaches to prevention (pp. 69–84). New York: New York Academy of Sciences.

DeVries, R., Hildebrandt, C., & Zan, B. (2000). Constructivist early education for moral development. *Early Education and Development, 11*(1), 9–35.

Dibble, N. (2006). Decision-making model for ethical-legal dilemmas. In N. Dibble (Ed.), *Wisconsin School Social Work Practice Guide* (pp. 61–62). Madison: Wisconsin Department of Public Instruction.

Dibble, N. (2007). School social work services and the privacy of minor students. In N. Dibble (Ed.), *Wisconsin school social work practice guide* (pp. 55–68). Madison: Wisconsin Department of Public Instruction.

Dickey, S. B., Kiefner, J., & Beidler, S. M. (2002). Consent and confidentiality issues among school-age children and adolescents. *Journal of School Nursing, 18*(3), 179–186.

Dishion, T., McCord, J., & Poulin, F. (1999). When interventions harm: Peer groups and problem behavior. *American Psychologist, 54*(9), 755–764.

Dishion, T. J., & Stormshak, E. A. (2007). *Intervening in children's lives: An ecological, family-centered approach to mental health care.* Washington, DC: American Psychological Association.

Dixon, A. L., & Tucker, C. (2008). Every student matters: Enhancing strengths-based school counseling through the application of mattering. *Professional School Counseling, 12*(2), 123–126.

Doe v. Renfrow, 451 U.S. 1022 (1981).

Doss, A. J. (2005). Evidence-based diagnosis: Incorporating diagnostic instruments into clinical practice. *Journal of the American Academy of Child and Adolescent Psychiatry, 44*(9), 947–952.

Doverspike, W. F. (2008). *Risk management: Clinical, ethical, and legal guidelines for successful practice.* Sarasota, FL: Professional Resource Press.

Doyle, C. (2003). Child emotional abuse: The role of educational professionals. *Educational and Child Psychology, 20*(1), 8–21.

Dubé, J. E., & Normandin, L. (2007). Mental activity and referential activity of beginning therapists: A construct validity study of the Countertransference Rating Scale (CRS). *American Journal of Psychotherapy, 61*(4), 351–374.

Duke, D. L. (2004). *The role and influence of ethics consultation in psychotherapy.* Doctoral dissertation. Auburn University, Alabama. Retrieved June 25, 2009, from Dissertations & Theses: Full Text database (Publication No. AAT 3135990).

Dupper, D. R., & Dingus, A. E. M. (2008). Corporal punishment in U.S. public schools : A continuing challenge for school social workers. *Children and Schools, 30*(4), 243–250.

Durodoye, B. A. (2006). Ethical issues in multicultural counseling. In C. C. Lee (Ed.), *Multicultural issues in counseling: New approaches to diversity* (3rd ed., pp. 357–368). Alexandria, VA: American Counseling Association.

Earl-Brooks, E., Buri, J., Byrne, E. A., & Hudson, M. C. (1962). Socioeconomic factors, parental attitudes, and school attendance. *Social Work, 7*, 103–128.

Edmondson, A. C. (2004). Learning from mistakes is easier said than done: Group and organizational influences on the detection and correction of human error. *Journal of Applied Behavioral Science, 40*(1), 66–90.

Edwards, O. W., Mumford, V. E., Shillingford, M. A., & Serra-Roldan, R. (2007). Developmental assets: A prevention framework for students considered at risk. *Children and Schools*, *29*(3), 143–153.

Edwards, S., & Harries, M. (2007). No-suicide contracts and no-suicide agreements: A controversial life. *Australasian Psychiatry*, *15*(6), 484–489.

Eisel v. Board of Education of Montgomery County, 324 Md. 376, 597 A.2d 447 (Md Ct. App., 1991).

Eisenberg, N., Wentzel, M., & Harris, J. D. (1998). The role of emotionality and regulation in empathy-related responding. *School Psychology Review*, *27*(4), 506–521.

Emerich v. Philadelphia Center for Human Development, 720 A.2d 1032 (1998).

Enebrink, P., Langstrom, N., Hulten, A., & Gumpert, C. H. (2006). Swedish validation of the Early Assessment Risk List for Boys (EARL-20B), a decision aid for use with children presenting with conduct-disordered behaviour. *Nordic Journal of Psychiatry*, *60*(6), 438–446.

Engle v. Vitale, 370 U.S. 421 (1962).

Erlen, J. A., & Frost, B. (1991). Nurses' perceptions of powerlessness in influencing ethical decisions. *Western Journal of Nursing Research*, *13*(3), 397–407.

Eshel, N., Nelson, E. E., Blair, R. J., Pine, D. S., & Ernst, M. (2007). Neural substrates of choice selection in adults and adolescents: Development of the ventrolateral prefrontal and anterior cingulated cortices. *Neuropsychologia*, *45*(6), 1270–1279.

Eskin, M. (2003). A cross-cultural investigation of the communication of suicidal intent in Swedish and Turkish adolescents. *Scandinavian Journal of Psychology*, *44*(1), 1–6.

Essex, N. L. (2003). Intrusive searches can prove troublesome for public school officials. *The Clearing House*, *76*(4), 195–197.

Evans, I. M. (2008). Ethical issues. In D. Reitman (Ed.), *Handbook of psychological assessment, case conceptualization, and treatment: Vol. 2 Children and adolescents* (pp. 176–195). Hoboken, NJ: John Wiley & Sons.

Fannif, A. M., & Becker, J. V. (2006). Specialized assessment and treatment of adolescent sex offenders. *Aggression and Violent Behavior*, *11*(3), 265–282.

Faunce, T. A., & Bolsin, S. N. (2005). Fiduciary disclosure of medical mistakes: The duty to promptly notify patients of adverse health care events. *Journal of Law and Medicine*, *12*(4), 478–482.

Fein, R. A., Vossekuil, B., Pollack, W. S., Borum, R., Modzeleski, W., & Reddy, M. (2002). *Threat assessment in schools: A guide to managing threatening situations and to creating safe school climates*. Washington, DC: U.S. Secret Service & U.S. Department of Education. Retrieved July 14, 2009, from http://www.secretservice.gov/ntac/ssi_guide.pdf

Figner, B., Mackinlay, R. J., Wilkening, F., & Weber, E. U. (2009). Affective and deliberative processes in risky choice: Age differences in risk taking in the Columbia Card Task. *Journal of Experimental Psychology*, *35*(3), 709–730.

Findlay, L. C., Girardi, A., & Coplan, R. J. (2006). Links between empathy, social behavior, and social understanding in early childhood. *Early Childhood Research Quarterly*, *21*(3), 347–359.

Finkelstein, D., Wu, A. W., Holtzman, N. A., & Smith, M. K. (1997). When a physician harms a patient by medical error: Ethical, legal, and risk-management considerations. *Journal of Clinical Ethics*, *8*(4), 330–335.

Finken, L. (2009). "What should I do?" How consultants impact adolescents' risky decisions [Special issue on Adolescent decision making]. *The Prevention Researcher, 16*(2), 12–16.

Fisher, C. B. (2004). Informed consent and clinical research involving children and adolescents: Implications of the revised APA Code of Ethics and HIPAA. *Journal of Clinical Child and Adolescent Psychology, 33*(4), 832–839.

Foltz, M-L., Kirby, P. C., & Paradise, L. V. (1989). The influence of empathy and negative consequences on ethical decisions in counseling situations. *Counselor Education and Supervision, 28*(3), 219–228.

Fontes, L. A. (2005). *Child abuse and culture: Working with diverse families.* New York: Guilford.

Fontes, L. A., & O'Neill-Arana, M. R. (2008). Assessing for child maltreatment in culturally diverse families. In L. A. Suzuki & J. G. Ponterotto (Eds.), *Handbook of multicultural assessment: Clinical, psychological and educational applications* (3rd ed., pp. 627–650). San Francisco: Jossey-Bass.

Ford, R. C. (1987). Cultural awareness and cross-cultural counseling. *International Journal for the Advancement of Counselling, 10*(1), 71–78.

Foshee, V. A., & Reyes, H. L. M. (2009). Primary prevention of adolescent dating abuse perpetration: When to begin, whom to target, and how to do it. In D. J. Whitaker & J. R. Lutzker (Eds.), *Preventing partner violence: Research and evidence-based intervention strategies* (pp. 141–168). Washington, DC: American Psychological Association.

Foster-Harrison, E. S. (1995). Peer helping in the elementary and middle grades: A developmental perspective. *Elementary School Guidance and Counseling, 30*(2), 94–104.

Francis, R. D. (2002). The need for a professional ethic: International perspectives. *Educational and Child Psychology, 19*(1), 7–15.

Franklin, C., Gerlach, B., & Chanmugam, A. (2008). School social work. In B. W. White, K. M. Sowers, & C. N. Dulmus (Eds.), *Comprehensive handbook of social work and social welfare, Vol. 1: The profession of social work* (pp. 205–225). Hoboken, NJ: John Wiley & Sons.

Franklin v. Gwinnett County Public Schools, 503 U.S. 60 (1992).

Frazier, T. W., Demeter, C. A., Youngstrom, E. A., Calabrese, J. R., Stansbrey, R. J., McNamara, N. K., & Findling, R. L. (2007). Evaluation and comparison of psychometric instruments for pediatric bipolar disorders in four age groups. *Journal of Child and Adolescent Psychopharmacology, 17*(6), 853–866.

Freed, C., & Pena, R. (2002). Minority education and analytical thinking skills: Traditionalizing disempowerment. *The High School Journal, 85*(2), 24–32.

Freedberg, S. (2009). *Relational theory for social work practice: A feminist perspective.* New York: Routledge.

French, J. R. P., & Raven, B. (1968). The bases of social power. In D. Cartwright & A. Zander (Eds.), *Group dynamics* (pp. 259–268). New York: Harper & Row.

Freud, S., & Krug, S. (2002). Beyond the Code of Ethics, Part I: Complexities of ethical decision making in social work practice. *Families in Society, 83*(5–6), 474–482.

Frieman, B. B. (1994). Children of divorced parents: Action steps for the counselor to involve fathers. *Elementary School Guidance & Counseling, 28*(3), 197–205.

Friedman, I. A. (1995). Student behavior patterns contributing to teacher burnout. *Journal of Educational Research, 88*(5), 281–289.

Friedman, S., & Gelso, C. J. (2000). The development of the Inventory of Counter-transference Behavior. *Journal of Clinical Psychology, 56*(9), 1221–1235.

Fry, S., & Veatch, R. (2000). *Case studies in nursing ethics* (2nd ed.). Sudbury, MA: Jones and Bartlett Publishers.

Fulenwider, T. (2007). *The application of ethical principles in decision-making between beginning, intermediate, and journeyman educational administrators.* Doctoral dissertation, University of the Pacific, Stockton, California. Retrieved August 29, 2009 from Dissertations & Theses: Full text (Publication No. 3302231).

Funk, B. A., III, Huebner, E. S., & Valois, R. F. (2006). Reliability and validity of a Brief Life Satisfaction Scale with a high school sample. *Journal of Happiness Studies, 7*(1), 41–54.

Gabbard, G. O. (1997). Lessons learned from the study of sexual boundary violations. *Australian and New Zealand Journal of Psychiatry, 31*(3), 321–327.

Gabbard, G. (2006). Sexual and nonsexual boundary violations in psychoanalysis and psychotherapy. In S. Akhtar (Ed.), *Interpersonal boundaries: Variations and violations* (pp. 39–48). Lanham, MD: Jason Aronson.

Gabriel, L., & Davies, D. (2000). The management of ethical dilemmas associated with dual relationships. In C. Neal & D. Davies (Eds.), *Issues in therapy with lesbian, gay, bisexual and transgender clients* (pp. 35–54). Maidenhead, England: Open University Press.

Galassi, J. P., & Akos, P. (2007). *Strengths-based school counseling: Promoting student development and achievement.* Mahwah, NJ: Lawrence Erlbaum.

Gambetti, E., & Giusberti, F. (2009). Trait anger and anger expression style in children's risky decisions. *Aggressive Behavior, 35*(1), 14–23.

Gambrill, E. (2005). *Critical thinking in clinical practice: Improving the quality of judgements and decisions.* Hoboken, NJ: John Wiley & Sons.

Gammelgard, M., Koivisto, A-M., Eronen, M., & Kaltiala-Heino, R. (2008). The predictive validity of the Structured Assessment of Violence Risk in Youth (SAVRY) among institutionalized adolescents. *Journal of Forensic Psychiatry and Psychology, 19*(3), 352–370.

Gandhi, M. K. (1948). *Non-violence in peace and war.* Ahmedabadi, India: Narajivan.

Garcetti v. Ceballos, 126 S. Ct. 1951.

Gardner, M., & Steinberg, L. (2005). Peer influence on risk taking, risk preference, and risky decision making in adolescence and adulthood: An experimental study. *Developmental Psychology, 41*(4), 625–635.

Garner, B. A. (2009). *Black's law dictionary* (9th ed.). St. Paul, MN: Thomson/West.

Gellerman, D. M., & Suddath, R. (2005). Violent fantasy, dangerousness, and the duty to warn and protect. *Journal of the American Academy of Psychiatry and the Law, 33*(4), 484–495.

Gentile, M. G., Manna, G. M., Ciceri, R., & Rodeschini, E. (2008). Efficacy of inpatient treatment in severely malnourished anorexia nervosa patients. *Eating and Weight Disorders, 13*(4), 191–197.

Germain, C. B. (2006). An ecological perspective on social work in the schools. In C. R. Massat, R. Constable, S. McDonald, & J. P. Flynn (Eds.), *School social work: Practice, policy, and research* (6th ed., pp. 28–39). Chicago, IL: Lyceum Books.

Gewirth, A. (1978). The Golden Rule rationalized. *Midwest Studies in Philosophy, 3,* 133–147.

Giesbrecht, N. D. (2008). Caregiving in sociocultural context. In B. Fehr, S. Sprecher, & L. G. Underwood (Eds.), *The science of compassionate love: Theory, research, and applications* (pp. 373–401). Hoboken, NJ: Wiley-Blackwell.

Giles, H. C. (2005). Three narratives of parent-educator relationships: Toward counselor repertoires for bridging the urban parent-school divide. *Professional School Counseling, 8*(3), 228–235.

Gilligan, C. (1982). *In a different voice: Psychological theory and women's development.* Cambridge, MA: University Press of America.

Glaser, B. A., & Cohen, P. J. (2005). Treating juvenile substance abuse in the institutional setting. In B. Sims (Ed.), *Substance abuse treatment with correctional clients: Practical implications for institutional and community settings* (pp. 197–210). New York: Haworth.

Gleason, E. T. (2007). A strengths-based approach to the social developmental study. *Children and Schools, 29*(1), 51–59.

Glosoff, H. (2002). Privacy and confidentiality in school counseling. *Professional School Counseling, 6*(1), 20–27.

Goldie, P. (1999). How we think of others' emotion. *Mind and Language, 14*(4), 394–423.

Goldstein, H. (1998). Education for ethical dilemmas in social work practice. *Families in Society, 79*(3), 241–253.

Goldstein, S., & Brooks, R. (2002). *Raising resilient children: A curriculum to foster strength, hope, and optimism in children.* Baltimore, MD: Paul H. Brookes.

Gonzaga University v. Doe, 536 U.S. 273 (2002).

Goss v. Lopez, 419 U.S. 565 (1975).

Graybeal, C. (2001). Strengths based social work assessment: Transforming the dominant paradigm. *Families in Society, 82*(3), 233–242.

Green, A., & Keys, S. (2001). Expanding the developmental school counseling paradigm: Meeting the needs of the 21st century student. *Professional School Counseling, 5*(2), 84–95.

Griffin, J. (1986). *Well-being: Its meaning, measurement, and moral importance.* Oxford, England: Clarendon Press.

Grinberg, I., Dawkins, M., Dawkins, M. P., & Fullilove, C. (2005). Adolescents at risk for violence: An initial validation of the Life Challenges Questionnaire and Risk Assessment Index. *Adolescence, 40*(159), 573–599.

Gun-Free School Zones Act of 1990, Pub. L. No. 101-647.

Gun-Free Schools Act of 1994. Pub. L. No. 103-382.

Gupta, S., Roesgen, S., Cohen, E., Quijano, E., & Toobin, J. (May 30, 2009). A collision of medicine, law, and ethics: What are your medical rights? *CNN: House Call with Dr. Sanjay Gupta* [Electronic version, Accession #: 32U3182841717CNSG]

Gutheil, T. G. (2006). Commentary: Systems, sensitivity, and "sorry". *Journal of the American Academy of Psychiatry and the Law, 34*(1), 101–102.

Gutierrez, P. M., Osman, A., Kopper, B. A., & Barrios, F. X. (2004). Appropriateness of the Multi-Attitude Suicide Tendency Scale for non-White individuals. *Assessment, 11*(1), 73–84.

Guttmacher Institute. (2009, August 1). State policies in brief: Minors' access to contraceptive services. Retrieved August 7, 2009, from http:www.guttmacher.org/statecenter/spibs/spib_MACS.pdf

Halpern-Felsher, B. (2009). Adolescent decision making: An overview [Special issue on Adolescent decision making]. *The Prevention Researcher, 16*(2), 3–7.

Hanks, J. C. (2004). Weapons in schools. In J. C. Hanks (Ed.), *School violence: From discipline to due process* (pp. 15–30). Chicago: Section of State and Local Government Law, American Bar Association.

Harrison, R. (1983). *Bentham*. London: Routledge & Kegan Paul.

Hastings, R. P., & Bham, M. S. (2003). The relationship between student behaviour patterns and teacher burnout. *School Psychology International, 24*(1), 115–127.

Hatfield, M. (2009, December 29). Ceres takes on truant students: Strategies range from parenting advice to fines. *Modesto Bee* [Electronic version]. Accession #: 2W62417349474.

Hathaway, W. L. (2001). Common sense professional ethics: A Christian appraisal. *Journal of Psychology and Theology, 29*(3), 225–234.

Haynes, C. (1998). Muslim students' needs in public school. *Update on Law-Related Education, 22*(1), 17–21.

Hazelwood School District v. Kuhlmeier, 484 U.S. 260 (1988).

Healy, L. M. (2007). Universalism and cultural relativism in social work ethics. *International Social Work, 50*(1), 11–26.

Hedlund v. Superior Court of Orange County, 34 Cal.3d 995; 669 P.2d 41 (1983).

Held, V. (2006). The ethics of care. In D. Copp (Ed.), *The Oxford handbook of ethical theory* (pp. 537–566). New York: Oxford University Press.

Helms, J. L. (2003). Barriers to help-seeking among 12th graders. *Journal of Educational and Psychological Consultation, 14*(1), 27–40.

Henderson, D. H. (1986). Constitutional implications involving the use of corporal punishment in the public schools: A comprehensive review. *Journal of Law and Education, 15*(4), 255–269.

Hendin, H., Maltsberger, J. T., & Haas, A. P. (2004). A physician's suicide - Reply. *American Journal of Psychiatry, 161*(12), 2330–2331.

Hepworth, D. H., Rooney, R. H., Rooney, G. D., Stom-Gottfried, K., & Larsen, J. A. (2006). *Direct social work practice: Theory and skills* (7th ed.). Belmont, CA: Thomson-Brooks/Cole.

Herlihy, B., & Watson, Z. E. (2003). Ethical issues and multicultural competence in counseling. In F. D. Harper, & J. McFadden (Eds.), *Culture and counseling: New approaches* (pp. 363–378). Needham Heights, MA: Allyn & Bacon.

Hick, J. (1996). A pluralist view. In J. Hick, C. H. Pinnock, A. E. McGrath, R. D. Geivett, & W. G. Phillips. *Four views on salvation in a pluralistic world* (pp. 29–59). Grand Rapids, MI: Zondervan.

Hill, T. E., Jr. (2006). Kantian normative ethics. In D. Copp (Ed.), *The Oxford handbook of ethical theory* (pp. 480–514). New York: Oxford University Press.

H.L. v. Matheson, 450 U.S. 398 (1981).

Hoagwood, K. E., Olin, S. S., Kerker, B. D., Kratochwill, T. R., Crowe, M., & Saka, N. (2007). Empirically based school interventions targeted at academic and mental health functioning. *Journal of Emotional and Behavioral Disorders, 15* (2), 66–92.

Hoge, R. D., & Andrews, D. A. (2002). *Youth Level of Service/Case Management Inventory (YLS/CMI). Users manual*. North Tonowanda, NY: Multi-Health Systems.

Hoida, J. A. (2007). *Family-school relationships and satisfaction of parents of students with emotional/behavioral disorders*. Doctoral dissertation, Indiana University, Bloomington. Retrieved May 19, 2009, from Dissertations & Theses: Full text database (Publication No. AAT3281646).

Holland, T. P., & Kilpatrick, A. C. (1991). Ethical issues in social work: Toward a grounded theory of professional ethics. *Social Work, 36*(2), 138–144.

Hollen, P. J., Hobbie, W. L., Donnangelo, S. F., Shannon, S., & Erickson, J. (2007). Substance abuse risk behaviors and decision-making skills among cancer-surviving adolescents. *Journal of Pediatric Oncology Nursing, 24*(5), 264–273.

Holmes, C. (2005). *The paradox of countertransference: You and me, here and now.* New York: Palgrave/Macmillan.

Holsinger, A. M., Lowenkamp, C. T., & Latessa, E. J. (2006). Predicting institutional misconduct using the Youth Level of Service/Case Management Inventory. *American Journal of Criminal Justice, 30*(2), 267–284.

Honig v. Doe, 484 U.S. 305 (1988).

Hook, K. G., & White, G. B. (2001). Code of Ethics for Nurses with interpretive statements: An independent study module. Retrieved May 19, 2009, from http://www.nursingworld.org/mods/mod580/code.pdf

Hooker, B. (2000). *Ideal code, real world: A rule-consequentialist theory of morality.* New York: Oxford University Press.

Hooper, C. J., Luciana, M., Wahlstrom, D., Conklin, H. M., & Yarger, R. S. (2008). Personality correlates of Iowa Gambling Task performance in health adolescents. *Personality and Individual Differences, 44*(3), 598–609.

Horesh, N., Zalsman, G., & Apter, A. (2004). Suicidal behavior and self-disclosure in adolescent psychiatric inpatients. *Journal of Nervous and Mental Disease, 192*(12), 837–842.

Horton, C. B. (1996). Children who molest other children: The school psychologist's response to the sexually aggressive child. *School Psychology Review, 25*(4), 540–557.

Houser, R., Wilczenski, F. L., & Ham, M-A. (2006). *Culturally relevant ethical decision-making in counseling.* Thousand Oaks, CA: Sage.

Huebner, E. S. (1994). Preliminary development and validation of a multidimensional life satisfaction scale for children. *Psychological Assessment, 6*(2), 149–158.

Huebner, E. S., Suldo, S. M., Valois, R. F., & Drane, J. W. (2006). The Brief Multidimensional Students' Life Satisfaction Scale: Sex, race, and grade effects for applications with middle school students. *Applied Research in Quality of Life, 1*(2), 211–216.

Huizenga, H. M., Crone, E. A., & Jansen, B. J. (2007). Decision-making in health children, adolescents and adults explained by the use of increasingly complex proportional reasoning rules. *Developmental Science, 10*(6), 814–825.

Hunn, D. (2009, April 12). How social worker Jane M. Buri saved $1.4 million, then gave it all away. *St. Louis Post-Dispatch.* Retrieved April 15, 2010, from http://videos.stltoday.com/p/video?id=3723050

Hunter, B. (2000). The unpopular issues of poverty and isolation. *School Administrator, 56*(4), 54.

Hurka, T. (2006). Value theory. In D. Copp (Ed.), *The Oxford handbook of ethical theory* (pp. 357–379). New York: Oxford University Press.

Hursthouse, R. (1999). *On virtue ethics*. New York: Oxford University Press.

Hus, S. N. (2001). Navigating the quagmire of inherent ethical dilemmas present in elementary school counseling programs. In D. S. Sandhu (Ed.), *Elementary school counseling in the new millennium* (pp. 15–25). Alexandria, VA: American Counseling Association.

Huth-Bocks, A. C., Kerr, D. C. R., Ivey, A. Z., Kramer, A. C., & King, C. A. (2007). Assessment of psychiatrically hospitalized suicidal adolescents: Self-report instruments as predictors of suicidal thoughts and behavior. *Journal of the American Academy of Child and Adolescent Psychiatry, 46*(3), 387–395.

Hyman, I. A. (1989). The make-believe world of 'Lean on Me.' *Educational Digest, 55*(3), 20.

Hyman, I. A., & Perone, D. C. (1998). The other side of school violence: Educator policies and practices that may contribute to student misbehavior. *Journal of School Psychology, 36*(1), 7–27.

Ichikawa, D. P. (1997). An argument on behalf of children. *Child Maltreatment, 2*(3), 202–211.

In re Gault, 387 U.S. 1 (1967).

Individuals with Disabilities Education Improvement Act of 2004, Pub. L. No. 108-446, 118 Stat. 2647 (2004).

Ingraham v. Wright, 430 U.S. 651 (1977).

Irving Independent School District v. Tatro, 468 U.S. 883, 104 S. Ct. 3371 (1984).

Isaacs, M. (1999). School counselors and confidentiality: Factors affecting professional choices. *Professional School Counseling, 2*(4), 258–266.

Jacob, S. (2008). Best practices in developing ethical school psychological practice. In A. Thomas & J. Grimes (Eds.), *Best practices in school psychology, V* (Vol. 6, pp. 1921–1932). Bethesda, MD: National Association of School Psychologists.

Jacob, S., & Hartshorne, T. S. (2007). *Ethics and law for school psychologists* (5th ed.). Hoboken, NJ: John Wiley & Sons.

Jaffee v. Redmond, 518 U.S. 1 (1996).

Jennings, L. (1988, January 20). Love him or not: Joe Clark stirs emotions. *Education Week, 7*(17), p. 10.

Jennings, L., Sovereign, A., Bottoroff, N., Mussell, M. P., & Vye, C. (2005). Nine ethical values of master therapists. *Journal of Mental Health Counseling, 27*(1), 32–47.

Jensen, A. L., & Weisz, J. R. (2002). Assessing match and mismatch between practitioner generated and standardized interview-generated diagnoses for clinic-referred children and adolescents. *Journal of Consulting and Clinical Psychology, 70*(1), 158–168.

Jerome, R., & Grout, P. (2002, June 17). Cheat wave. *People, 57*(23), 83–84.

Jimerson, S. R., Sharkey, J. D., Nyborg, V., & Furlong, M. J. (2004). Strengths-based assessment and school psychology: A summary and synthesis. *California School Psychologist, 9*, 9–19.

Jobes, D. A., & O'Connor, S. S. (2009). The duty to protect suicidal clients: Ethical, legal, and professional considerations. In J. L. Werth, Jr., E. R. Welfel, & G. A. H. Benjamin (Eds.), *The duty to protect: Ethical, legal, and professional considerations for mental health practitioners* (pp. 163–180). Washington, DC: American Psychological Association.

Joint Commission on Accreditation of Healthcare Organizations. (2007, July 22). *Standards sampler for ambulatory surgery centers*. Oakbrook Terrace, IL: Author. Retrieved April 7, 2009, from http://www.jointcommission.org/NR/rdonlyres/A88E7A36-0C20-4C37-B67D-CD8638538E09/0/ASC_stdsampler_07.pdf

Jones v. Clear Creek Independent School District, 977 F.2d 963 (5th Cir. 1992).

Josephson Institute. (2008). *The ethics of American youth*. Retrieved August 20, 2009, from http://charactercounts.org/pdf/reportcard/2008/Q_all.pdf

Jue, S., & Lewis, S. Y. (2001). Cultural considerations in HIV ethical decision making: A guide for mental health practitioners. In J. R. Anderson & B. Barret (Eds.), *Ethics in HIV-related psychotherapy: Clinical decision making in complex cases* (pp. 61–82). Washington, DC: American Psychological Association.

Kagle, J. D., & Kopels, S. (2008). *Social work records* (3rd ed.). Long Grove, IL: Waveland Press.

Kaigler, M. F. (1997) *Factors related to the ethical decision making of teachers*. Doctoral dissertation, University of New Orleans, Louisiana. Retrieved August 29, 2009, from Dissertations & Theses: Full text (Publication No. AAT 9807501).

Kant, I. (2002). *Grounding for the metaphysics of morals* (T. E. Hill, Jr. & A. Zweig, Eds. & Trans.). Oxford, England: Oxford University Press.

Karcher, M. J. (2008). The cross-age mentoring program: A developmental intervention for promoting intervention for promoting students' connectedness across grade levels. *Professional School Counseling, 12*(2), 137–143.

Kaser-Boyed, N., Adelman, H. S., & Taylor, L. (1985). Minors' ability to identify risks and benefits of therapy. *Professional Psychology: Research and Practice, 16*(3), 411–417.

Kawamura, N., Suzuki, H., & Iwai, K. (2004). Influence of negative feelings of junior high school teachers in disciplinary situations [Japanese/English abstract]. *Japanese Journal of Educational Psychology, 52*(1), 1–11.

Keller, J. (1997). Autonomy, relationality, and feminist ethics. *Hypatia, 12*(2), 179–202.

Kelley, G. A. (2002). Living at the sharp end: Moral obligations of nurses in reporting and disclosing errors in health care. *Critical Care Nursing Clinics of North America, 14*(4), 401–405.

Kertesz, R. (2002). Dual relationships in psychotherapy in Latin America. In A. A. Lazarus & O. Zur (Eds.), *Dual relationships and psychotherapy* (pp. 329–334). New York: Springer.

Kester, H. M., Sevy, S., Yechiam, E., Burdick, K. E., Cervellione, K. L., & Kumra, S. (2006). Decision-making impairments in adolescents with early-onset schizophrenia. *Schizophrenia Research, 85*(1-3), 113–123.

Kidder, R. M., & Born, P. (1998). Resolving ethical dilemmas in the classroom. *Educational Leadership, 56*(4), 38–41.

Kim, B. S. K., Hill, C. E., Gelso, C. J., Goates, M. K., Asay, P. A., & Harbin, J. M. (2003). Counselor self-disclosure, East Asian American client adherence to Asian cultural values, and counseling process. *Journal of Counseling Psychology, 50*(3), 324–332.

King, M. L. (1958). *Stride toward freedom*. San Francisco: Harper & Row.

Knapp, S., & VandeCreek, L. (1997). Jaffee v. Redmond: The Supreme Court recognizes a psychotherapist-patient privilege in federal courts. *Professional Psychology: Research and Practice, 28*(6), 567–572.

Knapp, S. J., & VandeCreek, L. D. (2006). *Practical ethics for psychologists: A positive approach*. Washington, DC: American Psychological Association.

Kocet, M. M. (2005). Ethical challenges in a complex world: Highlights of the 2005 ACA Code of Ethics. *Journal of Counseling and Development, 84*(2), 228–234.

Kochanska, G., & Aksan, N. (2006). Children's conscience and self-regulation. *Journal of Personality, 74*(6), 1578–1618.

Kochanska, G., Coy, K. C., & Murray, K. T. (2001). The development of self-regulation in the first four years of life. *Child Development, 72*(4), 1091–1111.

Kohlberg, L. (1969). Stage and sequence: The cognitive-developmental approach to socialization. In D. A. Goslin (Ed.), *Handbook of socialization theory and research* (pp. 347–480). Chicago: Rand McNally.

Koocher, G. P. (2006). Ethical issues in forensic assessment of children and adolescents. In S. N. Sparta & G. P. Koocher (Eds.), *Forensic mental health assessment of children and adolescents* (pp. 46–63). New York: Oxford University Press.

Koocher, G. P., & Keith-Spiegel, P. (2008). *Ethics in psychology and the mental health professions: Standards and cases* (3rd ed.). New York: Oxford University Press.

Kooyman, L., & Barret, B. (2009). The duty to protect: Mental health practitioners and communicable diseases. In J. L. Werth, Jr., E. R. Welfel, & G. A. H. Benjamin (Eds.), *The duty to protect: Ethical, legal, and professional considerations for mental health practitioners* (pp. 141–159). Washington, DC: American Psychological Association.

Kopels, S. (2007). Student rights and control of behavior. In P. Allen-Meares (Ed.), *Social work services in schools* (5th ed., pp. 108–144). Boston: Pearson/Allyn & Bacon.

Kopels, S., & Kagle, J. D. (1993). Do social workers have a duty to warn? *Social Service Review, 67*(1), 10–26.

Kopels, S., & Lindsey, B. (2006). The complexity of confidentiality in schools today: The school social worker context, (Special 100th anniversary issue). *School Social Work Journal,* 61–78.

Kovacs, M. (1992). *Children's Depression Inventory manual*. North Tonawanda, NY: Multi-Health Systems.

Kraft, A. D. (1986). Some theoretical considerations on confidential adoption - IV: Countertransference. *Child and Adolescent Social Work Journal, 3*(1), 3–14.

Kraman, S. S., & Hamm, G. (1999). Risk management: Extreme honesty may be the best policy. *Annals of Internal Medicine, 131*(12), 963–967.

Krivda, L. A. (2005). *Beliefs regarding confidentiality amongst parents and children receiving counseling through a school-based mental health clinic*. Doctoral dissertation. University of Arizona, Tucson. Retrieved January 11, 2009, from Dissertations & Theses (Publication No. AAT 3185661).

Küng, H. (1976). *On being a Christian*. (Trans: E. Quinn). Garden City, NJ: Doubleday.

Kurtz, L., & Derevensky, J. L. (1993). Stress and coping in adolescents: The effects of family configuration and environment on suicidality. *Canadian Journal of School Psychology, 9*(2), 204–216.

Kutchins, H. (1991). The fiduciary relationship: The legal basis for social workers' responsibility to clients. *Social Work, 36*(2), 106–113.

Kuther, T. L. (2003). Medical decision-making and minors: Issues of consent and assent. *Adolescence, 38*(150), 343–358.

Kyriacou, D., Anglin, D., Taliaferro, E., Stone, S., Tubb, T., Linden, J., Muelleman, R., Barton, E., & Kraus, J. (1999). Risk factors for injury to women from domestic abuse. *New England Journal of Medicine, 341*(25), 1892–1898.

Laible, D., Eye, J., & Carlo, G. (2008). Dimensions of conscience in mid-adolescence: Links with social behavior, parenting, and temperament. *Journal of Youth and Adolescence, 37*(7), 875–887.

Lambie, G. W., & Rokutani, L. J. (2002). A systems approach to substance abuse identification an intervention for school counselors. *Professional School Counseling, 5*(5), 353–359.

Lashley, C. (2007). Principal leadership for special education: An ethical framework. *Exceptionality, 15*(3), 177–187.

Lashway, L. (2006). Ethical leadership. In S. C. Smith & P. K. Piele (Eds.), *School leadership: Handbook for excellence in student learning* (4th ed., pp. 130–152). Thousand Oaks, CA: Corwin.

Lasser, J & McGarry Klose, L. (2007). School psychologists' ethical decision making: implications from selected social psychological phenomena. *Social Psychological Review, 36*(3), 484-500.

Latham, P. S., Latham, P. H., & Mandlawitz, M. R. (2008). *Special education law.* Boston: Pearson/Allyn & Bacon.

Lee, B. (1997). *The power principle: Influence with honor.* New York: Simon & Schuster.

Leming, J. S. (2001). Integrating a structured ethical reflection curriculum into high school community service experiences: Impact on students' sociomoral development. *Adolescence, 36*(141), 33–45.

Lemon v. Kurtzman, 403 U.S. 602 (1971).

Lerner, M. (2009, May 7). Trial will determine if family can reject son's cancer treatment. *Star Tribune.* [Electronic version, Accession #: 2W63133213276].

Levenson, H. (1981). Differentiating among internality, powerful others, and chance. In H. M. Lefcourt (Ed.), *Research with the locus of control construct: Vol. 1. Assessment methods* (pp. 15–63). New York: Academic Press.

Lewczyk, C. M., Garland, A. F., Hurlburt, M. S., Gearity, J., & Hough, R. L. (2003). Comparing DISC-IV and clinician diagnoses among youth receiving public mental health services. *Journal of the American Academy of Child and Adolescent Psychiatry, 42*(3), 349–356.

Lewis, C., Watson, M., & Schnaps, E. (2003). Building community in school: The Child Development Project. In M. J. Elias, H. Arnold, C. S. Hussey (Eds.), *EQ + IQ = Best leadership practices for caring and successful schools* (pp. 100–108). Thousand Oaks, CA: Corwin.

Link, R. (1991). Social work services to schools in the Midwestern United States and in London: A comparative study of guest status. *Social Work in Education, 13*(5), 278–294.

Linzer, N. (1999). *Resolving ethical dilemmas in social work practice.* Boston: Allyn & Bacon.

Lodewijks, H. P. B., Doreleijers, T. A. H., de Ruiter, C., & Borum, R. (2008). Predictive validity of the Structured Assessment of Violence Risk in Youth (SAVRY) during residential treatment. *International Journal of Law and Psychiatry, 31*(3), 263–271.

Loewenberg, F. M., Dolgoff, R., & Harrington, D. (2000). *Ethical decisions for social work practice* (6th ed.). Itasca, IL: Peacock.

Logan, W. L., & Scarborough, J. L. (2008). Connections through clubs: Collaboration and coordination of a school-wide program. *Professional School Counseling, 12*(2), 157–161.

Luce, J. M. (2006). Acknowledging our mistakes. *Critical Care Medicine, 34*(5), 1575–1576.

Lundgren, J., & Ciccone, J. R. (2009). No duty to warn, but common law duty of care. *Journal of the American Academy of Psychiatry and the Law, 37*(2), 260–262.

Market Street Associates Ltd. Partnership v. Frey, 941 F.2d 588, C.A.7 (Wis. 1991).

Maroda, K. J. (2007). Ethical considerations of the home office. *Psychoanalytic Psychology, 24*(1), 173–179.

Martenson, E. K., & Fagerskiold, A. M. (2008). A review of children's decision-making competence in health care. *Journal of Clinical Nursing, 17*(23), 3131–3141.

Masty, J., & Fisher, C. (2008). A goodness-of-fit approach to informed consent for pediatric intervention research. *Ethics and Behavior, 18*(2–3), 139–160.

Mattison, M. (2000). Ethical decision making: The person in the process. *Social Work, 45*(3), 201–212.

Mattison, M. (2006). Professional ethical codes: Applications to common ethical dilemmas. In C. Franklin, M. B. Harris, & P. Allen-Meares (Eds.), *The school services sourcebook: A guide for school-based professionals* (pp. 921–927). New York: Oxford University Press.

Mazor, K. M., Simon, S. R., Yood, R. A., Martinson, B. C., Gunter, M. J., Reed, G. W., et al. (2004). Health plan members' views about disclosure of medical errors. *Annals of Internal Medicine, 140*(6), 409–423.

McCabe, M., Tollerud, T., & Axelrod, J. (2006). A state mandate for social-emotional literacy: Implications for school counselors. In J. Pellitteri, R. Stern, C. Shelton, B. Muller-Ackerman (Eds.), *Emotionally intelligent school counseling* (pp. 239–251). Mahwah, NJ: Lawrence Erlbaum.

McCarthy, M. (2005). Corporal punishment in public schools: Is the United States out of step? *Educational Horizons, 83*(4), 235–240.

McIntosh v. Milano, 403 A.2d 500 (NJ 1979).

McKay, M. J. (2002, May 31). *Cheating in the heartland? Cheating scandal divides Kansas town.* Retrieved September 24, 2009, from http://www.cbsnews.com/stories/2002/05/31/48hours/main510772.shtml

McMahon, S. D., Wernsman, J., & Parnes, A. L. (2006). Understanding prosocial behavior: The impact of empathy and gender among African American adolescents. *Journal of Adolescent Health, 39*(1), 135–137.

McMyler, C., & Pryjmachuk, S. (2008). Do 'no-suicide' contracts work? *Journal of Psychiatric and Mental Health Nursing, 15*(6), 512–522.

McNamara, K. (2008). Best practices in the application of professional ethics. In A. Thomas & J. Grimes (Eds.), *Best practices in school psychology, V* (Vol. 6, pp. 1933–1941). Bethesda, MD: National Association of School Psychologists.

McNaughton, D., & Rawling, P. (2006). Deontology. In D. Copp (Ed.), *The Oxford handbook of ethical theory* (pp. 424–458). New York: Oxford University Press.

Meador, E. (2005). The making of marginality: Schooling for Mexican immigrant girls in the rural southwest. *Anthropology and Education Quarterly, 36*(2), 149–164.

Meer, D., & VandeCreek, L. (2002). Cultural considerations in release of information. *Ethics and Behavior, 12*(2), 143–156.

Melville, H. (1967). *Moby Dick: An authoritative text.* New York: W. W. Norton.

Merali, N. (2002). Culturally informed ethical decision making in situations of suspected child abuse. *Canadian Journal of Counselling, 36*(3), 233–244.

Merriken v. Cressman, 364 F. Supp. 913 (E.D.Pa 1973).

Metheny, J., McWhirter, E. H., & O'Neil, M. E. (2008). Measuring perceived teacher support and its influence on adolescent career development. *Journal of Career Assessment, 16*(2), 218–237.

Meyer-Adams, N., & Conner, B. T. (2008). School violence: Bullying behaviors and the psychosocial school environment in middle schools. *Children and Schools, 30*(4), 211–221.

Milfont, T. L., Merry, S., Robinson, E., Denny, S., Crengle, S., & Ameratunga, S. (2008). Evaluating the short form of the Reynolds Adolescent Depression Scale in New Zealand adolescents. *Australian and New Zealand Journal of Psychiatry, 42*(11), 950–954.

Miller, W. R., & Rollnick, S. (2002). *Motivational interviewing: Preparing people for change.* New York: Guilford.

Milson, A. J. (2003). Teachers' sense of efficacy for the formation of students' character. *Journal of Research in Character Education, 1*(2), 89–106.

Milson, A. J., & Mehlig, L. M. (2002). Elementary school teachers' sense of efficacy for character education. *Journal of Educational Research, 96*(1), 47–53.

Miranda v. Arizona, 384 U.S. 436 (1966).

Mitchell, R. W. (2007). *Documentation in counseling records: An overview of ethical, legal, and clinical issues* (3rd ed.). Alexandria, VA: American Counseling Association.

Monkman, M. M. (2009). The characteristic focus of the social worker in the public schools. In C. R. Massat, R. Constable, S. McDonald, & J. P. Flynn (Eds.), *School social work: Practice, policy, and research* (7th ed., pp. 30–48). Chicago, IL: Lyceum Books.

Monshi, B., & Zieglmayer, V. (2004). The problem of privacy in transcultural research: Reflections on an ethnographic study in Sri Lanka. *Ethics and Behavior, 14*(4), 305–312.

Moore, J. (2009, September 5). Daniel Hauser's chemo is finished. *Star Tribune.* [Electronic version, Accession #: 2W62433288753].

Moran, G., & Diamond, G. (2008). Generating nonnegative attitudes among parents of depressed adolescents: The power of empathy, concern, and positive regard. *Psychotherapy Research, 18*(1), 97–101.

Morrison, L. L., & Downey, D. L. (2000). Racial differences in self-disclosure of suicidal ideation and reasons for living: Implications for training. *Cultural Diversity and Ethnic Minority Psychology, 6*(4), 374–386.

Mueller, T. G., Singer, G. H., & Draper, L. M. (2008). Reducing parental dissatisfaction with special education in two school districts: Implementing conflict prevention and alternative dispute resolution. *Journal of Educational and Psychological Consultation, 18*(3), 191–233.

Mullis, F., & Otwell, P. S. (1998). Who gets the kids? Consulting with parents about child custody decisions? *Professional School Counseling, 2*(2), 103–109.

Munoz, M. A., & Vanderhaar, J. E. (2006). Literacy-embedded character education in a large urban district: Effect of the Child Development Project on elementary students and teachers. *Journal of Research in Character Education, 4*(1–2), 47–64.

Murphy, J. J. (2008). *Solution-focused counseling in schools* (2nd ed.). Alexandria, VA: American Counseling Association.

Mussen, P., & Eisenberg, N. (2001). Prosocial development in context. In A. C. Bohart & D. J. Stipek (Eds.), *Constructive and destructive behavior: Implications for family, school, and society* (pp. 103–126). Washington, DC: American Psychological Association.

Nabors, L. A., & Prodente, C. A. (2002). Evaluation of outcomes for adolescents receiving school-based mental health services. *Children's Services: Social Policy, Research, and Practice, 5*(2), 105–112.

Nadelson, C. C. (1993). Ethics, empathy, and gender in health care. *American Journal of Psychiatry, 150*(9), 1309–1314.

Nagy, T. F. (2005). *Ethics in plain English: An illustrative casebook for psychologists* (2nd ed.). Washington, DC: American Psychological Association.

Nassar-McMillen, S., & Post, P. (1998, March). Ethics reconsidered. Presentation at the 28th Annual North Carolina Counseling Association Conference, Chapel Hill, NC.

National Association of Elementary School Principals. (1976). *Statement of Ethics for School Administrators.* Alexandria, VA: Author.

National Association of School Nurses. (2002). *Code of Ethics.* Silver Spring, MD: Author. Retrieved May 19, 2009, from http://www.nasn.org/Default.aspx?tabid=512

National Association of School Psychologists. (2000). *Professional conduct manual; Principles for professional ethics; Guidelines for the Provision of School Psychological Services.* Bethesda, MD: Author.

National Association of Secondary School Principals. (2001). *Ethics for School Administrators.* Reston, VA: Author.

National Association of Social Workers. (2008). *Code of Ethics.* Silver Spring, MD: Author.

National Association of Social Worker Commission on Education. (1991). The school social worker and confidentiality. Washington, DC: Author. Also available in the *School Social Work Journal, 17*(1), 38–46.

National Education Association. (1975). *Code of Ethics.* Retrieved July 8, 2009, from http://www.nea.org/home/30442.htm

National Research Council. (2002). *Minority students in special and gifted education.* Washington, DC: National Academy Press.

Negrón, F. M., Jr. (2009). A foot in the door? The unwitting move towards a "new" student welfare standard in student speech after Morse v. Frederick. *American University Law Review, 58,* 1221–1241.

Nelson, J. A., & Bustamante, R. M. (2008). The School-Wide Cultural Competence Observation Checklist for professional school counselors: An assessment tool for leading culturally and linguistically diverse schools. In G. R. Walz, J. C. Bleuer, & R. K. Yep (Eds.), *Compelling counseling interventions: Celebrating VISTA's fifth anniversary* (pp. 211–220). Alexandria, VA: American Counseling Association.

New Jersey v. TLO, 469 U.S. 325, 105 S. Ct. 733 (1985).

Newhill, C. E. (2003). *Client violence in social work practice: Prevention, intervention, and research*. New York: Guilford.

No Child Left Behind Act of 2001, Pub. L. No. 107-110, 115 Stat. 1425 (2002).

Noddings, N. (2005). *The challenge to care in schools: An alternative approach to education* (2nd ed.). New York: Teachers College Press.

Norcross, J. C. (Ed.). (2002). *Psychotherapy relationships that work: Therapist contributions and responsiveness to patient needs*. New York: Oxford University Press.

Norman, M. (1988, January 27). Lessons: Can every student be saved? Why Joe Clark's discipline troubles many educators. *New York Times*, p. B-8.

Norris, J. A. (2008). Using social and emotional learning to address conflicts in the classroom. In C. Franklin, M. B. Harris, & P. Allen-Meares (Eds.), *The school practitioners' concise companion to preventing violence and conflict* (pp. 83–95). New York: Oxford University Press.

Nozick, R. (1989). *The examined life: Philosophical meditations*. New York: Simon & Schuster.

Obidah, J. E., Jackson-Minot, M., Monroe, C. R., & Williams, B. (2004). Crime and punishment: Moral dilemmas in the inner-city classroom. In V. S. Walker & J. R. Snarey (Eds.), *Race-ing moral formation: African American perspectives on care and justice* (pp. 111–129). New York: Teachers College Press.

O'Donohue, W., & Henderson, D. (1999). Epistemic and ethical duties in clinical decision-making. *Behavior Change, 16*(1), 10–19.

Ofek, H., Weizman, T., & Apter, A. (1998). The Child Suicide Potential scale: Inter-rater reliability and validity in Israeli in-patient adolescents. *Israel Journal of Psychiatry and Related Sciences, 35*(4), 253–261.

Olsen, D. P. (1991). Empathy as an ethical and philosophical basis for nursing. *Advances in Nursing Science, 14*(1), 62–75.

Onifade, E., Davidson, W., Campbell, C., Turke, G., Malinowski, J., & Turner, K. (2008). Predicting recidivism in probationers with the Youth Level of Service/Case Management Inventory (YLS/CMI). *Criminal Justice and Behavior, 35*(4), 474–483.

Opotow, S. (2006). Rationalities and levels of analysis in complex social issues: The examples of school overcrowding and poverty. *Social Justice Research, 19*(1), 135–150.

Orbach, I., Milstein, I., Har-Even, D., Apter, A., Tiano, S., & Elizur, A. (1991). A Multi-Attitude Suicide Tendency Scale for adolescents. *Psychological Assessment, 3*(3), 398–404.

O'Reilly, B. (2002, February 11). Impact: Interview with Christine Pelton. *O'Reilly Factor* (FOX News electronic version). Accession #: 32U3625477532FX2

Osman, A., Barrios, F. X., Grittmann, L. R., & Osman, J. R. (1993). The Multi-Attitude Suicide Tendency Scale: Psychometric characteristics in an American sample. *Journal of Clinical Psychology, 49*(5), 701–708.

Osman, A., Barrios, F. X., Gutierrez, P. M., Williams, J. E., & Bailey, J. (2008). Psychometric properties of the Beck Depression Inventory-II in nonclinical adolescent samples. *Journal of Clinical Psychology, 64*(1), 83–102.

Osmo, R., & Landau, R. (2006). The role of ethical theories in decision making by social workers. *Social Work Education*, *25*(8), 863–876.

O'Toole, M. E. (1999, July). *The school shooter: A threat assessment perspective*. Quantico, VA: U.S. Department of Justice/Federal Bureau of Investigation. Retrieved May 19, 2008, from http://www.fbi.gov/publications/school/school2.pdf

Owasso Independent School District v. Falvo, 534 U.S. 426 (2002).

Owen, S. S. (2005). The relationship between social capital and corporal punishment in schools: A theoretical inquiry. *Youth and Society*, *37*(1), 85–112.

Pabian, Y. L., Welfel, E., & Beebe, R. S. (2009). Psychologists' knowledge of their states' laws pertaining to Tarasoff-type situations. *Professional Psychology: Research and Practice*, *40*(1), 8–14.

Palmer, N., & Kaufman, M. (2003). The ethics of informed consent: Implications for multicultural practice. *Journal of Ethnic and Cultural Diversity in Social Work*, *12*(1), 1–26.

Palombo, J., & Berenberg, A. H. (1997). Psychotherapy for children with nonverbal learning disabilities. In B. S. Mark & J. A. Incorvaia (Eds.), *The handbook of infant, child, and adolescent psychotherapy, Vol. 2: New directions in integrative treatment* (pp. 25–67). Lanham, MD: Jason Aronson.

Parham, T. A. (1997). An African-centered view of dual relationships. In B. Herlihy & G. Corey (Eds.), *Boundary issues in counseling: Multiple roles and responsibilities* (pp. 109–112). Alexandria, VA: American Counseling Association.

Patrasso, C. J. (2005). Questions in the evaluation for threat assessment in schools. *The Forensic Examiner*, *14*(4), 6–12.

Pearson, J. (2006). Personal control, self-efficacy in sexual negotiation and contraceptive risk among adolescents: The role of gender. *Sex Roles*, *54*(9–10), 615–625.

Peck v. Counseling Service of Addison County, 499 A.2d 422 (1985).

Pelt, J. L., & Faldmo, L. P. (2008). Physician error and disclosure. *Clinical Obstetrics and Gynecology*, *51*(4), 700–708.

Perry, H. W., Jr. (2005). Writ of certiori. In K. L. Hall (Ed.-in-Chief)., *The Oxford companion to the Supreme Court of the United States* (2nd ed., pp. 154–155). New York: Oxford University Press.

Pescosolido, B. A., Fettes, D. L., Martin, J. K., Monahan, J., & McLeod, J. D. (2007). Perceived dangerousness of children with mental health problems and support for coerced treatment. *Psychiatric Services*, *58*(5), 619–625.

Petrosino, A., Turpin-Petrosino, C., & Buehler, J. (2003). Scared Straight and other juvenile awareness programs for preventing juvenile delinquency: A systematic review of the randomized experimental evidence. *Annals of the American Academy of Political and Social Science*, *589*, 41–62.

Pettifor, J. L. (2004). School psychology: How universal are ethical principles approved by international associations? *Canadian Journal of School Psychology*, *19*(1–2), 137–148.

Pettifor, J. L., & Sawchuk, T. R. (2006). Psychologists' perceptions of ethically troubling incidents across international borders. *International Journal of Psychology*, *41*(3), 216–225.

Pfeffer, C. R., Coute, H. R., Plutchik, R., & Jerett, I. (1979). Suicidal behavior in latency age children: An empirical study. *Journal of the American Academy of Child and Adolescent Psychiatry*, *18*(4), 679–692.

Pickering v. Board of Education of Township High School District 205, Will County, 391 U.S. 563 (1968).

Pierce v. Society of Sisters, 268 U.S. 510 (1925)

Pinnock, R., & Crosthwaite, J. (2005). When parents refuse to consent to treatment for children and young persons. *Journal of Paediatrics and Child Health, 41*(7), 369–373.

Pipes, R. B., Holstein, J. E., & Aguirre, M. G. (2005). Examining the personal-professional distinction: Ethics codes and the difficulty of drawing a boundary. *American Psychologist, 60*(4), 325–334.

Pitcairn, M. & Phillips, K. (2005). Ethics, laws, and adolescents – Confidentiality, reporting, & conflict. Retrieved April 7, 2010, from http://counselingoutfitters.com/vistas/vistas05/Vistas05.art14.pdf

Planned Parenthood of Central Missouri v. Danforth, 428 U.S. 52 (1976).

Plessy v. Ferguson, 163 U.S. 537 (1896).

Poland, S., & Lieberman, R. (2002). Best practices in suicide intervention. In A. Thomas & J. Grimes (Eds.), *Best practices in school psychology, IV* (Vol. 2, pp. 1151–165). Bethesda, MD: National Association of School Psychologists.

Polowy, C. I., Morgan, S., & Gilbertson, J. (2005). *Social workers and subpoenas.* Washington, DC: National Association of Social Workers.

Pompili, M., Girardi, P., Ruberto, A., & Tatarelli, R. (2006). Suicide in anorexia nervosa and bulimia nervosa. In P. I. Swain (Ed.), *Anorexia nervosa and bulimia: New research* (pp. 1–26). Hauppauge, NY: Nova Science.

Pope, K. S. & Bajt, T. R. (1988). When laws and values conflict: A dilemma for psychologists. *American Psychologist, 43*(10), 828–829.

Pope, K. S., & Vasquez, M. J. T. (2007). *Ethics in psychotherapy and counseling: A practical guide* (3rd ed.). San Francisco: Jossey-Bass.

Pope, K. S., & Vetter, V. A. (2003). Ethical dilemmas encountered by members of the American Psychological Association: A national survey. In D. N. Bersoff (Ed.), *Ethical conflicts in psychology* (3rd ed., pp. 3–25). Washington, DC: American Psychological Association.

Power, T. J., & Bartholomew, K. L. (1987). Family-school relationship patterns: An ecological assessment. *School Psychology Review, 16*(4), 498–512.

Poznanski, E. O., & Mokros, H. B. (1995). *Children's Depression Rating Scale, Revised manual.* Los Angeles: Western Psychological Services.

Prasse, D. P. (2008). Best practices in school psychology and the law. In A. Thomas & J. Grimes (Eds.), *Best Practices in School Psychology* (5th ed., pp. 1903–1920). Bethesda, MD: National Association of School Psychologists.

Prilleltensky, I., Peirson, L., & Nelson, G. (1997). The application of community psychology values and guiding concepts to school consultation. *Journal of Educational and Psychological Consultation, 8*(2), 153–173.

Prochaska, J. O., & DiClemente, C. C. (2005). The transtheoretical approach. In J. C. Norcross & M. R. Goldfried (Eds.), *Handbook of psychotherapy integration* (2nd ed., pp. 147–171). New York: Oxford University Press.

Protection of Pupil Rights Amendment, Pub. L. No. 95–561, 92 Stat. 2355

Prout, S. M., DeMartino, R. A., & Prout, H. T. (1999). Ethical and legal issues in psychological interventions with children and adolescents. In H. T. Prout & D. T. Brown (Eds.), *Counseling and psychotherapy with children and adolescents: Theory and practice for school and clinical settings* (3rd ed., pp. 26–48). Hoboken, NJ: John Wiley & Sons.

Quattrocchi, M. R., & Schopp, R. F. (2005). Tarasaurus Rex: A standard of care that could not adapt. *Psychology, Public Policy, and Law, 11*(1), 109–137.

Racker, H. (1968). *Transference and countertransference.* New York: International Universities Press.

Raines, J. C. (1990). Empathy in clinical social work. *Clinical Social Work Journal, 18*(1), 57–72.

Raines, J. C. (1996a). Self-disclosure in clinical social work. *Clinical Social Work Journal, 24*(4), 357–375.

Raines, J. C. (1996b). Appropriate vs. least restrictive: Educational policies and students with disabilities. *Social Work in Education, 18*(2), 113–127.

Raines, J. C. (2002). Brainstorming hypotheses for functional behavioral assessment: The link to effective behavioral intervention plans. *School Social Work Journal, 26*(2), 30–45.

Raines, J. C. (2004). To tell or not to tell: Ethical issues regarding confidentiality. *School Social Work Journal, 28*(2), 61–78.

Raines, J. C. (2006). The new IDEA: Reflections on the reauthorization. *School Social Work Journal, 31*(1), 1–18.

Raines, J. C. (2008). *Evidence-based practice in school mental health.* New York: Oxford University Press.

Raines, J. C. (2009). The process of ethical decision making in school social work: Confidentiality. In C. R. Massat, R. Constable, S. McDonald, & J. P. Flynn (Eds.), *School social work: Practice, policy, and research* (pp. 71–94). Chicago: Lyceum Books.

Raines, J. C., & Ahlman, C. (2004). No substitute for competence: How to survive and thrive as a substitute school social worker. *School Social Work Journal, 28*(2), 37–52.

Rasmussen, C., & Wyper, K. (2007). Decision making, executive functioning and risky behavior in adolescents with prenatal alcohol exposure. *International Journal on Disability and Human Development, 6*(4), 405–416.

Rawls, J. (1971). *A theory of justice.* Cambridge, MA: Harvard University Press.

Reamer, F. G. (2003). Boundary issues in social work: Managing dual relationships. *Social Work, 48*(1), 121–133.

Reamer, F. G. (2005a). Ethical and legal standards in social work: Consistency and conflict. *Families in Society, 86*(2), 163–169.

Reamer, F. G. (2005b). Update on confidentiality issues in practice with children: Ethics risk management. *Children and Schools, 27*(2), 117–120.

Reamer, F. G. (2006). *Ethical standards in social work: A review of the NASW Code of Ethics* (2nd ed.). Washington, DC: NASW Press.

Reamer, F. G. (2008). Social workers' management of error: Ethical and risk management issues. *Families in Society, 89*(1), 61–68.

Reddy, M., Borum, R., Berglund, J., Vossekuil, B., Fein, R., & Modzeleski, W. (2001). Evaluating risk for targeted violence in schools: Comparing risk assessment, threat assessment, and other approaches. *Psychology in the Schools, 38*(2), 157–172. Retrieved July 14, 2009, from http://www.secretservice.gov/ntac/ntac_threat_postpress.pdf

Reiner, S. M. (2007). *Teacher perceptions of the professional school counselor role: Value, effectiveness, and collaborative willingness.* Doctoral dissertation, University of Connecticut, Storrs. Retrieved June 19, 2009, from Dissertations & Theses: Full Text Database (Publication No. AAT 3265793).

Reyna, V. F., & Rivers, S. E. (2008). Current theories of risk and rational decision making. *Developmental Review, 28*(1), 1–11.

Reynolds, W. M. (1987). *The Suicidal Ideation Questionnaire: SIQ form HS.* Odessa, FL: Psychological Assessment Resources.

Reynolds, W. M. (1989). *Reynolds Child Depression Scale: Professional manual.* Odessa, FL: Psychological Assessment Resources.

Reynolds, W. M. (2002). *Reynolds Adolescent Depression Scale: Professional manual* (2nd ed.). Odessa, FL: Psychological Assessment Resources.

Rich, P. (2009). *Juvenile sex offenders: A comprehensive guide to risk evaluation.* Hoboken, NJ: John Wiley.

Ridley, C. R., Liddle, M. C., Hill, C. L., & Li, L. C. (2001). Ethical decision making in multicultural counseling. In J. G. Ponterotto, J. M. Casas, L. A. Suzuki, & C. M. Alexander (Eds.), *Handbook of multicultural counseling* (2nd ed., pp. 165–188). Thousand Oaks, CA: Sage.

Rimer, S. (January 14, 1988). Paterson principal: A man of extremes. *New York Times,* p. B1-2.

Rivers, S. E., Reyna, V. F., & Mills, B. (2008). Risk taking under the influence: A fuzzy-trace theory of emotion in adolescence. *Developmental Review, 28,* 107–144.

Roberts, A. R. (2006). School-based, adolescent suicidality: Lethality assessments and crisis intervention. In C. Franklin, M. B. Harris, & P. Allen-Meares (Eds.), *The school services sourcebook: A guide for school-based professionals* (pp. 3–13). New York: Oxford University Press.

Roberts, R. E., Attkinson, C. C., & Rosenblatt, A. (1998). Prevalence of psychopathology among children and adolescents. *American Journal of Psychiatry, 155*(6), 715–722.

Robinson, W., & Reeser, L. C. (2000). *Ethical decision making in social work.* Boston: Allyn & Bacon.

Roncker v. Walter, 700 F.2d 1058 (1999).

Rones, M., & Hoagwood, K. (2000). School-based mental health services: A research review. *Clinical Child and Family Psychology Review, 3*(4), 223–241.

Roou, D. (2004). Fighting the lunchroom bully. *Principal Leadership, 4*(5), 27–29.

Ross, J., & Walsh, P. (2009, May 22). Chief Deputy: Sheriff in Hauser chemo case heads to California, but not to find boy. *Star Tribune.* [Electronic version, Accession #: 2W63350025233].

Ross, W. D. (1930). *The right and the good.* Oxford: Clarendon Press.

Rossiter, A. (1996). Learning from broken rules: Individualism, bureaucracy and ethics. *Ethics and Behavior, 6*(4), 307–320.

Royal, C. W., & Baker, S. B. (2005). Effects of a deliberate moral education program on parents of elementary school students. *Journal of Moral Education, 34*(2), 215–230.

Rudd, M. D., Berman, A. L., Joiner, T. E., Jr., Nock, M. K., Silverman, M. M., Mandrusiak, M., Van Orden, K., & Witte, T. (2006). Warning signs for suicide: Theory, research, and clinical applications. *Suicide and Life-Threatening Behavior, 36*(3), 255–262.

Rudd, M. D., Mandrusiak, M., & Joiner, T. E., Jr. (2006). The case against no-suicide contracts: The commitment to treatment statement as a practice alternative. *Journal of Clinical Psychology, 62*(2), 243–251.

Ruuska, J., Kaltiala-Heino, R., Rantanen, P., & Koivisto, A-M. (2005). Psychopathological distress predicts suicidal ideation and self-harm in adolescent eating disorder patients. *European Child and Adolescent Psychiatry, 14*(5), 276–281.

Saad, L. (2008, November 24). Nurses shine, bankers slump in ethics ratings. Retrieved May 19, 2009, from http://www.gallup.com/poll/112264/Nurses-Shine-While-Bankers-Slump-Ethics-Ratings.aspx

Saarni, C. (2007). The development of emotional intelligence: Pathways for helping children to become emotionally intelligent. In R. Bar-On, J. G. Maree, & M. J. Elias (Eds.), *Educating people to be emotionally intelligent* (pp. 15–35). Westport, CT: Praeger.

Safford Unified School District v. Redding, 557 U.S. __ (2009), 129 S. Ct. 2633

Saleebey, D. (Ed.). (2002). *The strengths perspective in social work practice* (3rd ed.). Boston: Allyn & Bacon.

Samuels, C. A. (2008, June 18). States found moving to head-off due process hearings. *Education Week, 27*(42), 12.

San Antonio Independent School District v. Rodriguez, 411 U.S. 1 (1973).

Sanchez-Queija, I., Olivia, A., & Parra, A. (2006). Empathy and prosocial behaviour during adolescence [Spanish]. *Revista de Psicologia Social, 21*(3), 259–271.

Satterly, B. A. (2006). Therapist self-disclosure from a gay male perspective. *Families in Society, 87*(2), 240–247.

Sava, F. A. (2002). Causes and effects of teach conflict-inducing attitudes towards pupils: A path analysis model. *Teaching and Teacher Education, 18*(8), 1007–1021.

Schacter, D., Kleinman, I., & Harvey, W. (2005). Informed consents and adolescents. *Canadian Journal of Psychiatry, 50*(9), 534–540.

Schaffer, M. A., Cameron, M. E., & Tatley, E. B. (2000). The value, be, do ethical decision-making model: Balancing students' needs in school nursing. *Journal of School Nursing, 16*(5), 44–49.

Schaper, D. (2009, May 27). Youth killings reach crisis level in Chicago. *National Public Radio: All things considered.* Retrieved July 18, 2009, from http://www.npr.org/templates/story/story.php?storyId=104566915

Scheffler, S. (1992). *Human morality.* New York: Oxford University Press.

School SW of the Year 1989. Midwest School Social Work Council archives stored at Illinois State University, School of Social Work, Normal, IL 61790–4650.

Seifert, K., Phillips, S., & Parker, S. (2001). Child and Adolescent Risk for Violence (CARV): A tool to assess juvenile risk. *Journal of Psychiatry and Law, 29*(3), 329–346.

Seitsinger, A. M., Felner, R. D., Brand, S., & Burns, A. (2008). A large-scale examination of the nature and efficacy of teachers' practices to engage parents: Assessment, parental contact, and student-level impact. *Journal of School Psychology, 46*(4), 477–505.

Selman, R. L., & Schultz, L. H. (1998). *Making a friend in youth: Developmental theory and pair therapy.* New York: Aldine de Gruyter.

Sendor, B. (2001). A shock to the conscience. *American School Board Journal, 188*(4), 62–63, 78.

Shaffer, D., Scott, M., Wilcox, H., Maslow, C., Hicks, R., Lucas, C. P., Garfinkel, R., & Greenwald, S. (2004). The Columbia Suicide screen: Validity and reliability of a screen for youth suicide and depression. *Journal of the American Academy of Child and Adolescent Psychiatry, 43*(1), 71–79.

Shapiro, J. P., & Stefkovich, J. A. (2005). *Ethical leadership and decision making in education: Applying theoretical perspectives to complex dilemmas* (2nd ed.). Mahwah, NJ: Lawrence Erlbaum.

Shaw, L. R., & Lane, F. J. (2008). Ethical consultation: Content analysis of the Advisory Achive of the Commission on Rehabilitation Counselor Certification. *Rehabilitation Counseling Bulletin, 51*(3), 170–176.

Sheridan, S. M., & Gutkin, T. B. (2000). The ecology of school psychology: Examining and changing our paradigm for the 21st century. *School Psychology Review, 29*(4), 485–501.

Sherwood, D. (2003). Is the case method bad for your ethics? Exploring ethical, theoretical, and factual justifications for practice. *Social Work and Christianity, 30*(2), 117–127.

Simone, S., & Fulero, S. M. (2005). Tarasoff and the duty to protect. *Journal of Aggression, Maltreatment and Trauma, 11*(1–2), 145–168.

Simpson, M. D. (2002). Taking a stand for integrity: NEA member resigns over school board vote to ignore plagiarism. *NEA Today, 20*(8), 20.

Singer, M. G. (1963). The Golden Rule. *Philosophy, 38*, 293–314.

Sink, C. A., & Spencer, L. R. (2007). Teacher version of the My Class Inventory-Short Form: An accountability tool for elementary school counselors. *Professional School Counseling, 11*(2), 129–139.

Sklare, G. B. (2005). *Brief counseling that works: A solution-focused approach for school counselors and administrators* (2nd ed.). Thousand Oaks, CA: Corwin.

Skolnick, J. H., & Leo, R. A. (1992). The ethics of deceptive interrogation. *Criminal Justice Ethics, 11*(1), 3–12.

Slavkin, M. L. (2004). Predictive validity of the ego triad: The myth of enuresis, firesetting, and cruelty to animals. In S. P. Shohov (Ed.), *Advances in psychology research, 31* (pp. 199–206). Hauppauge, NY: Nova Science Publishers.

Smith, S. (2009). Mandatory reporting of child abuse and neglect. Retrieved July 31, 2009, from http://www.smith-lawfirm.com/mandatory_reporting.htm

Smith v. Seibly, 431 P.2d 719, 723 (Washington, 1967).

Society for Adolescent Medicine. (2003). Corporal punishment in schools. *Journal of Adolescent Health, 32*(5), 385–393.

Son Hing, L. S., Bobocel, D. R., Zanna, M. P., & McBride, M. V. (2007). Authoritarian dynamics and unethical decision making: High social dominance orientation leaders and high right-wing authoritarianism followers. *Journal of Personality and Social Psychology, 92*(1), 67–81.

Soper, P. (2002). *The ethics of deference: Learning from law's morals.* New York: Cambridge University Press.

Sori, C. F., & Hecker, L. L. (2006). Ethical and legal considerations when counseling children and families. In C. F. Sori (Ed.), *Engaging children in family therapy: Creative approaches to integrating theory and research in clinical practice* (pp. 159–174). New York: Routledge/Taylor & Francis.

Spear, H. J. (2002). Reading, writing, and having babies: A nurturing alternative school program. *Journal of School Nursing, 18*(5), 293–300.

Spengler, J. O. (2003). School punishment and physical education. *Journal of Physical Education, Recreation and Dance, 74*(2), 12–13.

Sprinkle, J. E. (2008). Animals, empathy, and violence: Can animals be used to convey principles of prosocial behavior to children? *Youth Violence and Juvenile Justice, 6*(1), 47–58.

Stadler, H. A. (1986). Making hard choices: Clarifying controversial ethical issues. *Counseling and Human Development, 19*(1), 1–10.

Staller, K. M., & Kirk, S. A. (1997). Unjust freedom: The ethics of client self-determination in runaway youth shelters. *Child and Adolescent Social Work Journal, 14*(3), 223–242.

Stapleton, L. M., Sander, J. B., & Stark, K. D. (2007). Psychometric properties of the Beck Depression Inventory for Youth in a sample of girls. *Psychological Assessment, 19*(2), 230–235.

Staral, J. M. (2003). Introducing Ignatian spirituality: Linking self-reflection with social work ethics. *Social Work and Christianity, 30*(1), 38–51.

Stewart, A., & Tan, J. (2007). Ethical and legal issues. In B. Lask & R. Bryant-Waugh (Eds.), *Eating disorders in childhood and adolescence* (3rd ed., pp. 335–359). London: Routledge/Taylor & Francis.

Stirrat, G. M., & Gill, R. (2005). Autonomy in medical ethics after O'Neill. *Journal of Medical Ethics, 31*(3), 127–130.

Steadman, S. (2004). *Assessing advanced practice psychiatric nurses' boundary violations in psychotherapy: Survey results with the Exploitation Index.* Ph.D. Dissertation, University of Utah.

Steege, M. W., Mace, F. C., Brown-Chidsey, R. (2007). Functional behavioral assessment of classroom behavior. In S. Goldstein, & R. B. Brooks (Eds.), *Understanding and managing children's classroom behavior: Creating sustainable, resilient classrooms* (2nd ed., pp. 43–63). Hoboken, NJ: John Wiley.

Stewart, A., & Tan, J. (2007). Ethical and legal issues. In B. Lask, & R. Bryant-Waugh (Eds.), *Eating disorders in childhood and adolescence* (3rd ed., pp. 335–359). New York: Routledge/Taylor & Francis.

Stockdale, K. C. (2008). *The validity and reliability of the Violence Risk Scale-Youth Version (VRS-VY).* Unpublished doctoral dissertation. University of Saskatchewan, Saskatoon. Retrieved July 17, 2009, from http://library2.usask.ca/theses/available/etd-08292008-113213/unrestricted/12Sep08_Revised_Dissertation_KStockdale.pdf

Stone, C. (2005). *School counseling principles: Ethics and law.* Alexandria, VA: American School Counselor Association.

Strean, H. S. (1997). Comment on James C. Raines' "Self-disclosure in clinical social work." *Clinical Social Work Journal, 25*(3), 365–366.

Strean, H. (2001). Resolving some therapeutic impasses by disclosing countertransference. In H. S. Strean (Ed.), *Controversies on countertransference* (pp. 109–132). Lanham, MD: Jason Aronson.

Strike, K. (2007). *Ethical Leadership in schools: Creating community in an environment of accountability*. Thousand Oaks, CA: Corwin.

Strom-Gottfried, K. (2007). *Straight talk about professional ethics*. Chicago: Lyceum.

Strom-Gottfried, K. (2008). *The ethics of practice with minors*. Chicago: Lyceum.

Sue, D. W. (1997). Multicultural perspectives on multiple relationships. In B. Herlihy & G. Corey (Eds.), *Boundary issues in counseling* (pp. 106–109). Alexandria, VA: American Counseling Association.

Sugai, G., & Horner, R. H. (2007). Is school-wide Positive Behavior Support an evidence-based practice? Retrieved April 7, 2010, from http://www.pbis.org/research/default.aspx

Sukemune, S. (1992). The development of prosocial behavior in Japanese children. In U. P. Gielen, L. L. Adler, & N. A. Milgram (Eds.), *Psychology in international perspective: 50 years of the International Council of Psychologists* (pp. 249–255). Lisse, Netherlands: Swets & Zeitlinger.

Sumner, L. W. (1996). *Welfare, happiness, and ethics*. Oxford: Clarendon Press.

Supreme Court upholds social work privilege: Majority of seven cites NASW legal brief. (1996). *NASW News, 41*(8), 1–10.

Swahn, M. H., & Potter, L. B. (2001). Factors associated with the medical severity of suicide attempts in youths and young adults. *Suicide and Life-Threatening Behavior, 32*(Suppl. 1), 21–29.

Szmukler, G., & Appelbaum, P. S. (2008). Treatment pressures, leverage, coercion, and compulsion in mental health care. *Journal of Mental Health, 17*(3), 233–244.

Szyndrowski, D. (1999). The impact of domestic violence on adolescent aggression in the schools. *Preventing School Failure, 44*(1), 9–11.

Tansey, M. J., & Burke, W. F. (1995). *Understanding countertransference: From projective identification to empathy*. Hillsdale, NJ: Analytic Press.

Tarasoff v. Board of Regents of the University of California, 529 P.2d 553 (1974); 551 P.2d 334 (1976).

Tarvydas, V. (1998). Decision making models in ethics: Models for increased clarity and wisdom. *Journal of Applied Rehabilitation Counseling, 18*(4), 50–52.

Tarvydas, V. M., Leahy, M. J., & Saunders, J. L. (2004). A comparison of the ethical beliefs of certified rehabilitation counselors and national certified counselors. *Rehabilitation Counseling Bulletin, 47*(4), 234–246.

Tasapoulos-Chan, M., Smetana, J. G., & Yau, J. P. (2009). How much do I tell thee? Strategies for managing information to parents among American adolescents from Chinese, Mexican, and European backgrounds. *Journal of Family Psychology, 23*(3), 364–374.

Taylor, L. & Adelman, H. (1989). Reframing the confidentiality dilemma to work in children's best interests. *Professional Psychology: Research and Practice, 20*(2), 1–5.

Taylor, L., & Adelman, H. S. (2003). Reframing the confidentiality dilemma to work in children's best interests. In D. N. Bersof (Ed.), *Ethical conflicts in psychology* (3rd ed., pp. 195–197). Washington, DC: American Psychological Association. (Originally published in 1989).

Teall, B. (2000). Using solutions focused interventions in an ecological frame: A case illustration. *Social Work in Education, 22*(1), 54–61.

Tenbusch, J. P. (2002, Spring). Stem the tide of technology-assisted plagiarism and tackle incidents properly when they occur. *Administrator Magazine*. Retrieved September 24, 2009, from http://www2.scholastic.com/browse/article.jsp?id=462

Tercyak, K. P., Beville, K. W., Walker, L. R., Prahlad, S., Cogen, F. R., Sobel, D. O., & Streisand, R. (2005). Health attitudes, beliefs, and risk behaviors among adolescents and young adults with Type 1 diabetes. *Children's Health Care, 34*(3), 165–180.

Terjesen, M. D., Jacofsky, M., Froh, J., & DiGiuseppe, R. (2004). Integrating positive psychology into schools: Implications for practice. *Psychology in the Schools, 41*(1), 163–172.

Termini, K. A., & Golden, J. A. (2007). Moral behaviors: What can behaviorists learn from the developmental literature? *International Journal of Behavioral Consultation and Therapy, 3*(4), 477–493.

Thapar v. Zezulka, 994 S.W.2d 635 (Tex. 1999).

Theriot, M. T. (2008). Conceptual and methodological considerations for assessment and prevention of adolescent dating violence and stalking at school. *Children and Schools, 30*(4), 223–233.

Thomas, J. T. (2005). Licensing board complaints: Minimizing the impact on the psychologist's defense and clinical practice. *Professional Psychology, 36*(4), 426–433.

Thompson v. County of Alameda, 27 Cal. 3d 741, 167 Cal. Rptr. 70, 614 P.2d 728 (1980).

Thompson, A. P., & Pope, Z. (2005). Assessing juvenile offenders: Preliminary data for the Australian adaptation of the Youth Level of Service/Case Management Inventory. *Australian Psychologist, 40*(3), 207–214.

Thompson, K. L., & Gullone, E. (2008). Prosocial and antisocial behaviors in adolescents: An investigation into associations with attachment and empathy. *Anthrozoos, 21*(2), 123–137.

Thoreau, H. D. (1960). *Walden and civil disobedience*. Boston: Houghton Mifflin. (Originally published in 1849).

Thornberg, R. (2006). Hushing as a moral dilemma in the classroom. *Journal of Moral Development, 35*(1), 89–104.

Tillich, P. (1955). *The new being*. New York: Scribner.

Timbremont, B., Braet, C., & Dreessen, L. (2004). Assessing depression in youth: Relation between the Children's Depression Inventory and a structured interview. *Journal of Clinical Child and Adolescent Psychology, 33*(1), 149–157.

Tinker v. Des Moines Independent School District, 393 U.S. 503 (1969).

Tirri, K. (1999). Teachers' perceptions of moral dilemmas at school. *Journal of Moral Education, 28*(1), 31–47.

Tjosvold, D., Yu, Z-Y., Hui, C. (2004). Team learning from mistakes: The contribution of cooperative goals and problem-solving. *Journal of Management Studies, 41*(7), 1223–1245.

Tolstoy, L. (1951). *The kingdom of God is within you* (L. Wiener, Trans.). Boston: Page (Originally published in 1894).

Tolstoy, L. (2005). Letter to Ernest Howard Crosby. In R. L. Holmes & B. L. Gan (Eds.), *Nonviolence in theory and practice* (2nd ed., pp. 69–76). Long Grove, IL: Waveland. (Originally published in 1896).

Towbin, K. E., & Campbell, P. A. (1995). Ethical conflicts in their management in inpatient child and adolescent psychiatry. *Child and Adolescent Psychiatric Clinics of North America, 4*(4), 747–767.

Tymchuk, A. (1986). Guidelines for ethical decision making. *Canadian Psychology, 27*(1), 36–43.

United Nations General Assembly. (1948). *Universal declaration of human rights.* New York: United Nations Department of Public Information.

United Nations General Assembly. (1989). *Convention on the rights of the child.* New York: United Nations Department of Public Information.

Ursano, R. J., Sonnenberg, S. M., & Lazar, S. G. (2004). *A concise guide to psychodynamic psychotherapy.* Washington, DC: American Psychiatric Association.

U.S. Department of Education. (2007a). Balancing student privacy and school safety: A guide to the Family Educational Rights and Privacy Act for elementary and secondary schools. Retrieved July 22, 2009, from http://www.ed.gov/policy/gen/guid/fpco/brochures/elsec.pdf

U.S. Department of Education (2008, December 9). Family Educational Rights and Privacy: Final Rule, 34 CFR Part 99, *Federal Register, 73*(237), 74806-74855. Retrieved July 6, 2009, from http://www.ed.gov/legislation/FedRegister/finrule/2008-4/120908a.pdf

U.S. Department of Education, National Center for Education Statistics. (2007b). *The condition of education 2007* (NCES 2007-064). Washington, DC: U.S. Government Printing Office. Retrieved December 5, 2009, from http://nces.ed.gov/pubs2007/2007064.pdf

U.S. Department of Education & U.S. Department of Justice. (2000). *1999 annual report on school safety.* Washington, DC: Authors.

U.S. Department of Health, Human Services & U.S. Department of Education. (2008, November). *Joint guidance on the application of the Family Educational Rights and Privacy Act (FERPA) and the Health Insurance Portability and Accountability Act of 1996 (HIPAA) to student health records.* Retrieved from July 14, 2009, http://www.ed.gov/policy/gen/guid/fpco/doc/ferpa-hipaa-guidance.pdf

Van Biema, D., & Moses, G. (1989). His pupils want someone to lean on, but Joe Clark may simply want out. *People, 31*(12), 51–53.

Van Divner, B., & Champ Morera, C. (2007). Ethical DECISIONS Model for School Psychologists. *InSight, 27*(2). Lititz, PA: Association of School Psychologists of Pennsylvania.

van Lang, N. D. J., Ferdinand, R. F., Oldehinkel, A. J., Ormel, J., & Verhulst, F. C. (2005). Concurrent validity of the DSM-IV scales affective problems and anxiety problems of the Youth Self-Report. *Behaviour Research and Therapy, 43*(11), 1485–1494.

Van Leijenhorst, L., Westenberg, P. M., & Crone, E. A. (2008). A developmental study of risky decisions on the cake gambling task: Age and gender analyses of probability estimation and reward evaluation. *Developmental Neuropsychology, 33*(2), 179–196.

VanVoorhis, C. R. W., & Blumentritt, T. L. (2007). Psychometric properties of the Beck Depression Inventory-II in a clinically-identified sample of Mexican American adolescents. *Journal of Child and Family Studies, 16*(6), 789–798.

Varnham, S. (2005). Seeing things differently: Restorative justice and school discipline. *Education and the Law, 17*(3), 87–104.

Velasquez, M., Moberg, D., Meyer, M. J., Shanks, T., McLean, M. R., DeCosse, D., et al. (2009). A framework for thinking ethically. Originally published in *Issues in Ethics, 1*(2). Retrieved May 19, 2009, from the Santa Clara University Web site: http://www.scu.edu/ethics/practicing/decision/framework.html

Verhulst, F. C. (2002). Editorial. *Journal of Child Psychology and Psychiatry, 43*(6), 693–694.

Viljoen, J. L., Scalora, M., Cuadra, L., Bader, S., Chavez, V., Ullman, D., & Lawrence, L. (2008). Assessing risk for violence in adolescents who have sexually reoffended: A comparison of the J-SOAP-II, J-SORRAT-II, and SAVRY. *Criminal Justice and Behavior, 35*(1), 5–23.

Volling, B. L., Kolak, A. M., & Kennedy, D. E. (2008). Empathy and compassionate love in early childhood: Development and family influence. In B. Fehr, S. Sprecher, & L. G. Underwood (Eds.), *The science of compassionate love: Theory, research, and applications* (pp. 161–200). Hoboken, NJ: Wiley-Blackwell.

Vreeke, G. J., & van der Mark, I. L. (2003). Empathy, an integrated model. *New Ideas in Psychology, 21*(3), 177–207.

Vygotsky, L. S. (1978). Thinking and speech. In R. W. & A. S. Carton (Eds.), N. Minick, (Trans.), *The collected works of L. S. Vygotsky: Vol. 1., Problems of general psychology* (pp. 37–285). New York: Plenum. [Originally published in 1934.]

Wagner, E. F., & Austin, A. (2008). Substance abuse disorders. In M. Hersen & D. Reitman (Eds.), *Handbook of psychological assessment, case conceptualization, and treatment, Vol. 2: Children and adolescents* (pp. 444–470). Hoboken, NJ: John Wiley.

Walker, L. J. (1999). The family context for moral development. *Journal of Moral Education, 28*(3), 261–264.

Walsh-Bowers, R., Rossiter, A., & Prilleltensky, I. (1996). The personal is the organizational in the ethics of hospital social workers. *Ethics and Behavior, 6*(4), 321–335.

Watson, M. (2006). Long-term effects of moral/character education in elementary schools: In pursuit of mechanisms. *Journal of Research in Character Education, 4*(1–2), 1–18.

Wattles, J. (1996). *The Golden Rule.* New York: Oxford University Press.

Webb, L., & Brigman, G. A. (2007). Student success skills: A structured group intervention for school counselors. *Journal for Specialists in Group Work, 32*(2), 190–201.

Weiss, H. B. (1990). Beyond *parens patriae*: Building policies and programs to care for our own and others' children. *Children and Youth Services Review, 12*(4), 269–284.

Weithorn, L. A., & Campbell, S. B. (1982). The competency of children and adolescents to make informed treatment decisions. *Child Development, 53*(6), 1589–1598.

Welfel, E. R. (1998). *Ethics in counseling and psychotherapy: Standards, research, and emerging issues.* Pacific Grove, CA: Brooks/Cole.

White, J. M., & Klein, D. M. (2008). *Family theories.* Los Angeles: Sage.

Williams, A. D., & Baumeister, D. E. (1988). The evaluator's role in juvenile court: Similarities and differences. *American Journal of Forensic Psychology, 6*(3), 45–51.

Wilson, M., & Daly, M. (1993). Spousal homicide risk and estrangement. *Violence and Victims, 8*(1), 3–16.

Winett, R. A., & Winkler, R. C. (1972). Current behavior modification in the classroom: Be still, be quiet, be docile. *Journal of Applied Behavior Analysis, 5*(4), 499–504.

Winters, W. G., & Easton, F. (1983). *The practice of social work in schools: An ecological perspective.* New York: Free Press.

Wisconsin v. Yoder, 406 U.S. 205 (1972).

Wishnie, H. A. (2005). *Working in the countertransference: Necessary entanglements.* Lanham, MD: Rowman & Littlefield.

Wolfe, D. A., Jaffe, P. G., & Crooks, C. V. (2006). *Adolescent risk behaviors: Why teens experiment and strategies to keep them safe.* New Haven, CT: Yale University Press.

Wolfe, W. (2009a, May 20). Dad of boy resisting chemo - He's left the country: The father of Daniel Hauser said today he believes his son and his wife have left the country, but won't say where he thinks they may have gone to keep out of reach of authorities. *Star Tribune.* [Electronic version, Accession #: 2W62067147902].

Wolfe, W. (2009b, May 23). Judge rejects family's request to life order on teen with cancer. *Star Tribune.* [Electronic version, Accession #: 2W63025959758].

Wolfe, W., & Lerner, M. (2009, May 15). Judge orders boy, 13, to have cancer treatment: Daniel Hauser's parents say using chemotherapy to fight his Hodgkin's lymphoma is against their religion and beliefs. *Star Tribune.* [Electronic version, Accession #: 2W62184581410].

Wolthers, O. D. (2006). A questionnaire on factors influencing children's assent and dissent to non-therapeutic research. *Journal of Medical Ethics, 32*(5), 292–297.

Womontree, M. (2004). *Ethical concerns common to small community and rural mental health practice.* Doctoral dissertation. Adler School of Professional Psychology, Chicago, IL. Retrieved June 25, 2009, from Dissertations & Theses: Full Text database (Publication No. AAT 3131346).

Wong, W. S. (2004). Attitudes toward life and death among Chinese adolescents: The Chinese version of the Multi-Attitude Suicide Tendency Scale. *Death Studies, 28*(2), 91–110.

Wong, S. C. P., & Gordon, A. (2006). The validity and reliability of the Violence Risk Scale: A treatment-friendly violence risk assessment tool. *Psychology, Public Policy, and Law, 12*(3), 279–309.

Woodrich, D. L. (2004). Professional beliefs related to the practice of pediatric medicine and school psychology. *Journal of School Psychology, 42*(4), 265–284.

Yarnell, H. (1940). Firesetting in children. *American Journal of Orthopsychiatry, 10,* 272–287.

Zhong, C-B. (2007). *The ethical dangers of rational decision making.* Doctoral dissertation, Northwestern University, Illinois. Retrieved August 7, 2009, from Dissertations & Theses: Full text (Publication no. AAT 3287189).

Zimmerman, R. (2004). Doctors' new tool to fight lawsuits: Saying "I'm sorry": Malpractice insurers find owning up to errors soothes patient anger. *Journal of the Oklahoma State Medical Association, 97*(6), 245–247.

Zirkel, P. A. (2009a). Section 504: An update.

Zirkel, P. A. (2009b). What does the law say? New Section 504 student eligibility standards. *Teaching Exceptional Children, 41*(4), 68–71.

Zur, O. (2002). The truth about codes of ethics: Dispelling the rumors that dual relationships are unethical. In A. A. Lazarus & O. Zur (Eds.), *Dual relationships and psychotherapy* (pp. 55–63). New York: Springer.

Zur, O. (2007). Toward a better understanding of boundaries in therapy. In O. Zur (Ed.), *Boundaries in psychotherapy: Ethical and clinical explorations* (pp. 217–219). Washington, DC: American Psychological Association.

Index

Numbers in *italics* are in figures or tables.

Integrity, xiii–xiv, 3, 6, 12, 38, 42, 108–109, 135, 146, 149, 161, 165–166, 202

Jaffee v. Redmond, 93–94, 96, 98, 216
Jane Buri, 14–15, 28
Joe Clark, 9–11, 28
Journals
  student, 173

Malpractice, 70, 94, 96, 167, 202
Mandated reporting, 37, 156, 188
Medicaid, 85, 97, 185
Minors, 8, 31, 55, 60–61, 63, 123, 125, 127, 148, 181, 202
Mistakes
  managing, 59, 62, 74, 185–187, 195
Moral realism, 145, 202

Negligence, 34, 61, 63, 202
Norms, ix, xvi, xviii, 145, 202
Nonmaleficence, 3, 42, 109, 146–147, 202

Obligations, 4, 41, 52, 95, 97–98, 116–117, 165, 202
Orientation
  ethical, 58–59, 66, 67, 70, 96, 141, 148

Parens Patriae, 8, 203
Passive consent, 59, 203
Paternalism, 21, 142, 203
Permission
  parental, 47, 61, 89, 129, 148, 190, 203

Plagiarism, 39–40
Police officers, 23, 134, 135, 164–168, 181, 182–183, 183, 196, 211
Positive regard, 24, 25–27, 175
Power
  types, 47–49, 50, 52, 66, 71, 97, 187, 193, 203
Privilege (legal), 74, 86, 93, 93–94, 94–95, 203
Privacy, 3, 5, 42, 54, 84, 147, 169, 203
Profession, xiii, xix, xx, 1, 3–4, 15, 33, 44, 98, 126, 197, 203

Relativism, 145, 204
Religious issues, 26, 36–37, 63–65, 76, 77–78, 81, 101, 146–147, 206–211
Risk assessment, 131, 139, 153, 166, 171
Risk-benefit analysis, 7–8
Risk factors, 129, 143–144, 204

Safford v. Redding, 78, 79–80, 211
School expulsion, 9–11, 81, 189, 190, 192, 194–195
Self-determination, 8, 20, 42, 54, 56, 57, 117–119, 175, 181, 190, 204
Sex offenders, 164, 165–168
Sexually transmitted
  infections, 47, 55, 60, 119, 123, 155
Sexual orientation, 26–27
Special education, 82, 104–106, 168, 217

CPSIA information can be obtained
at www.ICGtesting.com
Printed in the USA
LVOW13s1242270618
582004LV00009B/40/P

9 780199 735853